R&AW
Then and Now

R&AW

Then and Now

Dr. C.P. Thakur

Neha Publishers & Distributors

Published by:
Neha Publishers & Distributors
4832/24, Prahlad Lane, S-207 Ansari Road,
Daryaganj, New Delhi-110002

ISBN: 978-93-80318-80-6

Price: 895/-

Typesetting: JEE-VEE Graphics

First Edition: 2024

Printed by: Neeta Press

Preface

Founded in 1968, RAW focused largely on Pakistan. Its formation was initially motivated by reports of Pakistan supplying weapons to Sikh militants, and providing shelter and training to guerrillas in Pakistan.

The Research and Analysis Wing (R&AW or RAW) is the primary foreign intelligence agency of India. Thus R&AW was formed in September 1968 under the guidance of its first Director, Rameshwar Nath Kao. RAW and Pakistan's spy agency, the Inter-Services Intelligence (ISI), have been engaged in covert operations against one other for over three decades.

Not much is known regarding the structure of RAW, say experts. The organization started with 250 people and about $400,000. It has since expanded to several thousand personnel, but its staffing and budget remain secret. However, an estimate by the U.S.-based Federation of American Scientists suggests that in 2000, RAW had about eight to ten thousand agents and a budget that experts place at $145 million.

The primary function of R&AW is collection of external intelligence and counter-terrorism. In addition, it is responsible for obtaining and analysing information about foreign governments, corporations and persons to advise

Indian policymakers. R&AW is an effective and one of the primary instrument of India's national power. It is also involved in the security of India's nuclear programme.

Most recently, RAW has gained attention for providing the US with intelligence on Al-Qaeda and Taliban targets for the war on terrorism in Afghanistan. Maps and photographs of terrorist training camps in Afghanistan and Pakistan, along with other evidence implicating Osama bin Laden in terrorist attacks, were given to US intelligence officials.

The book brings to light several lacunae in the functioning of the country's top intelligence agency, the most glaring being the anomalies in procurement of equipment, lack of accountability and our dependence on foreign sources, with the resultant threat to national security.Ihicia conet lam verspit odion comnis explamu saepernatur aut assum dis es auditios rem quis elit aut apellat.

—Author

Contents

1

Research and Analysis Wing

Research and Analysis Wing (RAW or R&AW) is the primary external intelligence agency of the Republic of India. It was formed in September 1968 under the helmsman-ship of its first Director, Rameshwar Nath Kao. Its creation was necessitated post the Sino-Indian War 1962 and Indo-Pakistani War of 1965 which posed various gaps in intelligence gathering undertaken by Intelligence Bureau (which then handled both internal and external intelligence). This convinced the Government of India that a specialised, independent agency was required for competent external intelligence gathering.

The primary function of R&AW is collection of external intelligence and counter-terrorism. In addition, it is responsible for obtaining and analysing information about foreign governments, corporations and persons to advise Indian policymakers. R&AW is an effective and one of the primary instrument of India's national power. It is also involved in the security of India's nuclear programme.

Headquartered in New Delhi, R&AW's current chief is Alok Joshi a 1976-batch IPS officer of Haryana cadre.

INTRODUCTION

The Research and Analysis Wing famously known as RAW, is India's foreign intelligence agency. RAW has become an effective instrument of Indian national power, and has assumed a significant role in carrying out India's domestic and foreign policies. RAW has engaged in spying against Pakistan and other neighbouring countries. It has enjoyed the backing of successive Indian governments in these efforts. Working directly under the Prime Minister, the structure and operations of the Research & Analysis Wing are kept secret from Parliament.

Founded in 1968, RAW focused largely on Pakistan. Its formation was initially motivated by reports of Pakistan supplying weapons to Sikh militants, and providing shelter and training to guerrillas in Pakistan.

Most recently, RAW has gained attention for providing the US with intelligence on Al-Qaeda and Taliban targets for the war on terrorism in Afghanistan. Maps and photographs of terrorist training camps in Afghanistan and Pakistan, along with other evidence implicating Osama bin Laden in terrorist attacks, were given to US intelligence officials.

The objectives of RAW include:

To monitor the political and military developments in adjoining countries, which have direct bearing on India's national security and in the formulation of its foreign policy.

To seek the control and limitation of the supply of military hardware to Pakistan, mostly from European countries, the USA and China.

The chief of the RAW is designated Secretary (Research) in the Cabinet Secretariat, which is part of the Prime Minister's Office (PMO). They also have the benefit of training in either US or the UK, and more recently in Israel.

The structure of the RAW is a matter of speculation, but brief overviews of the same are present in the public domain. Attached to the HQ of RAW at Lodhi Road, New Delhi are different regional headquarters, which have direct links to overseas stations and are headed by a controlling officer who keeps records of different projects assigned to field officers who are posted abroad.

Some officers of the RAW are members of a specialized service, the Research and Analysis Service (RAS), but several officers also serve on deputation from other services. The RAW has sub-organizations like the Aviation Research Center (ARC), the Radio Research Center (RRC) or the Electronics and Technical Service

(ETS), which have considerable capacity for technical intelligence gathering. Another important branch under the operational control of the RAW is the Directorate General of Security (DGS). This agency has oversight over organizations like the Special Frontier Force (SFF), the Special Services Bureau (SSB) etc... Liaison with the military is maintained through the Military Intelligence Advisory Group and the Military Advisor to the Director RAW.

HISTORICAL BACKGROUND OF R&AW

Background: 1933–68

Prior to the inception of Research and Analysis Wing, overseas intelligence collection was primarily the responsibility of the Intelligence Bureau (IB), which was created by the British. In 1933, sensing the political turmoil in the world which eventually led to the Second World War, the Intelligence Bureau's responsibilities were increased to include the collection of intelligence along India's borders.

In 1947, after independence, Sanjeevi Pillai took over as the first Indian Director of the IB. Having been depleted of trained manpower by the exit of the British, Pillai tried to run the bureau on MI5 lines.

In 1949, Pillai organised a small foreign intelligence operation, but the Indian debacle in the Sino-Indian war of 1962 showed it to be ineffective.

Foreign intelligence failure during the 1962 Sino-Indian War led then Prime Minister Jawaharlal Nehru to order a dedicated foreign intelligence agency to be established. After the Indo-Pakistani war of 1965, Indian Chief of Army Staff General Joyanto Nath Chaudhuri also called for more intelligence-gathering. Around the end of 1966 the concept of a separate foreign intelligence agency began to take concrete shape.

R&AW: 1968–present

In 1968, the Indira Gandhi administration decided that a full-fledged second security service was needed. R. N. Kao, then a deputy director of the Intelligence Bureau, submitted a blueprint for the new agency. Kao was appointed as the chief of India's first foreign intelligence agency, the Research and Analysis Wing.

The R&AW was given the responsibility for strategic external intelligence, human as well as technical, plus concurrent responsibility with the Directorate-General of Military Intelligence for tactical trans-border military intelligence up to a certain depth across the Line of control (LOC) and the international border.

R&AW started as a wing of the main Intelligence Bureau with 250 employees and an annual budget of 20 million (). In the early seventies, its annual budget had risen to 300 million () while its personnel numbered several thousand. In 1971, Kao had persuaded the Government to set up the Aviation Research Centre (ARC). The ARC's job was aerial reconnaissance.

It replaced the Indian Air Force's old reconnaissance aircraft and by the mid-1970s, R&AW, through the ARC, had high quality aerial pictures of the installations along the Chinese and Pakistani borders.

Presently, the budget of R&AW is speculated to be as high as US$150 million to as low as US$31 million. Slowly other child agencies like The Radio Research Center and Electronics & Tech. Services were added to R&AW in 1970s and 1990s.

In 1990s the Special Frontier Force became the paramilitary wing of R&AW, providing the requisite muscle for covert military operations. In 2004 Government of India added yet another intelligence agency called the National Technical Facilities Organisation (NTFO), which was later renamed as National Technical Research Organisation (NTRO). It is believed to be functioning under R&AW, although it remains autonomous to some degree. While the exact nature of the operations conducted by NTRO is classified, it is believed that it deals with research on imagery and communications using various platforms.

The Joint Intelligence Committee (JIC), under the Cabinet Secretariat, is responsible for coordinating and analysing intelligence activities between R&AW, the Intelligence Bureau and the Defence Intelligence Agency (DIA). In practice, however, the effectiveness of the JIC has been varied. With the establishment of the National Security Council in 1999, the role of the JIC has been merged with the NSC. R&AW's legal status is unusual, in that it is not an "Agency", but a "Wing" of the Cabinet Secretariat. Hence, R&AW is not answerable to the Parliament of India on any issue, which keeps it out of reach of the *Right to Information Act.* This exemption was granted through Section 24 read with Schedule II of the act. However, information regarding the allegations of corruption and human rights violations has to be disclosed.

Objectives

The present R&AW objectives include, and are not limited to:

- Monitoring the political, military, economic and scientific developments in countries which have direct bearing on India's national security and the formulation of its foreign policy.
- Moulding international public opinion with the help of the strong and vibrant Indian diaspora.
- Covert Operations to safe guard India's National interests.
- Anti – Terror Operations and neutralising terror elements posing a threat to India.

In the past, following the Sino-Indian war of 1962 and due to India's volatile relations with Pakistan, R&AW's objectives had also consisted the following:

- To watch the development of international communism and the schism between the two big communist nations, the Soviet Union and China. As with other countries, both these powers had direct access to the communist parties in India.
- To control and limit the supply of military hardware to Pakistan, from mostly European countries, America and more importantly from China.

Organisational Structure

R&AW has been organised on the lines of the CIA. The head of R&AW is designated "Secretary (Research)" in the Cabinet Secretariat. Most of the previous chiefs have been experts on either Pakistan or China. They also have the benefit of training in either the USA or the UK, and more recently in Israel. The "Secretary (R)", although is under direct command of Prime Minister, reports on an administrative basis to the Cabinet Secretary, who reports to the Prime Minister (PM). However, on a daily basis the "Secretary (R)" reports to the National Security Advisor. Reporting to the "Secretary (R)" are:

- An Additional Secretary responsible for the Office of Special Operations and intelligence collected from different countries processed by large number of Joint Secretaries, who are the functional heads of various specified desks with different regional divisions/areas/countries: Area one – Pakistan; Area two – China and Southeast Asia; Area three – the Middle East and Africa; and Area four – other countries. Two Special Joint Secretaries, reporting to the Additional Secretary, head the Electronics and Technical Department which is the nodal agency for ETS, NTRO and the RRC.
- The Director General of Security has two important sections - the Aviation Research Centre is headed by one Special Secretary and the Special Services Bureau controlled by two Special Secretaries.

The internal structure of the R&AW is a matter of speculation, but brief overviews of the same are present in the public domain. Attached to the Headquarters of R&AW at Lodhi Road, New Delhi are different regional headquarters, which have direct links to overseas stations and are headed by a controlling officer who keeps records of different projects assigned to field officers who are posted abroad. Intelligence is usually collected from a variety of sources by field officers and deputy field officers; it is either preprocessed by a senior field officer or by a desk officer. The desk officer then passes the information to the Joint Secretary and then on to the Additional Secretary and from there it is disseminated to the concerned end user. R&AW personnel are called "Research Officers" instead of the traditional "agents". There is a sizeable number of female officers in R&AW even at the operational level. In recent years, R&AW has shifted its primary focus from Pakistan to China and have started operating a separate desk for this purpose.

List of Secretaries of the Research and Analysis Wing

No.	Name	Took office	Left office
1	R. N. Kao	1968	1977
2	K. Sankaran Nair	1977	1977
3	N. F. Suntook	1977	1983
4	Girish Chandra Saxena	1983	1986
5	S. E. Joshi	1986	1987
6	A. K. Verma	1987	1990
7	G. S. Bajpai	1990	1991
8	N. Narasimhan	1991	1993
9	J. S. Bedi	1993	1993
10	A.S. Syali	1993	1996
11	Ranjan Roy	1996	1997
12	Arvind Dave	1997	1999
13	A. S. Dulat	1999	2000
14	Vikram Sood	13 December 2000	31 March 2003
15	C. D. Sahay	1 April 2003	31 January 2005
16	P. K. H. Tharakan	1 February 2005	31 January 2007
17	Ashok Chaturvedi	1 February 2007	31 January 2009
18	K. C. Verma	1 February 2009	30 December 2010
19	Sanjeev Tripathi	30 December 2010	29 December 2012
20	Alok Joshi	30 December 2012	Present

Most of the Directors/Secretaries of Research and Analysis Wing have been Indian Police Service (IPS) officers. RN Kao and Sankaran Nair belonged to the Imperial Police (IP), of the British colonial days which was renamed as the Indian Police Service after Indian Independence in 1947.

N.F.Suntook had served in the Indian Navy, then in the Indian Police Service and in the Indian Frontier Administration Service. Vikram Sood was from the Indian Postal Service and was later permanently absorbed in the RAS cadre.

Now he acts as Advisor to Fair Observer. A.S. Dulat was an Indian Police Service officer deputed from the Intelligence Bureau, while K.C. Verma is an ex-Intelligence Bureau officer. All the chiefs have been experts on China or Pakistan except for Ashok Chaturvedi, who is an expert on Nepal.

Designations at R&AW

Secretarial Level	*Analyst Level*	*Field Level*
Secretary (R)	Central Intelligence Officer	Senior Field Officer
Additional Secretary	Assistant Central Intelligence Officer	Field Officer
Special Secretary/ Joint Secretary	Junior Intelligence Officer	Deputy Field Officer
Director/Deputy Secretary/Attache	Assistant Field Officer	

Recruitment

Initially, R&AW relied primarily on trained intelligence officers who were recruited directly. These belonged to the external wing of the Intelligence Bureau. In times of great expansion, many candidates were taken from the military, police and other services. Later, R&AW began directly recruiting graduates from universities. However owing to allegations of nepotism in appointments, in 1983 R&AW created its own service cadre, the Research and Analysis Service (RAS) to absorb talent from other UPSC Group A officer cadre. Direct recruitment at Class I executive level is from Civil services officers undergoing Foundation course at Lal Bahadur Shastri National Academy of Administration.

At the end of the course, R&AW conducts a campus interview. Based on a selection of psychological tests and the interview, candidates are inducted into R&AW for a lien period of one year. During this period, they have an option of rejoining their parent service (if they wish to) after which they can be permanently absorbed into the Research and Analysis Service. Delhi-based security think tank Institute for Defence Studies and Analyses noted in one of its reports that R&AW suffered from the 'tail-end syndrome' where the 'bottom of the entrance lists' of those appearing for the UPSC examinations were offered jobs. Additionally, recruitment is also by lateral deputation from the Armed Forces or Civil Service Officers. The Civil and Defence Service Officers permanently resign their cadre and join the RAS. However, according to recent reports, officers can return to their parent cadre after serving a specific period in the agency if they wish to. Most of the secretaries have been officers from the IPS. R&AW also employs a number of linguists and other experts in various fields. The service conditions of R&AW officers is governed by the Research and Analysis Wing (Recruitment, Cadre and Service) Rules, 1975.

BASIC TRAININGOF R&AW

Basic training

Basic training commences with 'pep talks' to boost the morale of the new recruit. This is a ten-day phase in which the inductee is familiarised with the real world of intelligence and espionage, as opposed to the spies of fiction. Common usages, tradecraft techniques and classification of information are taught. Financial and economic analysis, Space Technology, Information Security, Energy Security and Scientific knowledge is imbibed to the trainees. The recruit is made to specialise in a foreign language and introduced to Geo strategic analysis. Case studies of other agencies like CIA, KGB, ISI, Mossad and Secret Intelligence Service are presented for study. The inductee is also taught that intelligence organisations do not identify who is friend and who is foe, the country's foreign policy does. Basic classroom training to R&AW officers are imparted at R&AW's Training Institute in Gurgaon. A multi-disciplinary school of economic intelligence is also being set up in Mumbai to train intelligence officers in investigating economic crimes like money laundering for terror purposes etc.

Advanced training

After completing 'Basic Training' the recruit is now attached to a Field Intelligence Bureau (FIB). His/her training here lasts for 1–2 years. He/she is given firsthand experience of what it was to be out in the figurative cold, conducting clandestine operations. During night exercises under realistic conditions, he/she is taught infiltration and exfiltration. He/she is instructed to avoid capture and if caught, how to face interrogation. He/she learns the art of reconnoitre, making contacts, and, the numerous skills of operating an intelligence mission. At the end of the field training, the new recruit is brought back to the school for final polishing. Before his deployment in the field, he is given exhaustive training in the art of self-defence mainly Krav Maga, and the use of technical espionage devices. He/she is also drilled in various administrative disciplines so that he could take his place in the foreign missions without arousing suspicion. He/she is now ready to operate under the cover of an Embassy to gather information, set up his own network of informers, moles or operatives as the task may require. Field training is provided in the Indian Military Academy Headquarters at Dehradun. The training model has been criticised as being 'archaic and too police-centric' and not incorporating 'modern technological advances in methods of communication' etc.

INDIAN RAW CRACKS DOWN ON MOSSAD OPERATIONS IN INDIA

An Israeli Chabad sect couple, Rabbi Sheneor Zalman and his wife Yaffa Shenoi, have been told by Kerala police to leave India in fifteen days. The two are suspected by the Indian intelligence, the Research and Analysis Wing (RAW) of being involved in a covert operation in India linked to the 2008 Mumbai terrorist attack in which six Chabad members were killed in a shootout between Dawood Ibrahim's Pakistan-based gangsters and the residents of Mumbai's Chabad House.

The incident was reported as a major act of terrorism when, in fact, it was score settling between Ibrahim's drug syndicate and Chabadniks who were seen as moving in on Ibrahim's control over the Mumbai drug trade.

WMR has previously reported that Chabad houses around the world are believed by multiple intelligence agencies to be centers for Mossad activity operating under religious "cover."

RAW agents apparently staked out the couple's pricey residence in Kochi as late night meetings were conducted with suspect individuals under Indian intelligence surveillance. The Israeli couple had lived in Kochi for almost two years. After being presented with evidence of espionage by the intelligence and police services, the Ernakulum District in Kochi decided to order the Israeli couple deported. Chabad Jews and Mossad were forced to leave their former base in Goa as a result of increased RAW and federal police surveillance of their activities, believed to include the shipment of heroin from Afghanistan to Southeast Asia in the east and the United Arab Emirates to the west. The Israeli Mossad and Chabad re-located their operations to Kochi, which had replaced Goa as a major drug trans-shipment point.

In addition, Mumbai bombing suspect David Headley is believed to have maintained contact with the Mossad station in Goa prior to the Mumbai terrorist attacks. Headley is believed to have also maintained links with Ibrahim's crime syndicate in Pakistan and the Lashkar-e-Taiba terrorist group in planning false flag terrorist attacks in India. Then the green light for the Mumbai attacks was given; Ibrahim's men decided to use the occasion to also attack their drug smuggling competitors at the Mumbai Chabad House. Kochi had, according to WMR's Indian intelligence sources, also served as a clandestine communications support facility for Israeli Dolphin-class submarines and their contingent of naval divers operating in the Indian Ocean and Arabian Sea. The submarines are believed to be targeting Iran in the event of an outbreak of hostilities between Israel and Iran.

Indian intelligence also believes the Israelis in Kochi were targeting the classified communications of the Indian naval base in Kochi, the headquarters for the Indian Navy's Southern Command. By targeting the Kochi naval base and the anti-submarine warfare intelligence elements there and at the Indian naval air station on Willingdon Island, the Israelis were capable of providing warning to Israeli forces of Indian, Chinese, American, British, and French warships transiting past the tip of southern India to the Arabian and Red Seas.

Rabbi Zalman and his wife denied all charges against them and insisted they were meeting people day and night as a service to the local Jewish community.

Our sources say that after years of being played by Mossad, RAW has finally taken action against a major Mossad cell operating in the country.

FUNCTIONS AND METHODS OF R&AW

Activities and functions of R&AW are highly confidential and declassification of past operations are uncommon unlike agencies like CIA, MI6 and Mossad who have many of their activities declassified. Foreign analysts have often referred to R&AW as one of the most feared intelligence agency operating in the region. The Secretary (R) reported to the Vohra Committee that R&AW offices abroad have limited strength and are largely geared to the collection of military, economic, scientific and political intelligence.

R&AW monitors the activities of certain organisations abroad only insofar as they relate to their involvement with narco terrorist elements and smuggling arms, ammunition, explosives, etc. into India. It does not monitor the activities of criminal elements abroad, which are mainly confined to normal smuggling without any links to terrorist elements. However, if there is evidence to suggest that certain organisations have links with Intelligence agencies of other countries, and that they are being used or are likely to be used by such countries for destabilising India's economy, it would become R&AW's responsibility to monitor their activities.

The primary mission of R&AW includes aggressive intelligence collection via espionage, psychological warfare, subversion, sabotage and assassinations. R&AW maintains active collaboration with other secret services in various countries. Its contacts with FSB of Russia, NDS, the Afghan agency, Israel's Mossad, the CIA and MI6 have been well-known, a common interest being Pakistan's nuclear programme. R&AW has been active in obtaining information and operating through third countries like Afghanistan, the United Kingdom, Hong Kong, Myanmar and Singapore.

R&AW obtains information critical to Indian strategic interests both by overt and covert means. The data is then classified and filed with the assistance of the computer networks. International business houses, information technology sector and media centres can easily absorb R&AW operatives and provide freedom of movement. A task force report prepared by a New Delhi based security think tank highlighted that R&AW operatives have inadequate non-official cover for overseas operations which 'limits access to spot real targets' and causes issues on handling 'high-value assets'.

Major operations

- ELINT operations in Himalayas: After China tested its first nuclear weapons on 16 October 1964, at Lop Nur, Xinjiang, India and the USA shared a common fear about the nuclear capabilities of China. Owing to the extreme remoteness of Chinese testing grounds, strict secrecy surrounding the Chinese nuclear programme, and the extreme difficulty that an Indian or American would have passing themselves off as Chinese, it was almost impossible to carry out any HUMINT operation. So, the CIA in the late 1960s decided to launch an ELINT operation along with RAW and ARC to track China's nuclear tests and monitor its missile launches. The operation, in the garb of a mountaineering expedition to Nanda Devi involved celebrated Indian climber M S Kohli who along with operatives of Special Frontier Force and the CIA – most notably Jim Rhyne, a veteran STOL pilot – was to place a permanent ELINT device, a transceiver powered by a plutonium battery, that could detect and report data on future nuclear tests carried out by China. The monitoring device was near successfully implanted on Nanda Devi, when an avalanche forced a hasty withdrawal. Later, a subsequent mountain operation to retrieve or replant the device was aborted when it was found that the device was lost. Recent reports indicate that radiation traces from this device have been discovered in sediment below the mountain. However, the actual data is not conclusive.
- Creation of Bangladesh and aftermath: In the early 1970s the army of Pakistan launched military crackdown in response to the Bangladesh independence movement. Nearly 10 million refugees fled to India. RAW was instrumental in the formation of the Bangladeshi guerilla organisation Mukti Bahini and responsible for supplying information, providing training and heavy ammunition to this organisation. It is also alleged that RAW planned and

executed the 1971 Indian Airlines hijacking as a false flag operation to ban overflight by Pakistani aircraft and disrupt Pakistani troop movement in East Pakistan. Special Frontier Force, the paramilitary wing of R&AW actively participated in military operations especially in the Chittagong Hill Tracts. The war ended in the successful creation of Bangladesh. However within months of independence of Bangladesh Mujibur Rahman was assassinated at his residence. RAW operatives claim that they had advance information about Mujib-ur-Rahman's assassination but Sheikh Mujib tragically ignored inputs. He was killed along with 40 members of his family. RAW thus failed to prevent the assassination which led to the loss of a charismatic leader who had a soft corner for India after all they had done for his country's independence. Later, RAW successfully thwarted plans of assassinating Sheikh Hasina Wazed, daughter of Mujibur Rahman, by Islamist extremists.

- Operation Smiling Buddha: Operation Smiling Buddha was the name given to India's nuclear programme. The task to keep it under tight wraps for security was given to RAW. This was the first time that RAW was involved in a project inside India. On 18 May 1974, India detonated a 15-kiloton plutonium device at Pokhran and became a member of the nuclear club.
- Amalgamation of Sikkim: In 1947 Sikkim became a protectorate under India, which controlled its external affairs, defence, diplomacy and communications. It is alleged that in 1972 RAW was authorised to install a pro-Indian democratic government there. After widespread rioting and demonstration against the King of Sikkim in 1975 a referendum was held in which 97.5% of the electorate (in a nation where 59% of the population could vote) voted to join the Indian Union. On 16 May 1975, Sikkim officially became the 22nd state of the Indian Union, and the monarchy was abolished.
- Kahuta's Blueprint: Kahuta is the site of the Khan Research

Laboratories (KRL), Pakistan's main nuclear weapons laboratory as well as an emerging centre for long-range missile development. The primary Pakistani fissile-material production facility is located at Kahuta, employing gas centrifuge enrichment technology to produce Highly Enriched Uranium (HEU). RAW first confirmed Pakistan's nuclear programs by analysing the hair samples snatched from the floor of barber shops near KRL; which showed that Pakistan had developed the ability to enrich uranium to weapons-grade quality. RAW agents knew of Kahuta Research Laboratories from at least early 1978, when the then Indian Prime Minister, Morarji Desai, accidentally thwarted RAW's operations on Pakistan's covert nuclear weapons program. In an indiscreet moment in a telephone conversation one day, Morarji Desai informed the then Pakistan President, Zia-ul-Haq, that India was aware of Pakistan's nuclear weapons program. According to later reports, acting on this "tip-off", Pakistani Intelligence eliminated RAW's sources on Kahuta, leaving India in the dark about Pakistan's nuclear weapons program from then on.

- Operation Meghdoot: RAW received information from the London company which had supplied Arctic-weather gear for Indian troops from Northern Ladakh region some paramilitary forces that Pakistan too had bought similar Arctic-weather gear. This information was shared with Indian Army which soon launched Operation Meghdoot to take control of Siachen Glacier with around 300 acclimatised troops were airlifted to Siachen before Pakistan could launch any operation resulting in Indian head start and eventual Indian domination of all major peaks in Siachen.
- Kanishka Bombing case: On 23 June 1985 Air India's Flight 182 was blown up near Ireland and 329 innocent lives were lost. On the same day, another explosion took place at Tokyo's Narita airport's transit baggage building where baggage was being transferred from Cathay Pacific Flight No CP 003 to Air India Flight 301 which was scheduled

for Bangkok. Both aircraft were loaded with explosives from Canadian airports. Flight 301 got saved because of a delay in its departure. This was considered as a major setback to RAW for failing to gather enough intelligence about the Khalistani terrorists.

- Special Operations: In the mid-1980s, RAW set up two covert groups, *Counterintelligence Team-X(CIT-X)* and *Counterintelligence Team-J(CIT-J)*, the first directed at Pakistan and the second at Khalistani groups. Rabinder Singh, the RAW double agent who defected to the United States in 2004, helped run CIT-J in its early years. Both these covert groups used the services of cross-border traffickers to ferry weapons and funds across the border, much as their ISI counterparts were doing. According to former RAW official and noted security analyst B. Raman, the Indian counter-campaign yielded results. "The role of our cover action capability in putting an end to the ISI's interference in Punjab", he wrote in 2002, "by making such interference prohibitively costly is little known and understood." These covert operations were discontinued during the tenure of IK Gujral and were never restarted. As per B Raman the former RAW cabinet secretary, such covert operations were successful in keeping a check on ISI and were "responsible for ending the Khalistani insurgency". He also notes that a lack of such covert capabilities, since they were closed down in 1997, has left the country even more vulnerable than before and says that developing covert capabilities is the need of the hour.
- Operation Cactus: In November 1988, the People's Liberation Organisation of Tamil Eelam (PLOTE), composed of about 200 Tamil secessionist rebels, invaded Maldives. At the request of the president of Maldives, Maumoon Abdul Gayoom, the Indian Armed Forces, with assistance from RAW, launched a military campaign to throw the mercenaries out of Maldives. On the night of 3 November 1988, the Indian Air Force airlifted the 6th parachute battalion of the Parachute Regiment from Agra

and flew them over 2,000 km to Maldives. The Indian paratroopers landed at Hulule and restored the Government rule at Malé within hours. The operation, labelled *Operation Cactus*, also involved the Indian Navy. Swift operation by the military and precise intelligence by RAW quelled the insurgency.

- Sri Lanka: RAW started training the LTTE to keep a check on Sri Lanka, which had helped Pakistan in the Indo-Pak War by allowing Pakistani ships to refuel at Sri Lankan ports. However, the LTTE created a lot of problems and complications and the then Prime Minister of India Rajiv Gandhi was forced to send the Indian Peace Keeping Force (IPKF) in 1987 to restore normalcy in the region. The disastrous mission of the IPKF was blamed by many on the lack of co-ordination between the IPKF and RAW. Its most disastrous manifestation was the Heliborne assault on LTTE HQ in the Jaffna University campus in the opening stages of Operation Pawan. The site was chosen without any consultation with the RAW. The dropping paratroopers became easy targets for the LTTE. A number of soldiers were killed. The assassination of Rajiv Gandhi is also blamed as a fallout of the failed RAW operation in Sri Lanka.
- Anti-Apartheid Movement: RAW trained the intelligence officers of many independent African countries and assisted the anti-apartheid struggles in South Africa and Namibia. Retired RAW officers were deputed to work in training institutes of intelligence agencies of some African states.
- Operation Chanakya: This was the RAW operation in the Kashmir region to infiltrate various ISI-backed Kashmiri separatist groups and restore peace in the Kashmir valley. RAW operatives infiltrated the area, collected military intelligence, and provided evidence about ISI's involvement in training and funding Kashmiri separatist groups. RAW was successful not only in unearthing the links between the ISI and the separatist groups, but also in infiltrating and neutralising the militancy in the Kashmir valley. RAW

is also credited for creating a split in the Hizb-ul-Mujahideen. Operation Chanakya also marked the creation of pro-Indian groups in Kashmir like the Ikhwan-ul-Muslimeen, Muslim Mujahideen etc. These counter-insurgencies consist of ex-militants and relatives of those slain in the conflict. Ikhwan-ul-Muslimeen leader Kokka Parrey was himself assassinated by separatists.

- Help to the Northern Alliance: After the rise of Pakistan backed Taliban in Afghanistan, India decided to side with the Northern Alliance By 1996, RAW had built a 25 bed military hospital at the Farkhor Air Base. This airport was used by the Aviation Research Centre, the reconnaissance arm of RAW, to repair and operate the Northern Alliance's aerial support. This relationship was further cemented in the 2001 Afgan war. India supplied the Northern Alliance high altitude warfare equipment worth around US$8–10 million. RAW was the first intelligence agency to determine the extent of the Kunduz airlift.
- Kargil War: RAW was heavily criticised in 1999, following the Pakistani incursions at Kargil. Critics accused RAW of failing to provide intelligence that could have prevented the ensuing ten-week conflict that brought India and Pakistan to the brink of a full-scale war. While the Army has been critical of the information they received, RAW has pointed the finger at the politicians, claiming they had provided all the necessary information. However, RAW was successful in intercepting a telephonic conversation between Pervez Musharraf, the then Pakistan Army Chief who was in Beijing and his chief of staff Lt. Gen. Mohammed Aziz in Islamabad. This tape was later published by India to prove Pakistani involvement in the Kargil incursion. In 2011, a think tank report stated that RAW had warned in its October 1998 assessment that Pakistan Army might launch a limited swift offensive with possible support of alliance partners, however the government ignored such reports.
- Operation Leech: Surrounded by Arakans and dense forest, Myanmar had always been a worrisome point for Indian

intelligence. As the major player in the area, India has sought to promote democracy and install friendly governments in the region. To these ends, RAW cultivated Burmese rebel groups and pro-democracy coalitions, especially the Kachin Independence Army (KIA). India allowed the KIA to carry a limited trade in jade and precious stones using Indian territory and even supplied them weapons. It is further alleged that KIA chief Maran Brang Seng met the RAW chief in Delhi twice. However, when the KIA became the main source of training and weapons for all northeastern rebel groups, RAW initiated an operation, code named *Operation Leech*, to assassinate the leaders of the Burmese rebels as an example to other groups. in 1998, six top rebel leaders, including military wing chief of National Unity Party of Arakans (NUPA), Khaing Raza, were shot dead and 34 Arakanese guerrillas were arrested and charged with gunrunning.

- War on Terror: Although RAW's contribution to the War on Terror is highly classified, the organisation gained some attention in the Western media after claims that it was assisting the United States by providing intelligence on Osama Bin Laden and the Taliban's whereabouts. Maps and photographs of terrorist training camps in Afghanistan and Pakistan along with other evidence implicating Osama bin Laden in terrorist attacks were given to US intelligence officials. RAW's role in the War on Terror may increase as US intelligence has indicated that it sees RAW as a more reliable ally than Pakistani intelligence. It has further come to light that a timely tip-off by RAW helped foil a third assassination plot against Pakistan's former President, General Pervez Musharraf.
- 2008 Mumbai attacks: About 2–6 months before 26/11 Mumbai attacks RAW had intercepted several telephone calls through SIGINT which pointed at impending attacks on Mumbai Hotels by Pakistan based terrorists, however there was a co-ordination failure and no follow up action was taken. Few hours before the attacks, a RAW technician monitoring satellite transmissions picked up conversations

between attackers and handlers, as the attackers were sailing toward Mumbai. The technician flagged the conversations as being suspicious and passed them on to his superiors. RAW believed that they were worrying and immediately alerted the office of the National Security Advisor. However the intelligence was ignored. Later, just after the terrorists had attacked Mumbai, RAW technicians started monitoring the six phones used by the terrorists and recorded conversations between the terrorists and their handlers. On 15 January 2010, in a successful snatch operation RAW agents nabbed Sheikh Abdul Khwaja, one of the handlers of the 26/11 attacks, chief of HuJI India operations and a most wanted terror suspect in India, from Colombo, Sri Lanka and brought him over to Hyderabad, India for formal arrest.

- Snatch operations with IB: In late 2009, investigative journal *The Week* ran a cover story on one of India's major clandestine operations that the RAW ran with Intelligence Bureau to nab terrorists infiltrating India, via Nepal and other neighbouring countries. To bypass the lengthy extradition process, RAW conducts snatch operations to nab suspects from various foreign countries. The suspect is brought to India, interrogated and is usually produced before a court. With emergence of Nepal as a terror transit point RAW and the IB started closely monitoring the movement of suspected terrorists in Nepal. According to The Week, in last decade there has been close to 400 successful snatch operations conducted by RAW and/or IB in Nepal, Bangladesh and other countries. Some famous snatches netted Bhupinder Singh Bhuda of the Khalistan Commando Force, Lashkar militant Tariq Mehmood and Abdul Karim Tunda, Sheikh Abdul Khwaja, one of the handlers of the 26/11 attacks etc. most of the suspects are kept at Tihar Jail.

Controversies

From its inception R&AW has been criticised for being an agency not answerable to the people of India (R&AW reports to

Prime Minister only). Fears arose that it could turn into the KGB of India. Such fears were kept at bay by the R&AW's able leadership (although detractors of R&AW and especially the Janata Party have accused the agency of letting itself be used for terrorising and intimidating opposition during emergencies). The main controversy which has plagued R&AW in recent years is over bureaucratisation of the system with allegations about favouritism in promotions, corruption, ego clashes, no financial accountability, inter-departmental rivalry etc. R&AW also suffers from ethnic imbalances in the officer level. Noted security analyst and former Additional Secretary B.Raman has criticised the agency for its asymmetric growth; "while being strong in its capability for covert action it is weak in its capability for intelligence collection, analysis and assessment. Strong in low and medium-grade intelligence, weak in high-grade intelligence. Strong in technical intelligence, weak in human intelligence. Strong in collation, weak in analysis. Strong in investigation, weak in prevention. Strong in crisis management, weak in crisis prevention."

- In the 8 February 2010 edition *Outlook Magazine* reported on former R&AW Chief, Ashok Chaturvedi, utilising Government of India funds to take his wife along on international trips. After retirement, Chaturvedi had a diplomatic passport issued for himself and his wife. Per *Outlook Magazine*: "Only grade 'A' ambassadors—usually IFS officers posted in key countries like the UK and US—are allowed to hold diplomatic passports after retirement. The majority, who do not fit that bill, hold passports issued to ordinary citizens. In fact, all former R&AW chiefs Outlook spoke to confirmed they had surrendered their diplomatic passports the day they retired. And their spouses weren't entitled to diplomatic passports even while they were in service."
- In September 2007, R&AW was involved in a controversy due to a high profile CBI raid at the residence of Major General (retired) V K Singh, a retired Joint Secretary of R&AW who has recently written a book on R&AW where it was alleged that political interference and corruption in the intelligence agency has made it vulnerable to defections.

One of the instances of corruption mentioned in the book was the preference given by R&AW departments towards purchasing intelligence from the Rohde and Schwarz company. A reason for such corruption as explained by the author is that "*...R&AW was not answerable to any outside agency – the control of the Prime Minister's Office was perfunctory, at best – many officers thought that they were not only above the law but a law unto themselves.*" A case under the Official Secrets Act has also been filed against V K Singh.

- On 19 August 2008 the R&AW Director (Language) who was also head of the R&AW Training Institute in Gurgaon from 2005 tried to commit suicide in front of Prime Minister's Office, alleging inaction and wrong findings to a sexual harassment complaint filed against a Joint Secretary, who was on deputation to R&AW. She was discharged from duty on the ground that she was mentally unfit and that her identity was disclosed. She was later separately charged with criminal trespass, human trafficking and for her repeated attempts to commit suicide. The Central Administrative Tribunal (CAT) ordered R&AW to reinstate her however R&AW filed an appeal against the CAT order which is pending before Delhi High Court. On 20 January 2011 she was sent for psychological evaluation and medical detention by a Delhi High Court judge when she tried to strip herself in the court protesting over the slow pace of her trial. The psychological evaluation report stated that 'she may be suffering a mental problem due to loss of job and her continuous run-ins at the courts, but she was certainly not suffering from any permanent or grave mental disorder.'
- A senior technical officer was arrested by CBI on graft charges, on 4 February 2009. The scientist, a Director level employee, worked in the division that granted export licenses to companies dealing in "sensitive" items, including defence-related equipment. He was accused of demanding and accepting a bribe of Rs. 100,000 from a

Chennai based manufacturer for obtaining an export license.

- In September 2009, seven Additional Secretaries from the RAS cadre had gone on protest leave after A. B. Mathur, an IPS officer, superseded them to the post of Special Secretary. Over the years the tussle between the RAS cadre and officers on deputation from IPS cadre has caused friction in the working of the agency.

Defections & spy scandals

- In early 1980s, K.V. Unnikrishnan, a 1962 batch IPS officer, who was posted at R&AW station in Colombo was honeytrapped by CIA. Between 1985–87 when he was deputed as the station chief at Chennai, co-ordinating Sri Lanka operations, he gave away information to his handler on training and arming Tamil groups including LTTE and the Indian government's negotiating positions on the peace accord with Sri Lanka. He was caught by IB counter-intelligence in 1987, spent a year in Tihar jail and was dismissed from IPS cadre.
- In 2004, there was spy scandal involving the CIA. Rabinder Singh, Joint Secretary and the head of R&AW's South East Asia department, defected to America on 5 June 2004. R&AW had already become suspicious about his movements and he was under surveillance for a very long time. Soon he was confronted by Counter Intelligence officials on 19 April 2004. Despite all precautions, Rabinder Singh managed to defect with 'sensitive files' he had allegedly removed from R&AW's headquarters in south New Delhi. This embarrassing fiasco and national security failure were attributed to weak surveillance, shoddy investigation and lack of co-ordination between the Counter Intelligence and Security (CIS), Intelligence Bureau (IB) and R&AW. According to unconfirmed reports, Singh has surfaced in Virginia, USA. Recently in an affidavit submitted to the court, R&AW deposed that Singh has been traced in New Jersey.

- In 2007, there was a spy scandal involving Bangladesh. A Bangladeshi DGFI agent concealed his nationality before joining R&AW, and was known by the name of Diwan Chand Mallik in the agency. He was known to have some important intel which was damaging for the national security. He joined the agency in 1999 and used to live in East Delhi. A case of cheating and forgery was filed against him at the Lodhi Colony police station on the basis of a complaint by a senior R&AW official.

In popular culture

Unlike Hollywood, which has portrayed FBI, CIA, MI6 etc. in quite a number of films and TV series, Bollywood has been shy to explore the area of espionage, especially R&AW. Unlike CBI, the federal investigative agency of India, whose existence is known to the majority of people, R&AW receives little to no attention from the populace, which seems to be unaware of the existence of such an organisation or even India's internal intelligence agency, the Intelligence Bureau (IB). Excessive secrecy surrounding activities and rare declassification of the information are considered to be the major reasons behind this.

Nevertheless, there were Bollywood films which refer to 'agents', 'espionage', 'terrorism' etc. like Aankhen *(1968, Ramanand Sagar Production, starring Dharmendra, Mala Sinha),* Prem Pujari *starring Dev Anand in 1970, and* Hindustan Ki Kasam *(starring Raaj Kumar, Priya Rajvansh in 1973). However since the late 1990s and early 2000 the following films have openly mentioning R&AW and its allied units, with the intelligence agencies at the centre of the plot.*

Year	*Name of the film*	*Director*
1998	*Such a Long Journey*	Sturla Gunnarsson
2002	*16 December*	Mani Shankar
2003	*The Hero: Love Story of a Spy*	Anil Sharma
2004	*Asambhav*	Rajiv Rai
2008	*Mission Istaanbul*	Apoorva Lakhia
2008	*Maan Gaye Mughal-e-Azam*	Sanjay Chhel
2008	*Chamku*	Kabeer Kaushik
2011	*Aazaan*	Prashant Chadha

2012	*Agent Vinod*	Sriram Raghavan
2012	*Ek Tha Tiger*	Kabir Khan
2013	*D-Day*	Nikhil Advani
2013	*Madras Cafe*	Shoojit Sircar

Apart from Bollywood, the other film industries of India have cashed in on the patriotic appeal of espionage. Telugu movie star Krishna's *Goodachari No. 1* explores the life of an undercover agent working to thwart ISI activities in India. Cine star Bala Krishna's film in the direction of Swarna Subba Rao, *Vijayendra Varma,* is based on a real life story of a R&AW agent; he donned the role of the R&AW officer. The Tamil movie *Ottran* casts Arjun Sarja as a R&AW officer. A 1990s Malayalam film *Highway* portrays Suresh Gopi as a R&AW agent investigating a bomb blast. Kamal Hasan in a film titled *Dasavathaaram* and later a dubbed Hindi version titled *Dashavatar* essayed the role of a Telugu (in original film)/ Bengali (in Hindi version) R&AW operative. *Thandavam* is based on the story of a R&AW agent. The role was played by Vikram (actor). Kamal Haasan played the character of R&AW agent Wisam Ahmed Kashmiri in multilingual *Vishwaroopam,* which explores the R&AW operation in Afghanistan and US to bring down terrorists affiliated to Al Queda.

The thriving entertainment channels in India have started to tap into the theme of Intelligence agencies. *2612* which used to air on Life OK, featured Cabir Maira as a R&AW agent Anand Swami who helps a STF officer Randeep Rathore to save the country from a terrorist attack. *Time Bomb 9/11,* a series aired on Zee TV, featured Rajeev Khandelwal in the role of a R&AW field officer who attempts to defuse a nuclear bomb set in India, as well as saving the life of the Indian prime minister. Zee Bangla featured a serial named *Mohona* where the chief protagonist is a R&AW officer. *Sajda Tere Pyar Mein* a series on Star Plus, features Shaleen Bhanot in the role of a R&AW officer who asks a young woman named Aliya for help in catching a spy named Mahendra Pratap.

2

Formation of R&AW

After the death of Lal Bahadur Shastri, Mrs Indira Gandhi became Prime Minister of India in early 1966. In 1968, she decided to form a separate external intelligence department based on CIA of the United States of America and MI6 of Britain. She selected Kao, who was then the Joint Director in the Intelligence Bureau (IB), for this job. She wanted a loyal man of known integrity. Kao had served as the personal security officer of Pandit Nehru and accompanied Queen Elizabeth and Chou En Lai as Security Officer when they visited India for the first time during Nehru's rule.

Many eyebrows were raised on the selection of Kao – he too was a Kashmiri Pandit like Mrs Gandhi – but she was firm in her decision. Indira Gandhi gave Kao free hand, except for two conditions; that the new organization should be a multi-disciplined one and should not draw its senior personnel exclusively from the IPS and secondly the top two posts could be filled on the discretion of the Prime Minister from within the organization or from outside. Kao prepared a blue print of new intelligence set-up based on detailed studies of CIA, MI6, French intelligence, Mossad and Japanese intelligence.

It was accepted by the Cabinet and the new external intelligence agency, Research and Analysis Wing (RAW), was created on September 21, 1968 with a skeleton staff of 250, which was taken from the IB. K Sankaran Nair, another able officer from IB, was selected as his deputy. The then Director of IB, M M Hooja, fought tooth and nail to deny the new agency the chattels of office, like buildings, furniture, accounts staff and food personnel but with the help of another capable army officer, I S Hassanwalia, RAW started firing on all cylinders within one year.

In the new outfit, Kao, introduced many new divisions based on his studies of various intelligence agencies of the world. Economic intelligence was a distant idea of that era because there was no such concept in the erstwhile IB. This division was then created to monitor various economic developments in the neighbouring countries which could affect the Indian interests, particularly in the field of defence, security and science and technology. Similarly, Information Division, Science and Technology Division, code breaking branch, Satellite Monitoring Division, were also the new chapters opened in RAW. Prior to this, Aviation Research Centre (ARC) and Special Security Bureau (SSB) were his brainchild in the IB after the 1962 war with China. Later on, in the early 1980s, terrorism in Punjab reached its peak and the government needed a guerrilla outfit. Kao created National Security Guards (NSG) in 1982 to address the needs of the government.

When Pakistan army started its brutality in East Pakistan in March, 1971, millions of refugees thronged to India and caused several major problems for the country. Mrs Indira Gandhi could not find a political solution to sort out this grievous situation and asked then Army Chief General Manekshaw to prepare the Indian army for the liberation of Bangladesh. General Manekshaw sought six months time for the preparations. Kao was asked by Mrs Gandhi to prepare ground work for the army before the final assault and use RAW to its optimum capacity in this operation. Kao, with the help of his able colleagues, build up a formidable guerilla force – Mukti Bahini – of more than one lakh Bangladesh refugees. Mukti Bahini created havoc for the Pakistani army in East Pakistan. Besides that, RAW penetrated deep into all the establishments of East and West Pakistan and when Indian army went for the final war on December 3, 1971, 95000 soldiers of Pakistan army were hauled up in Dacca and were made to surrender to the Indian Army before Lt General J S Aurora on December 16, 1971, i.e. within two weeks of the start of army action. This was the biggest and historical achievement for RAW under Kao in the intelligence history of India.

In the North East of India, Sikkim was a strategic state between India and China. There were some internal problems between the ruler of Sikkim and the local population which went beyond the control of the ruler. Kao advised Mrs. Indira Gandhi to annex Sikkim to which she agreed. Kao provided all sort of help to the local politicians of Sikkim who subsequently won the local elections and passed a resolution for accession by India, which was accepted by Indian Parliament. In this bloodless operation of RAW, Sikkim became a part of India as the 22nd State without the intervention of defence forces. This was another feather in the cap of R N Kao.

Nuclear explosion

In May, 1974, India exploded its first nuclear blast at Pokeran in Rajasthan to the utter surprise of many countries, particularly the US. CIA had received 26 reports in 1972 that India was on the verge of exploding a nuclear device or was capable of doing so. Kao was coordinating with the scientists on the operation of security matters. It must be to his credit that he kept the entire programme under wrap and did not allow other nations to penetrate it. Only after the explosion, Pakistan radio made a broadcast at 1 pm on that day and the rest of the world started probing the truth about it. This was another major achievement of this elite intelligence officer of India.

R N Kao had excellent rapport with his various counterparts in other countries. He was a good friend of George Bush Senior, who was Director of CIA in the mid-seventies. Likewise, Sir Maurice Old-field, head of MI6 during this period, was a personal friend of Kao and shared views with him on various art and culture matters besides the routine intelligence sharing. He was the model for 'M', James Bond's secret service chief in the 007 novels of Ian Fleming. He used to come on long vacations in India as personal guest of Kao in the mid-seventies and visited important towns like Jaipur and Jaisalmer on the verge of the desert for relaxation. Mossad chief and French Intelligence also had very excellent rapport with Kao during this period. When Sewsagar Ramgoolam, the Prime Minister of Mauritius visited India in the early seventies, he requested Mrs Gandhi to help his ruling party fight the movement of Militant Mauritian of Paul Beranger. Ramgoolam's party was largely ethnic Indian in composition while Beranger's was the party of the Ceroles, the Africans of the island who spoke "patoix", a mixture of French and African languages. K Sankaran Nair, the number two in RAW, was deputed by Kao to provide all sort of help to Ramgoolam and he won the next elections.

Wali Khan, son of Khan Abdul Ghaffar Khan, the Frontier Gandhi and a stalwart in the independence movement, was living in exile in London in the early-seventies. He was bitter opponent of Bhutto, the new Prime Minister of Pakistan because the North West Frontier Pathans were demanding autonomy which was oppressed by the central government of Pakistan. Wali Khan wanted moral, political and other support from Mrs Indira Gandhi. Kao sent his deputy Sankaran Nair to negotiate as the Indian representative. Since Pakistani Embassy in London was keeping watch on the movements of Wali Khan, the rendezvous was shifted to Copenhagen in Sweden where Nair and another RAW man of Indian mission, I S Hassanwalia, met Wali Khan. Subsequently all sort of support was given to Wali Khan by the Indian government till 1977 when Indira Gandhi lost election and Janta Party came to power.

Unsung hero

Mrs Indira Gandhi imposed emergency in India in June, 1975 and arrested most of the opposition leaders all over the country. There were charges of brutality and torture against these leaders. Ultimately, when in March, 1977, she lifted emergency and was routed in the subsequent parliamentary election. Morarji Desai of Janta Party became the new Prime Minister of India. Since, most of these leaders were recently released from jail they apprehended that RAW was misused by Mrs Indira Gandhi during emergency against these leaders. Kao, who was on an extension as RAW chief was unceremoniously asked by Mroraji Desai to proceed on leave because he suspected him as the prime accused for internal interference during Emergency. Charan Singh, the then Home

Minister of India, appointed a one men committee headed by S P Singh to find out the involvement of RAW in the internal affairs of the country during Emergency in 1975-77. This committee gave clean chit to RAW in this regard and Kao was honourably exonerated for his involvement in Emergency.

When Mrs Indira Gandhi again became Prime Minister in 1980, she recalled Kao from his retirement and appointed him as her senior advisor on internal and external developments. She used to consult him on political and intelligence matters. His professional guidance was of general nature. In one major development, when Mrs Gandhi wanted to go USA she was not getting her choice of appointment date with the US President through External Affairs Ministry channels. Kao through his friend George Bush Senior – who was then US Ambassador in China – arranged her meeting with the US President.

When Mrs Gandhi was assassinated, he was upset over her death and resigned on moral grounds. There were charges against Kao that he did not guide Mrs Gandhi against a possible assassination attack from her security guards which were not substantiated in the Judicial Commission which was appointed subsequently to probe the assassination.

Kao was very affectionately and emotionally linked to his younger brother. His brother had a heart attack and Kao went to see him in the hospital. He could not tolerate the condition of his brother and had a heart attack there. Kao died along with his brother on January 20, 2002.

This unsung hero was forgotten by the Indian Government for his big achievements for the country which had no parallel in this hidden society of Intelligence community. He gave lot to the country but got nothing from the government, though he got decorated so many of his juniors with various awards and rewards of the government.

THE STRUCTURE AND FUNCTION OF RAW

Not much is known regarding the structure of RAW, say experts. The organization started with 250 people and about $400,000. It has since expanded to several thousand personnel, but its staffing and budget remain secret. However, an estimate by the U.S.-based Federation of American Scientists suggests that in 2000, RAW had about eight to ten thousand agents and a budget that experts place at $145 million. Unlike the United States' Central Intelligence Agency (CIA) or Britain's MI6, RAW reports directly to the prime minister instead of the Ministry of Defense. The chief of RAW is designated secretary (research) in the Cabinet Secretariat, which is part of the prime minister's office. Some officers of RAW are members of a specialized service, the Research and Analysis Service, but several officers also serve on deputation from other services such as the Indian Police Service.

RAW had two priorities after its formation, writes B. Raman, a former RAW official, in the 2007 book, *The Kaoboys of R&AW: Down Memory Lane*. The organization worked to strengthen its capability for intelligence gathering on Pakistan and China and for covert action in East Pakistan (now Bangladesh). Some experts say that RAW's efforts in East Pakistan, which was created from the partition of the Indian state of Bengal and completely separated from the rest of Pakistan, was aimed at fomenting independence sentiment. Over time, RAW's objectives have broadened to include:

- Monitoring the political and military developments in adjoining countries, which have direct bearing on India's national security and in the formulation of its foreign policy.
- Seeking the control and limitation of the supply of military hardware to Pakistan, mostly from European countries, the United States, and China.

Experts disagree on the amount of influence RAW asserts on India's foreign policy.Sumit Ganguly, a professor of political science at Indiana University, says the agency has no influence on foreign policy. However, Dipankar Banerjee, a retired army official and founding director of the Institute of Peace and Conflict Studies, a New Delhi-based think tank, says the head of RAW has direct access to the head of state, to whom he provides input and analysis.

From the early days, RAW had a secret liaison relationship with the Mossad, Israel's external intelligence agency. The main purpose was to benefit from Israel's knowledge of West Asia and

North Africa, and to learn from its counterterrorism techniques, say experts.

THE RESEARCH AND ANALYSIS WING WAS NEVER RAW

There has been a great deal of discussion in the media about the effectiveness of our intelligence organizations following the blasts in Hyderabad during the last week of August, which killed 41 persons and injured over 60.

The blasts have followed similar explosions at the Mecca Masjid, also in Hyderabad in May. More intriguing has been the report that the Central Home Ministry knew that there was a distinct possibility of bomb attacks somewhere in the southern states of the country, but had no clue as to where and when it would happen.

There have been reports that the blasts have been engineered by the Inter-Services Intelligence of Pakistan and the Harkat-ul-Jehadi Islami which has its base in Bangladesh. A little over a year ago there were serial bomb blasts in Mumbai Metro Railways.

These tragic incidents have been taking place at regular intervals, in spite of the fact that the Indian Intelligence Bureau, which has been ranked the fourth among all intelligence agencies of the world, has been keeping the Government informed of the dangers facing the country.. The Research and Analysis Wing, (R and AW) responsible for collecting intelligence from outside the country, has enjoyed the reputation as one of the best in the region.

What are our weaknesses? There has been little informed discussion about the intelligence organizations in the country. When something goes wrong, like in Kargil in 1999, the intelligence agencies are blamed. Something similar happened in Sri Lanka in 1987 when the Government decided to send the Indian Peacekeeping Force on tasks which were not clear.

One should, therefore, welcome the recent book "The KAO Boys of the R and AW" by B. Raman, one of the country's outstanding strategic analysts, who was with the organization for 26 years. He has documented the achievements of the R and AW, as well as its 'failures' and has given his own assessment of the organisation.

While the country became independent, we had only one intelligence agency whose domain was all-pervasive. The Army, Navy and the Air Force had their intelligence set ups, but they were recipients of inputs from the Intelligence Bureau. The Research and Analysis Wing was created in 1968.

Following the Kargil War, a Defence Intelligence Organisation and a National Technical Research Organisation have been created. Para-military forces have also spruced up their own intelligence set ups. Some States also have their intelligence units. The different organizations have their own chain of command and are reluctant to share the information collected by them, except in exceptional circumstances.

There are suggestions that India needs a Federal Intelligence Agency on the pattern of the FBI of the United States, but would this be possible, given that states of the country have different political parties holding office, and most are reluctant to permit a Central Agency to look over their shoulders. Law and order being a State subject, the Centre will have difficulty in creating a Federal Intelligence Agency or creating a force which can 'act' against terrorist forces across the country.

The job of coordination is presently done by the National Security Advisor, who has a full time-job which includes strategic policy making. B. Raman says it is time to think in terms of a National Intelligence Advisor, directly answerable to the Prime Minister.

Raman's book could not have come at a better time. Raman himself was the head of the counter-terrorism wing of the R and AW, between 1988 and 1994 and narrowly missed being the head of the agency.

An original KAOBOY, as he calls officers who were recruited by the first head of the Research Wing, Rameshwar Nath Kao, when the agency was created, he has had the opportunity of being closely involved with many events and observing others during his tenure with the organization.

His first assignment in the agency was to keep an eye on developments in Burma. In that capacity, he collected information about the support given by China to Naga hostiles including giving them weapons and military training in remote areas of Burma. The Chinese efforts to promote insurgency in Nagaland and Mizoram, in association with Pakistan, came to an end only after the liberation of Bangladesh.

The Research and Analysis Wing came into limelight for the role it played during the liberation of Bangladesh. The organization had set up a psychological warfare unit, which created awareness both in East Pakistan and all over the world about the misdeeds of the Pakistan Army in the East.

As Raman says, the successful completion of the liberation of Bangladesh was the result of the struggle of people of then East Pakistan, supported by the Indian Army. It was also the R and AWs 'finest hour', and dozens of officers of the organization contributed to its 'brilliant performance under the leadership of Kao and K. Sankaran Nair, his No. 2. As Public Relations Officer of the Army in Delhi, I had the advantage of observing Kao in the office of General SHFJ Manekshaw, during those critical days.

The expansion of the agency, and the setting up of new offices within the country, gave it a larger than life image. It was rumored that the organization was 'spying' on political rivals of Indira Gandhi. When Indira Gandhi lost power after the elections in 1977, Morarji Desai cut down some units, particularly the Information and the Political Divisions. Raman points out that there have been efforts to revive the Information Division, but the adhoc steps have never been able to restore the vision that Kao had.

The Research and Analysis Wing has also had many critics within the bureaucracy. As Raman points out, when they are posted in Embassies abroad, they are given cover assignments. The officers' report directly to their desks at the Headquarters in Delhi, and this has invited criticism that the R and AW has been trying to function as a parallel Foreign Ministry.

The Agency played an important role in countering the Khalistan agitation, which had received ample support from

Pakistan, and even from organizations in the United States. The restrictions imposed on persons arriving in Delhi during the Asian Games and the Non-Aligned summit in 1983 angered Sikhs in Punjab, which provided fuel to the agitation.

The 'Khalistanis', in coordination with the ISI, successfully hijacked Indian Airlines aircraft, which gave a boost to the controversy. Raman reveals how the agency managed to arrest the hijackers on August 24, 1984 in the UAE with the assistance of Romesh Bhandari, then Secretary in the Ministry of External Affairs, which put an end to such attempts.

Raman discloses that the Agency representative had detailed discussions with those holed up in the Akal Takht as suggested by Prime Minister Indira Gandhi, to find a solution to the situation in the Golden Temple Amritsar. The Akal Takht was occupied by late Sant Bhindranwale, who had fortified the place, which was adjacent to the temple.

The Army was asked to clear the Akal Takht, causing the least damage to the structure.. Raman says that General Sunderji was overconfident during the Blue Star operations. He displayed similar overconfidence during the IPKF operations in Sri Lanka, by assuring Rajiv Gandhi, the LTTE could be controlled within a month, a task which the Indian Army could not accomplish for many months.

Raman has detailed the after-effects of Blue Star operations. Kao, who had retired as the head of the R and AW and was Advisor to Indira Gandhi, was away in China on that fateful day when she was shot by her own bodyguards. The assassination of Indira Gandhi, he says, is a 'dark chapter' in the history of the Indian intelligence and security establishment. He says: "She depended on us to protect her. We failed her."

Raman has also given instances when foreign intelligence agencies were able to penetrate the R and AW and the Prime Minister's Office. The defection of Raminder Singh, after he was found, sending information to the CIA is a recent incident.

Earlier, during Rajiv Gandhi's Prime Ministership, Raman discloses, the CIA was able to get from the French external intelligence agency - which had penetrated the office of the Principal

Secretary to the Prime Minister — copies of all reports on Sri Lanka being sent to the PMO by the IB and the R and AW.

Raman's book is candid in many respects. He says the R and AW has only partly fulfilled the purposes for which it was set up by Indira Gandhi and Kao. It is strong in its capability for covert action, weak in its capability for intelligence collection, analysis and assessment. One of its strong points is TECHINT, or technical intelligence. One recalls how it was able to intercept the conversation that General Musharraf, who was on a visit to China, had with his Chief of Staff in Rawalpindi, in 1999.

Among the many suggestions that Raman has made is that the R and AW should be ready to accept external auditing of its management and performance which could identify and eliminate inadequacies and bad practices.

The overall impression that one gets after going through Raman's ' memory lane' is that R and AW was a mature organization right from the beginning not at any time raw.

RAW LEFT WITH EGG ON ITS FACE AS TERROR PLOT UNRAVELS

The Research and Analysis Wing, India's external intelligence service, is facing allegations of incompetence after three Lashkar-e-Taiba operatives who, it claimed, were about to conduct a suicide-squad operation in western India turned out to be living at their homes in Lahore — and to be businessmen, not terrorists.

The Mumbai police issued warnings earlier this week after receiving information on what they said was an imminent plot to target two of India's largest OILrefineries: Reliance Industries' plant at Jamnagar in Gujarat and Mittal Energy's unit at Bhatinda, Punjab.

Five Pakistani Lashkar-e-Taiba operatives, the police alleged in briefings for the media on Wednesday, had infiltrated India to execute the operation.

Though periodic warnings have been issued on the threats to the plant — the last by the Intelligence Bureau in May — this warning was unusually specific, and accompanied by photographs of the Lashkar team.

Late on Wednesday evening though, a Pakistani television show host revealed that the men were living in Lahore: two running shops at the Hafeez shopping complex in Lahore's Gulberg district, and the third a guard employed on the premises.

The revelations led shopkeepers in Lahore to stage demonstrations in support of the two men, while the Jamaat-ud-Dawa said this showed that India falsified information on Pakistani involvement in terrorist strikes, including 26/11. Both men also moved the Lahore High Court on Thursday, seeking protection against any possible action by India, and have told *The Hindu* that they intended to petition the Indian High Commission in Islamabad to be formally exonerated.

No official explanation has been offered by New Delhi for the apparent debacle. A fresh alert was issued in Pune after local intelligence officials warned that the suicide squad could strike the city. The RAW officer with supervisory responsibility for issuing the alerts did not respond to a query from *The Hindu*.

Elusive answers

The testimony from the two men who spoke to *The Hindu* from Lahore threw up as many questions as it answered. Late on Wednesday, shopkeeper Mahtab Butt said he had on a whim used Google to search for the word 'India.' The search led him to an *India Today* group site. There, he discovered a photo of himself, fellow storeowner Atif Butt and night guard Muhammad Babar, illustrating a story on the alleged Mumbai terror plot.

Mr. Butt said he immediately called Pakistani television show host Mubashir Lucman — a controversial figure known for his dogged support of the religious right — with the news.

Three separate Google searches conducted by *The Hindu* did not lead to results with *India Today* on the first page, raising questions about this account —though, in all fairness, results using the site often vary by region.

Later that evening though, both Mr. Butt and Mr. Atif Butt provided *The Hindu* with a quite different version of events. The two men said they had learned of the report from a common friend, whom they identified as Khubaab.

Neither man could explain where the photographs of them — clearly personal in nature, rather than the kinds typically used in passport or driving-licence applications — were taken. Nor did they have any explanation for what led them, or their friend, to search for information on India late in the evening.

Duped by ISI?

Highly placed intelligence sources in New Delhi said the photographs had been obtained from an individual they described as a "trans-border source — a euphemism for smugglers who often conduct espionage in return for some degree of impunity from law-enforcement agencies. The sources noted that the first photographs of the suspects had been released on the Internet at 8.21 p.m., while Mr. Lucman revealed their true identities less than an hour later — fuelling suspicion that the photographs might have been planted by Pakistan's own intelligence services to discredit the RAW. The New Delhi-based intelligence officials said the affair pointed to underlying problems in India's post-26/11 intelligence reforms — key among them, pressure to circulate information before it could be thoroughly corroborated. The intelligence was passed on to the Mumbai police through the Intelligence Bureau-run Multi-Agency Centre — the core of the proposed National Counter-Terrorism Centre — but its credibility does not appear to have been questioned by other agencies.

The intelligence debacle, the RAW's worst fiasco in years, is the latest in a series of embarrassing intelligence failures, among them the listing of individuals held in Indian prisons in a government dossier on the alleged fugitives in Pakistan.

Though there was no corroboration of the threat from other agencies or communications intelligence, the Mumbai Police decided to make the information public. "The consensus," an officer present at the meetings told *The Hindu,* "was that it was best to get the information we had out there, in the hope of at least embarrassing the ISI into calling off the operation. No one wanted to be accused of withholding information, in case something happened."

3

R&AW: An Instrument of Indian Imperialism

The Research and Analysis Wing (RAW), created in 1968, has assumed a significant status in the formulation of India's domestic and foreign policies, particularly the later. Working directly under the Prime Minister, it has over the years become and effective instrument of India's national power. In consonance with Kautilya's precepts, RAW's espionage doctrine is based on the principle of waging a continuous series of battles of intrigues and secret wars.

RAW, ever since its creation, has always been a vital, though unobtrusive, actor in Indian policy-making apparatus. But it is the massive international dimensions of RAW operations that merit a closer examination. To the credit of this organization, it has in very short span of time mastered the art of spy warfare. Credit must go to Indira Gandhi who in the late 1970s gave it a changed and much more dynamic role. To suit her much publicized Indira Doctrine, (actually India Doctrine) Mrs. Gandhi specifically asked RAW to create a powerful organ within the organization which could undertake covert operations in neighbouring countries. It is this capability that makes RAW a more fearsome agency than its superior KGB, CIA, MI-6, BND and the Mossad.

Its internal role is confined only in monitoring events having bearing on the external threat. RAW's boss works directly under the Prime Minister. An Additional Secretary to the Government of India, under the Director RAW, is responsible for the Office of Special Operations (OSO), intelligence collected from different countries, internal security (under the Director General of Security), the electronic/technical section and general administration. The Additional Secretary as well as the Director General of Security is also under the Director of RAW. DG Security has two important sections: the Aviation Research Center (ARC) and the Special Services Bureau (SSB). The joint Director has specified desks with different regional divisions/areas (countries):

Area one. Pakistan: Area two, China and South East Asia: Area three, the Middle East and Africa: and Area four, other countries. Aviation Research Center (ARC) is responsible for interception, monitoring and jamming of target country's communication systems. It has the most sophisticated electronic equipment and also a substantial number of aircraft equipped with state-of- the art eavesdropping devices. ARC was strengthened in mid-1987 by the addition of three new aircraft, the Gulf Stream-3. These aircraft can reportedly fly at an altitude of 52,000 ft and has an operating range of 5000 kms. ARC also controls a number of radar stations located close to India's borders. Its aircraft also carry out oblique reconnaissance, along the border with Bangladesh, China, Nepal and Pakistan.

RAW having been given a virtual carte blanche to conduct destabilization operations in neighbouring countries inimical to India to seriously undertook restructuring of its organization accordingly. RAW was given a list of seven countries (Bangladesh, Sri Lanka, Nepal, Sikkim, Bhutan, Pakistan and Maldives) whom India considered its principal regional protagonists. It very soon systematically and brilliantly crafted covert operations in all these countries to coerce, destabilize and subvert them in consonance with the foreign policy objectives of the Indian Government.

RAW's operations against the regional countries were conducted with great professional skill and expertise. Central to the operations was the establishment of a huge network inside the target countries. It used and targeted political dissent, ethnic divisions, economic backwardness and criminal elements within these states to foment subversion, terrorism and sabotage. Having thus created the conducive environments, RAW stage-managed future events in these countries in such a way that military intervention appears a natural concomitant of the events. In most cases, RAW's hand remained hidden, but more often that not target countries soon began unearthing those "hidden hand". A brief expose of RAW's operations in neighbouring countries would reveal the full expanse of its regional ambitions to suit India Doctrine (Open Secrets. India's Intelligence Unveiled by M K Dhar. Manas Publications, New Delhi, 2005).

BANGLADESH

Indian intelligence agencies were involved in erstwhile East Pakistan, now Bangladesh since early 1960s. Its operatives were in touch with Sheikh Mujib for quite some time. Sheikh Mujib went to Agartala in 1965. The famous Agartala case was unearthed in 1967. In fact, the main purpose of raising RAW in 1968 was to organise covert operations in Bangladesh. As early as in 1968, RAW was given a green signal to begin mobilising all its resources for the impending surgical intervention in erstwhile East Pakistan. When in July 1971 General Manekshaw told Prime Minister Indira Gandhi that the army would not be ready till December to intervene in Bangladesh, she quickly turned to RAW for help. RAW was ready. Its officers used Bengali refugees to set up Mukti Bahini. Using this outfit as a cover, Indian military sneaked deep into Bangladesh. The story of Mukti Bahini and RAW's role in its creation and training is now well-known. RAW never concealed its Bangladesh operations.

Interested readers may have details in Asoka Raina's Inside RAW: the story of India's secret service published by Vikas Publishing House of New Delhi. The creation of Bangladesh was masterminded by RAW in complicity with KGB under the covert clauses of Indo-Soviet Treaty of Friendship and Co-operation (adopted as 25-year Indo-Bangladesh Treaty of Friendship and Co-operation in 1972).

RAW retained a keen interest in Bangladesh even after its independence. Mr. Subramaniam Swamy, Janata Dal MP, a close associate of Morarji Desai said that Rameswar Nath Kao, former Chief of RAW, and Shankaran Nair upset about Sheikh Mujib's assassination chalked a plot to kill General Ziaur Rahman. However, when Morarji Desai came into power in 1977 he was indignant at RAW's role in Bangladesh and ordered operations in Bangladesh to be called off; but by then RAW had already gone too far. General Zia continued to be in power for quite some time but he was assassinated after Indira Gandhi returned to power, though she denied her involvement in his assassination (Weekly Sunday,Calcutta,18 September, 1988).

RAW was involved in training of Chakma tribals and Shanti Bahini who carry out subversive activities in Bangladesh. It has also unleashed a well-organized plan of psychological warfare, creation of polarisation among the armed forces, propaganda by false allegations of use of Bangladesh territory by ISI, creation of dissension's among the political parties and religious sects, control of media, denial of river waters, and propping up a host of disputes in order to keep Bangladesh under a constant political and socio-economic pressure (" RAW and Bangladesh" by Mohammad Zainal Abedin, November 1995, RAW In Bangladesh: Portrait of an Aggressive Intelligence, written and published by Abu Rushd, Dhaka).

SIKKIM AND BHUTAN

Sikkim was the easiest and most docile prey for RAW. Indira Gandhi annexed the Kingdom of Sikkim in mid-1970s, to be an integral part of India. The deposed King Chogyal Tenzig Wangehuck was closely followed by RAW's agents until his death in 1992.

Bhutan, like Nepal and Sikkim, is a land-locked country, totally dependent on India. RAW has developed links with members of the royal family as well as top bureaucrats to implements its policies. It has cultivated its agents amongst Nepalese settlers and is in a position to create difficulties for the Government of Bhutan. In fact, the King of Bhutan has been reduced to the position of merely acquiescing into New Delhi's decisions and go by its dictates in the international arena.

SRI LANKA

Post-independence Sri Lanka, inspire of having a multi-sectoral population was a peaceful country till 1971 and was following independent foreign policy. During 1971 Indo-Pakistan war despite of heavy pressure from India, Sri Lanka allowed Pakistan's civil and military aircraft and ships to stage through its air and sea ports with unhindered re-fueling facilities. It also had permitted Israel to establish a nominal presence of its intelligence training set up. It permitted the installation of high powered transmitter by Voice of America (VOA) on its territory, which was resented by India.

It was because of these 'irritants' in the Indo-Sri Lanka relations that Mrs Indira Gandhi planned to bring Sri Lanka into the fold of the so-called Indira Doctrine (India Doctrine) Kao was told by Gandhi to repeat their Bangladesh success. RAW went looking for militants it could train to destabilize the regime. Camps were set up in Tamil Nadu and old RAW guerrillas trainers were dug out of retirement. RAW began arming the Tamil Tigers and training them at centers such as Gunda and Gorakhpur. As a sequel to this ploy, Sri Lanka was forced into Indian power-web when Indo-Sri Lanka Accord of 1987 was singed and Indian Peace-Keeping-Force (IPKF) landed in Sri Lanka.

The Ministry of External Affairs was also upset at RAW's role in Sri Lanka as they felt that RAW was still continuing negotiations with the Tamil Tiger leader Parabhakran in contravention to the Indian government's foreign policy. According to R Swaminathan, (former Special Secretary of RAW) it was this outfit which was used as the intermediary between Rajib Gandhi and Tamil leader Parabhakaran. The former Indian High Commissioner in Sri Lanka, J.N. Dixit even accused RAW of having given Rs. five corore to the LTTE. At a later stage, RAW built up the EPRLF and ENDLF to fight against the LTTE which turned the situation in Sri Lanka highly volatile and uncertain later on.

MALDIVES

Under a well-orchestrated RAW plan, on November 30 1988 a 300 to 400-strong well trained force of mercenaries, armed with automatic weapons, initially said to be of unknown origin, infiltrated in boats and stormed the capital of Maldives. They resorted to indiscriminate shooting and took high-level government officials as hostages. At the Presidential Palace, the small contingent of loyal national guards offered stiff resistance, which enabled President Maumoon Abdul Gayoom to shift to a safe place from where he issued urgent appeals for help from India, Pakistan, Sri Lanka, Britain and the United States.

The Indian Prime Ministe Rajiv Gandhi reacted promptly and about 1600 combat troops belonging to 50 Independent Para-Brigade in conjunction with Indian Naval units landed at Male under the code-name Operation Cactus. A number of IAF transport aircraft, escorted by fighters, were used for landing personnel, heavy equipment and supplies.

Within hours of landing, the Indian troops flushed out the attackers form the streets and hideouts. Some of them surrendered to Indian troops, and many were captured by Indian Naval units while trying to escape along with their hostages in a Maldivian ship, Progress Light. Most of the 30 hostages including Ahmed Majtaba, Maldives Minister of Transport, were released. The Indian Government announced the success of the Operation Cactus and complimented the armed forces for a good job done.

The Indian Defense Minister while addressing IAF personnel at Bangalore claimed that the country's prestige has gone high because of the peace-keeping role played by the Indian forces in Maldives.

The International Community in general and the South Asian states in particular, however, viewed with suspicious the over-all concept and motives of the operation. The western media described it as a display of newly-acquired military muscle by India and its growing role as a regional police. Although the apparent identification of the two Maldivian nationals could be a sufficient reason, at its face value, to link it with the previous such attempts by the mercenaries, yet other converging factors, indicative of involvement of external hand, could hardly be ignored. Sailing of the mercenaries from Manar and Kankasanturai in Sri Lanka, which were in complete control of IPKF, and the timing and speed of the Indian intervention proved their involvement beyond any doubt.

NEPAL

Ever since the partition of the sub-continent India has been openly meddling in Nepal's internal affairs by contriving internal strife and conflicts through RAW to destabilize the successive legitimate governments and prop up puppet regimes which would be more amenable Indian machinations. Armed insurrections were sponsored and abetted by RAW and later requests for military assistance to control these were managed through pro-India leaders. India has been aiding and inciting the Nepalese dissidents to collaborate with the Nepali Congress. For this they were supplied arms whenever the King or the Nepalese Government appeared to be drifting away from the Indian dictates and impinging on Indian hegemonic designs in the region. In fact, under the garb of the so-called democratization measures, the Maoists were actively encouraged to collect arms to resort to open rebellion against the legitimate Nepalese governments. The contrived rebellions provided India an opportunity to intervene militarily in Nepal, ostensibly to control the insurrections which were masterminded by the RAW itself. It was an active replay of the Indian performance in Sri Lanka and Maldives a few years earlier. RAW is particularly aiding the people of the Indian-origin and has been providing them with arms and ammunition. RAW has also infiltrated the ethnic Nepali refugees who have been extradited by Bhutan and have taken refuge in the eastern Nepal. RAW can exploit its links with these refugees in either that are against the Indian interest. Besides the Nepalese economy is totally controlled by the Indian money lenders, financiers and business mafia (RAW's Machination In South Asia by Shastra Dutta Pant, Kathmandu, 2003).

AFGHANISTAN

Since December 1979, throughout Afghan War, KGB, KHAD (WAD) (former Afghan intelligence outfit) and RAW stepped up their efforts to concentrate on influencing and covert exploitation of the tribes on both sides of the Pakistan-Afghanistan border. There was intimate co-ordination between the three intelligence agencies not only in Afghanistan but in destabilization of Pakistan through subversion and sabotage plan related to Afghan refugees and mujahideen, the tribal belt and inside Pakistan. They jointly organized spotting and recruitment of hostile tribesmen and their training in guerrilla warfare, infiltration, subversion, sabotage and establishment of saboteur force/terrorist organizations in the pro-Afghan tribes of Pakistan in order to carry out bomb explosions in Afghan refugee camps in NWFP and Baluchistan to threaten and pressure them to return to Afghanistan. They also carried out bomb blasts in populated areas deep inside Pakistan to create panic and hatred in the minds of locals against Afghan refugee mujahideen for pressurizing Pakistan to change its policies on Afghanistan.

PAKISTAN

Pakistan's size, strength and potential have always overawed the Indians. It, therefore, always considers her main opponent in her expansionist doctrine. India's animosity towards Pakistan is psychologically and ideologically deep-rooted and unassailable. India's war with Pakistan in 1965 over Kashmir and in 1971 which resulted in the dismemberment of Pakistan and creation of Bangladesh are just two examples.

Raw considers Sindh as Pakistan's soft under-belly. It has, therefore, made it the prime target for sabotage and subversion. RAW has enrolled and extensive network of agents and anti-government elements, and is convinced that with a little push restless Sindh will revolt. Taking fullest advantage of the agitation in Sindh in 1983 and the ethnic riots, which have continued till today, RAW has deeply penetrated and cultivated dissidents and secessionists, thereby creating hard-liners unlikely to allow peace to return to Sindh. Raw is also involved similarly in Balochistan.

RAW is also being blamed for confusing the ground situation is Kashmir so as to keep the world attention away from the gross human rights violations by India in India occupied Kashmir. ISI being almost 20 years older than RAW and having acquired much higher standard of efficiency in its functioning, has become the prime target of RAW's designs, ISI is considered to be a stumbling block in RAW's operations, and has, therefore, been made a target of all kinds of massive misinformation and propaganda campaign. The tirade against ISI continues unabated. The idea is to keep ISI on the defensive by fictionalising and alleging its hand is supporting Kashmiri Mujahideen and Sikhs in Punjab. RAW'S fixation against ISI has taken the shape of ISI-phobia, as in India everyone traces down the origin of all happenings and shortcomings to the ISI. Be it an abduction at Banglaore or a student's kidnapping at Cochin, be it a bank robbery at Calcutta or a financial scandal in Bombay, be it a bomb blast at Bombay or Bangladesh, they find an ISI hand in it (RAW :GLOBAL AND REGIONAL AMBITIONS" Edited by Rashid Ahmad Khan and Muhammad Saleem, Published by Islamabad Policy Research Institute, Asia Printers, slamabad, 2005).

RAW over the years has admirably fulfilled its tasks of destabilising target states through unbridled export of terrorism. The India Doctrine spelt out a difficult and onerous role for RAW. It goes to its credit that it has accomplished its assigned objectives due to the endemic weakness in the state apparatus of those nations and failure of their leaders.

RAW'S ROLE IN BANGLADESH, MYANMAR, AND SRI LANKA

RAW played a significant role in the formation of Bangladesh along with the Indian army and other Indian security and intelligence agencies. Besides providing intelligence to policymakers and the army, RAW trained and armed Mukti Bahini, a group of East Pakistanis fighting for the separate state of Bangladesh. Analysts say that RAW also facilitated the northeastern state of Sikkim's accession to India in 1975, and provided military assistance to groups hostile to the pro-China regime in Myanmar, such as the Kachin Independence Army. But it was the support for the Tamil separatist group, Liberation Tigers of Tamil Eelam (LTTE) in Sri Lanka, that brought RAW much criticism from human rights organizations. RAW helped train and arm the LTTE in the 1970s, but after the group's terrorist activities grew in the 1980s-including its alliances with separatist groups in the southern Indian state of Tamil Nadu-RAW withdrew this support. In 1987, New Delhimade a pact with the Sri Lankan government to send peacekeeping troops to the island, and Indian forces ended up fighting the group RAW had armed. In 1991, Rajiv Gandhi, prime minister of India at the time of the peacekeeping force deployment, was assassinated by an LTTE suicide bomber.

It was the support for the Tamil separatist group, Liberation Tigers of Tamil Eelam in Sri Lanka, that brought RAW much criticism from human rights organizations.

Covert Action in Afghanistan and Pakistan

Since its inception in 1968, RAW has had a close liaison relationship with KHAD, the Afghan intelligence agency, due to the intelligence it has provided RAW on Pakistan. This relationship was further strengthened in the early 1980s when the foundation was laid for a trilateral cooperation involving RAW, KHAD, and the Soviet KGB. Raman says RAW valued KHAD's cooperation for monitoring the activities of Sikh militants in Pakistan's tribal areas. Sikhs in the Indian state of Punjab were demanding an independent state of Khalistan. According to Raman, Pakistan's ISI set up clandestine camps for training and arming Khalistani recruits in Pakistan's Punjab Province and North West Frontier Province. During this time, the ISI received large sums from Saudi Arabia and the CIA for arming the Afghan mujahadeen against Soviet troops in Afghanistan. "The ISI diverted part of these funds and arms and ammunition to the Khalistani terrorists," alleges Raman.

In retaliation, in the mid-1980s, RAW set up two covert groups of its own, Counter Intelligence Team-X (CIT-X) and Counter Intelligence Team-J (CIT-J), the first targeting Pakistan in general and the second directed at Khalistani groups. The two groups were responsible for carrying out terrorist operations inside Pakistan, writes Pakistani military expert Ayesha Siddiqa. Indian journalist, Praveen Swami, writes that a "low-grade but steady campaign of bombings in major Pakistani cities, notably Karachi and Lahore" was carried out. This forced the head of ISI to meet his counterpart in RAW and agree on the rules of engagement as far as Punjab was concerned, writes Siddiqa. The negotiation was brokered by then-Jordanian Crown Prince Hassan bin-Talal, whose wife, Princess Sarvath, is of Pakistani origin. "It was agreed that

Pakistan would not carry out activities in the Punjab as long as RAW refrained from creating mayhem and violence inside Pakistan," Siddiqa writes.

In the past, Pakistan also accused RAW of supporting Sindhi nationalists demanding a separate state, as well as Seraikis calling for a partition of Pakistan's Punjab to create a separate Seraiki state. India denies these charges. However, experts point out that India has supported insurgents in Pakistan's Balochistan, as well as anti-Pakistan forces in Afghanistan. But some experts say India no longer does this. As this Backgrounder explains, Pakistan is suspicious of India's influence in Afghanistan, which it views as a threat to its own interests in the region. Experts say although it is very likely that India has active intelligence gathering in Afghanistan, it is difficult to say whether it is also involved in covert operations.

Relations with the CIA

The CIA assisted in the creation of RAW, says South Asia expert Stephen P. Cohen of the Brookings Institution. However, India's intelligence relations with the CIA started even before the existence of RAW, note experts. After India's war with China in 1962, CIA instructors trained Establishment 22, a "covert organisation raised from among Tibetan refugees in India, to execute deep-penetration terror operations in China," wrote Swami.

But the CIA's operations with the ISI to fight the Soviets in Afghanistan in the 1980s made RAW very wary. However, it did not stop RAW from seeking the CIA's assistance in counterterrorism training. Raman writes: "One had one more bizarre example of how international intelligence cooperation works." The CIA trained the officers of the ISI in the use of terrorism against an adversary, and at the same time, he writes, it trained RAW and IB officers "in some of the techniques of countering that terrorism." India's intelligence agencies also feel the lack of an equal relationship with the CIA, say experts. Swami says RAW's grievance is that they get little information on Pakistan from the United States; however, Washington expects New Delhi to provide it with intelligence on Afghanistan.

In 1997, Prime Minister I.K. Gujral shut down both the CITs aimed at Pakistan on moral grounds. Before Gujral, Prime Minister P.V. Narasimha Rao had ended RAW's eastern operations in the early 1990s, as part of his efforts to build bridges with China and Myanmar, say analysts.

Successive RAW leaders attempted to gain fresh authorization for deterrent covert operations, but without success, says Swami. Siddiqa wrote: "The Indian government probably realized that encouraging covert warfare would not only destabilize bilateral relations but was also dangerous for the peace and stability of the entire region."

R.A.W.: AN INSTRUMENT OF INDIAN IMPERIALISM

India's intelligence agency Research and Analysis Wing (R.A.W.), created in 1968, has assumed a significant status in the formulation of the country's domestic and foreign policies, particularly the latter. Working directly under the prime minister, it has over the years become an effective instrument of India's national power. In consonance with Kautilya's precepts, R.A.W.'s espionage doctrine is based on the principle of waging a continuous series of battles of intrigues and secret wars. (Kautilya, or more popularly, Chânakya, was an ancient Indian political theorist.)

Since its creation, R.A.W. has been a vital, though unobtrusive, actor in the Indian policy-making apparatus. But it is the massive international dimensions of R.A.W. operations that merit a closer examination. To the credit of this organization, it has in a very short span of time mastered the art of spy warfare. Credit must go to Indira Gandhi who in the late 1970's gave it a changed and much more dynamic role. To suit her much publicized Indira Doctrine (India Doctrine), Gandhi specifically asked R.A.W. to create a powerful organ within the organization that could undertake covert operations in neighbouring countries. It is this capability that makes R.A.W. a more fearsome agency than the superior K.G.B., C.I.A., M.I.6, B.N.D., or Mossad.

Its internal role is confined only to monitoring events that have a bearing on the external threat. R.A.W.'s boss works directly under the prime minister. An Additional secretary to the government of India, under the director of R.A.W., is responsible for the Office of Special Operations, intelligence collected from different countries, internal security (under the director general of security), the electronic/technical section, and general administration. The additional secretary as well as the director general of security is also under the director of R.A.W. The director of security has two important sections: the Aviation Research Center and the Special Services Bureau. The joint director has specified desks with different regional divisions/areas (countries): area one, Pakistan; area two, China and Southeast Asia; area three, the Middle East and Africa; and area four, other countries.

The Aviation Research Center (A.R.C.) is responsible for interception, monitoring and jamming of a target country's communication systems. It has the most sophisticated electronic equipment and also a substantial number of aircraft equipped with state-of-the-art eavesdropping devices. A.R.C. was strengthened in mid-1987 by the addition of three new aircraft, all Gulf Stream-3s. These aircraft can reportedly fly at an altitude of 52,000 feet and have an operating range of 5,000 kilometers. A.R.C. also controls a number of radar stations located close to India's borders. Its aircraft also carry out oblique reconnaissance, along the border with Bangladesh, China, Nepal, and Pakistan.

Having been given virtual carte blanche to conduct destabilization operations in neighbouring countries inimical to India, R.A.W. seriously undertook restructuring of its organization accordingly. R.A.W. was given a list of seven countries—Bangladesh, Sri Lanka, Nepal, Sikkim, Bhutan, Pakistan, and Maldives—that India considered its principal regional protagonists. It very soon systematically and brilliantly crafted covert operations in all these countries to coerce, destabilize, and subvert them in consonance with the foreign policy objectives of the Indian government.

R.A.W.'s operations against the regional countries were conducted with great professional skill and expertise. Central to the operations was the establishment of a huge network inside the target countries. It used and targeted political dissent, ethnic divisions, economic backwardness, and criminal elements within these states to foment subversion, terrorism, and sabotage. Having thus created conducive environments, R.A.W. stage-managed future events in these countries in such a way that military intervention appears a natural concomitant of the events. In most cases, R.A.W.'s hand remained hidden, but more often than not target countries soon began unearthing this "hidden hand." A brief expose of R.A.W.'s operations in neighbouring countries, "Open Secrets: India's Intelligence Unveiled " by M. K. Dhar (Manas Publications, New Delhi, 2005), revealed the full expanse of its regional ambitions to suit the India Doctrine.

Bangladesh

Indian intelligence agencies were involved in erstwhile East Pakistan, now Bangladesh, beginning in the early 1960's. Its operatives were in touch with Sheikh Mujib for quite some time. Sheikh Mujib went to Agartala in 1965. The famous Agartala case was unearthed in 1967. In fact, the main purpose of raising R.A.W. in 1968 was to organize covert operations in Bangladesh. As early as 1968, R.A.W. was given a green light to begin mobilizing all its resources for the impending surgical intervention in erstwhile East Pakistan. When in July 1971 General Manekshaw told Prime Minister Indira Gandhi that the army would not be ready until December to intervene in Bangladesh, she quickly turned to R.A.W. for help. R.A.W. was ready. Its officers used Bengali refugees to set up the guerilla force Mukti Bahini. Using this outfit as a cover, the Indian military sneaked deep into Bangladesh. The story of Mukti Bahini and R.A.W.'s role in its creation and training is now well known. R.A.W. never concealed its Bangladesh operations. (See Asoka Raina's "Inside R.A.W.: the story of India's Secret Service, Vikas Publishing House of New Delhi.)

The creation of Bangladesh was masterminded by R.A.W. in complicity with the K.G.B. under the covert clauses of the Indo-Soviet Treaty of Friendship and Cooperation (adopted as the 25-Year Indo-Bangladesh Treaty of Friendship and Cooperation in 1972).

R.A.W. retained a keen interest in Bangladesh even after its independence. Subramaniam Swamy, Janata Dal member of

Parliament, a close associate of Morarji Desai, said that Rameswar Nath Kao, former chief of R.A.W., and Shankaran Nair were upset about Sheikh Mujib's assassination and chalked a plot to kill Gen. Ziaur Rahman. However, when Desai came to power in 1977 he was indignant at R.A.W.'s role in Bangladesh and ordered operations in Bangladesh to be called off; but by then R.A.W. had already gone too far. General Zia continued in power for quite some time but was assassinated after Indira Gandhi returned to power, though she denied involvement in his assassination (*Weekly Sunday*, Calcutta, Sept. 18, 1988).

R.A.W. was involved in training of Chakma tribes and Shanti Bahini, who carried out subversive activities in Bangladesh. It also unleashed a well-organized plan of psychological warfare, created polarization among the armed forces, propagated false allegations of the use of Bangladesh territory by Pakistan's Inter-Services Intelligence agency, created dissension among the political parties and religious sects, controlled the media, denied the use of river waters, and propped up a host of disputes in order to keep Bangladesh under constant political and socio-economic pressure (See "R.A.W. and Bangladesh" by Mohammad Zainal Abedin, November 1995, and "R.A.W. in Bangladesh: Portrait of an Aggressive Intelligence," written and published by Abu Rushd, Dhaka).

Sikkim and Bhutan

Sikkim was the easiest and most docile prey for R.A.W. Indira Gandhi annexed the Kingdom of Sikkim in the mid-1970's. The deposed King Chogyal Tenzig Wangehuck was closely followed by R.A.W.'s agents until his death in 1992.

Bhutan, like Nepal and Sikkim, is a land-locked country totally dependent on India. R.A.W. developed links with members of the royal family as well as top bureaucrats to implements its policies. It cultivated agents from among Nepalese settlers and put itself in a position to create difficulties for the government of Bhutan. In fact, the king of Bhutan has been reduced to the position of merely acquiescing to New Delhi's decisions and goes by its dictates in the international arena.

Sri Lanka

Post-independence Sri Lanka, despite having a multi-sectoral population, was a peaceful country until 1971 and was following an independent foreign policy. During the 1971 Indo-Pakistan war, despite heavy pressure from India, Sri Lanka allowed Pakistan's civil and military aircraft and ships to stage through its air and seaports with unhindered refueling facilities. It had also permitted Israel to establish a nominal intelligence presence and permitted the installation of a high-powered transmitter by Voice of America, which was resented by India.

It was because of these "irritants" that Indira Gandhi planned to bring Sri Lanka into the fold of the so-called Indira Doctrine (India Doctrine). Kao was told by Gandhi to repeat their Bangladesh success. R.A.W. went looking for militants it could train to destabilize the regime. Camps were set up in Tamil Nadu and old R.A.W. guerrilla trainers were dug out of retirement. R.A.W. began arming the Tamil Tigers and training them at centers such as Gunda and Gorakhpur. As a sequel to this ploy, Sri Lanka was forced into the Indian power web when the Indo-Sri Lanka Accord of 1987 was singed and the Indian Peacekeeping Force landed in Sri Lanka. The Ministry of External Affairs was upset at R.A.W.'s role in Sri Lanka as they felt that R.A.W. was continuing negotiations with Tamil Tiger leader Parabhakaran in contravention to the Indian government's foreign policy. According to R. Swaminathan, (former special secretary of R.A.W.) it was this outfit that was used as the intermediary between Rajib Gandhi and Tamil leader Parabhakaran. Former Indian high commissioner in Sri Lanka J. N. Dixit even accused R.A.W. of having given 10 million rupees to the L.T.T.E. (Liberation Tigers of Tamil Eelam). At a later stage, R.A.W. built up the E.P.R.L.F. (Eelam People's Revolutionary Liberation Front) and E.N.D.L.F. (Eelam National Democratic Liberation Front) to fight against the L.T.T.E., which made the situation in Sri Lanka highly volatile and uncertain later on.

Maldives

Under a well-orchestrated R.A.W. plan, on Nov. 30, 1988, a 300- to 400-strong well-trained force of mercenaries armed with automatic weapons, initially said to be of unknown origin, infiltrated in boats and stormed the capital of Maldives. They resorted to indiscriminate shooting and took high-level government officials hostage. At the Presidential Palace, the small contingent of loyal national guards offered stiff resistance, which enabled President Maumoon Abdul Gayoom to move to a safe place where he issued urgent appeals for help from India, Pakistan, Sri Lanka, Britain, and the United States.

Indian Prime Minister Rajiv Gandhi reacted promptly and about 1,600 combat troops belonging to the 50th Independent Para-Brigade in conjunction with Indian naval units landed at Male, the capital of Maldives, under the code name Operation Cactus. A number of Indian air force transport aircraft, escorted by fighters, were used for landing personnel, heavy equipment, and supplies. Within hours of landing, Indian troops flushed out the attackers from the streets and hideouts. Some of them surrendered to Indian troops, and many were captured by Indian naval units while trying to escape with their hostages in a Maldivian ship, Progress Light. Most of the 30 hostages, including Ahmed Majtaba, Maldives' minister of transport, were released. The Indian government announced the success of Operation Cactus and complimented the armed forces for a good job done.

The Indian defense minister, while addressing air force personnel at Bangalore, claimed that the country's prestige had been raised because of the peace-keeping role played by Indian forces in Maldives. The international community in general and South Asian states in particular, however, viewed with suspicion the over-all concept and motives of the operation. The Western media described it as a display by India of its newly acquired military muscle and its growing role as a regional police force. Although the apparent identification of two Maldivian nationals among the mercenaries, at face value, link it with previous such attempts, other converging factors indicative of external involvement could hardly be ignored. That the mercenaries sailed from Manar and Kankasanturai in Sri Lanka, which were in complete control of the Indian Peacekeeping Force, and the timing and speed of India's intervention proved its involvement beyond any doubt.

Nepal

Since the partition of the subcontinent, India has openly meddled in Nepal's internal affairs by contriving internal strife and conflicts through R.A.W. to destabilize the successive legitimate governments and prop up puppet regimes that would be more amenable to Indian machinations. Armed insurrections were sponsored and abetted by R.A.W. and later requests for military assistance to control these conflicts were managed through pro-India leaders. India has been aiding and inciting the Nepalese dissidents to collaborate with the Nepali Congress. For this they were supplied arms whenever the king or the Nepalese government appeared to be drifting away from India's dictates and impinging on India's hegemonic designs in the region. In fact, under the garb of the so-called democratization measures, the Maoists were actively encouraged to collect arms and resort to open rebellion against the legitimate Nepalese governments. The contrived rebellions provided India an opportunity to intervene militarily in Nepal, ostensibly to control the insurrections, which were masterminded by R.A.W. itself. It was an active replay of the Indian performance in Sri Lanka and Maldives a few years earlier. R.A.W. is particularly aiding the people of Indian origin and has been providing them with arms and ammunition. R.A.W. has also infiltrated the ethnic Nepali refugees who have been extradited by Bhutan and taken refuge in eastern Nepal. R.A.W. can exploit its links with these refugees whenever either country goes against Indian interests. Besides, the Nepalese economy is totally controlled by Indian moneylenders, financiers, and business mafia. (See "R.A.W.'s Machinations in South Asia" by Shastra Dutta Pant, Kathmandu, 2003.)

Afghanistan

Since December 1979, throughout the Afghan War, the K.G.B., K.H.A.D. (W.A.D.) (a former Afghan intelligence outfit), and R.A.W. stepped up their efforts to concentrate on influencing and covertly exploiting the tribes on both sides of the Pakistan-Afghanistan border. There was intimate coordination between the three intelligence agencies not only in Afghanistan but also in Pakistan, where destabilization was sought through a subversion and sabotage plan related to Afghan refugees and mujahideen in the tribal belt and inside Pakistan. They jointly organized spotting and recruitment of hostile tribesmen and trained them in guerrilla warfare, infiltration, subversion, sabotage, and the establishment of saboteur forces/terrorist organizations in the pro-Afghan tribes of Pakistan in order to carry out bombings in Afghan refugee camps in the Northwest Frontier province (NWFP) and Baluchistan to threaten and pressure them to return to Afghanistan. They also carried out bomb blasts in populated areas deep inside Pakistan to create panic and hatred in the minds of locals against Afghan refugee mujahideen to pressure Pakistan to change its policies on Afghanistan.

Pakistan

Pakistan's size, strength, and potential have always overawed India. It has always considered Pakistan to be the main opponent to its expansionist doctrine. India's animosity toward Pakistan is psychologically and ideologically deep-rooted and unassailable. India's 1965 and 1971 wars with Pakistan over Kashmir, which resulted in the dismemberment of Pakistan and the creation of Bangladesh, are just two examples.

R.A.W. considers Sindh province to be Pakistan's soft underbelly. It has made it the prime target for sabotage and subversion. R.A.W. has enrolled an extensive network of agents and antigovernment elements and is convinced that with a little push restless Sindh will revolt. Taking full advantage of the agitation in Sindh in 1983, and the periodic ethnic riots, which have continued to today, R.A.W. has deeply penetrated Sindh and cultivated dissidents and secessionists, thereby creating hard-liners unlikely to allow peace to return to Sindh. R.A.W. is also similarly involved in Baluchistan.

R.A.W. is also being blamed for confusing the ground situation is Kashmir so as to keep the world's attention away from the gross human rights violations in Indian-occupied Kashmir. Pakistan's Inter-Services Intelligence agency (I.S.I.), being almost 20 years older than R.A.W. and having acquired a much higher standard of efficiency in its functioning, has become the prime target of R.A.W.'s designs. The I.S.I. is considered to be a stumbling block in R.A.W.'s operations and has been made a target of massive misinformation and propaganda campaigns. The tirade against I.S.I. continues unabated. The idea is to keep I.S.I. on the defensive by alleging that it has had a hand in supporting the Kashmiri mujahideen and the Sikhs in Punjab. R.A.W.'s fixation on I.S.I. has taken the shape of I.S.I.-phobia, as in India everyone traces the origin of all happenings and shortcomings to the I.S.I. Whenever and wherever there is a kidnapping, a bank robbery, a financial scandal, a bomb blast, or what have you, the I.S.I. is deemed to have had a hand in it. (See "R.A.W.: Global and Regional Ambitions" edited by Rashid Ahmad Khan and Muhammad Saleem, Islamabad Policy Research Institute, Asia Printers, Islamabad, 2005).

In summary, R.A.W. over the years has admirably fulfilled its tasks of destabilizing target states through the unbridled export of terrorism. The Indira Doctrine spelt out a difficult and onerous role for R.A.W. It goes to its credit that it has accomplished its assigned objectives due to the endemic weakness in the state apparatus of these nations and the failures of their leaders.

INDIAN ENCROACHMENT IN AFGHANISTAN: A NEW IMPERIALISM IN THE MAKING

Geo-Strategic and geo-political landscape of the South Asia over the past sixty-one years has mostly remained turbulent mainly because of Indian hegemonic designs towards its neighbors. India is one of the very rare countries, if not the only country, that has inimical relationship with all of its neighbors. Assuming itself a dominant power in this Indo-centric region where all states of South Asia are sharing physical borders with India, India, as policy objectives, has not only been strengthening itself militarily in order to assert her dominant position but also preventing outsiders from encouraging the regional powers that may challenge India's hegemonic ambitions. Strategic thinking of the Indian foreign policy revolved around the obsession that its politico-strategic boundary runs via Kandahar and Kabul. A glance over its policy moves, clearly points to its imperialistic mind-set whereby she seems anxious to dominate the entire region by imposing its will. Following the footprints of American Empire, it introduced Indira Doctrine, Rajeve Doctrine and Gujral Doctrine to keep all of its neighbours under influence of its hard and soft power and deprived them of any out side help. Under the self assumed responsibility of regional policeman, India with her coercive diplomacy has successfully brought almost all South Asian states such as, Nepal, Bhutan, and Sri Lanka within ambit of its informal regional security system through formal treaties, agreements and accords. Probably Pakistan is the only country that has refused to be browbeaten. Rajiv Gandhi, in 1987, sent Indian troops to Sri Lanka to suppress Tamil freedom fighters, which his mother and he trained and armed earlier on. Though Bangladesh and Maldives are apparently out of Indian security system, but for all practical purposes, both of these states are covertly dove-tailed to Indian strategic plans. Amongst all the South Asian states, India has been the only country that has frequently used forces against its neighbours. Pakistan alone has been resolutely guarding its sovereignty and vehemently resisting Indian nefarious imperialistic designs. Since India never accepted open heartedly the creation of Pakistan therefore it has all along been busy in interfering and destabilizing this country. India combined all tools including sabotage, internal dissention, coercion and enflaming ethnic issues and discords of other states with Pakistan.

India could not feel satisfied even after the dismemberment of East Pakistan and stepped up its efforts in Afghanistan to make Pakistan worried about its Western borders as well. Indian hegemonic pursuits involve the outsiders and non-regional powers when needed even though she vehemently denies the same privileges to other states in the region. Indian doctrine of imperialism and hygmonism with respect to its weaker neighbors is in play till today. Not only should countries in South Asia seek military assistance from India first when they have a need but they should also get India's approval for conducting peace talks to settle their internal conflicts. However, Pakistan has to face multi-directional and multi dimensional intrigues/threats to its security as a cost of challenging the hegemonic tendencies of India. India's misguided pursuit of regional supremacy, desire for politico-military hegemony over Pakistan, its obsession for control over South Asia are the main causes that have motivated her to lay tentacles in Afghanistan against Pakistan. Indian support of the US invasion of Afghanistan was motivated by anti-Pakistan sentiments and were not meant for ending terrorism there, as was proclaimed in its public statements. Indian Prime Minister, Jawaharlal Nehru once remarked about Indian relations with Afghanistan:

'Ever since India's independence, we have grown closer to each other, for a variety of reasons. The long memory of our past was there, and the moment it was possible to renew them, we renewed them. And then came mutual interest, (our common hostility towards Pakistan) which is a powerful factor.'

Indian Objectives in Afghanistan: Because of its geo-strategic location, Afghanistan has remained the focus of Indian regional policy. However, its geopolitical significance and its latent hostility towards Pakistan has overshadowed all other factors. India's economic interests in Afghanistan are secondary to its strategic interests. Apart from the desire to restore Pakistan's two-front problem, some of the Indian objectives in Afghanistan are:

- Support Pakistan's Afghan adversaries with a view to counter- balancing Pakistan's help to Kashmiries and other insurgencies in India. India went all out to fuel Kabul's claims to represent all ethnic-Pashtuns and supported Afghanistan's rejection of the Durand Line, the colonial-era border that divides Pakistan from Afghanistan.
- Resurgence of Islamic independence movement and their successes have the potential to undermine the social fabric of India by providing cannon fodder to oppressed minorities particularly the Sikhs and the Kashmiri Muslims. Resurgent Taliban are seen as an immediate source that may infuse the spirit of freedom amongst the Sikhs, Kashmiries and other movements in India. This is the reason why India supports the so-called democratisation in Afghanistan and strengthens the Karazai rule in Afghanistan. This arrangement, they persume, could

frustrate the Taliban movement (and by implication other freedom movements) and marginalize their role in Kabul affairs. Indian provision of technical assistance in education, and other so-called nation-building activities are part of Indo-US strategy of preventing the return of Taliban to power and isolating Pakistan in Afghanistan. Hence, Indian reconstruction efforts in Afghanistan are not aimed at social stabilization and providing assistance to the people. Instead, its a strategy for acquiring legitimacy for Karzai's government and wiping out the Taliban from the corridors of power.

- India realizes the fact that, being an immediate and strategically tied neighbours Pakistan's influence in Afghanistan will always surpass that of Indian. If both of the Muslim neighbours are allowed to work together, then there are possibilities that they may reach on agreed solutions of the problems like infiltration across porous borders, drug trafficking, Durand Line, Afghan refugees etc. India, does not want these neighbours to resolve their disputes amicably.
- From a geo-strategic and geo-economic point of view India takes control over Afghanistan as the threshold to Central Asian oil and gas pipelines to be constructed to markets in Pakistan, India and else where in the world. Indian solid positioning in Afghanistan politics would enable India to become a formidable part of Central Asian oil and gas distribution network thereby acquiring a strong foothold in the region and marginalizing Pakistan's unique position in this regard. India by virtue of its high publicity has succeeded in presenting herself as a counterweight to China and thus has increased its influence in the region. India's posture as counterweight to China compliments U.S. objectives of preventing Chinese or Russian influence over the newly independent Central Asian republics, helping these states develop alternative exit routes for their oil and gas other than through Russia or Iran. Resultantly in a bid to reinforce India's strategic relevance in the region, the United States has in turn encouraged Indian trade,

investment, and assistance to the Central Asian states and Afghanistan. Afghanistan's entry into SAARC and signing of Indo-Afghan free trade area should be seen in this backdrop

- Indian presence in Afghanistan and Central Asia and its unconditional support to U.S. in its War on Terror has helped India in realization of her long drawn dream of replacing Pakistan as the America's strategic ally and sweeps-out Pakistani influence in the region. A cursory look over the post cold war events in general and post 9/11 in particular reveals that there is not only abstract cooperation rather there exists solid coordination between two countries with complimenting goals and congruence of strategies anchored not on principles but on commonality of interests. Indo-US commonalities of interests that helped in fomenting Indo-US strategic partnership symbolized by the Malabar joint naval exercises, agreement 123 on civilian nuclear cooperation, securing Indian interests in Afghanistan and other collaborations on range of regional and global issues, include:
    - o Protecting their interests, primacy and security obligations by preventing key South Asian, Southeast Asian and Central Asian states from becoming strategically dependent on China. Maintaining and increasing of their military presence in these regions will preempt any such move from China that if materialized will serve their common strategic interests.
    - o U.S. objectives also include the containment of anti-American regional powers, such as Iran and Syria, and limiting their access to WMD capabilities. This latter objective is shared by India, which also supports the U.S. goal of promoting pluralist democratic governments in the region. India by using American shoulders seeks to strike a balance between maintaining its access to Israeli military technology and its older (though currently decreasing) commitment to Arab causes in the region.

- o The United States and India seek to prevent the use of the ocean's transit routes for the movement of weapons of mass destruction and associated materials, in addition to protecting the littoral island states from internal and external threats and from exporting instability. Both countries maintain a strong naval presence in the region: the U.S. Navy maintains bases in Diego Garcia and the Persian Gulf, while the Indian Navy maintains a significant presence throughout the northern Indian Ocean. In addition, both have invested significant political, military and diplomatic capital on maintenance of cooperative security relationships with various littoral states as well as other key regional actors such as Japan and Singapore. The goals and strategies pursued by the two countries are thus clearly complementary.

India's Afghan Policy: An Overview

Afghanistan remained the focus of Indian regional policy because of its geo-strategic proximity to Pakistan, and having potential of becoming its rival from the West. Since Indian foreign policy was centered on maintaining very cordial relations with Afghanistan therefore, to enhance Indian influence it did architect "Friendship Treaty" in 1950 and signed various agreements and protocols to promote bilateral co-operation alienating Pakistan further. After the Soviet invasion in 1979 India doubled up its efforts to further strengthen its relations with Afghanistan by co-operating in industrial, irrigation, and hydroelectric projects. The diplomatic table in Afghanistan was turned against India with the Soviet withdrawal and its disintegration 1991, Mujahideens control of Kabul and overthrow of Najibullah in April 1992. India tried to regain its dwindling influence in the Burhanuddin Rabbani government however that was short lived till the rise of Taliban and closed its embassy in September 1996.

History testifies that India and Pakistan had competing strategic agendas in Afghanistan. Pakistan visualizes Indian influence in Afghanistan as part of a threatening Indian double envelopment movement, and a source of fueling Pashtun separatism inside

Pakistan. And Pakistan's friendly relations with Kabul can provide "strategic depth" to Pakistan. On the other hand, India perceives Afghanistan as an important geopolitical constraint on Pakistan, as well as the gateway to Central Asia.

Indian friendly Afghanistan will not only deny most crucial strategic depth to Pakistan against Indian long range missiles and blitzkrieg/ pincer movements, rather would offer another front to dissipate and over-stretch Pakistan's defence resources to fight on two different fronts. During the cold war period, Indian hand was found involved behind each and every estrangement between both nations and during the post cold war America has joined India in this regard.

Both India and USA are playing their game of divide and rule to full fill their Imperialistic designs. Both are looking to strip off Pakistan from its strategic assets including its nuclear deterrence capabilities. Both are working to control Afghanistan so as to command access to the Central Asian oil and gas reserves. Both are struggling to undermine Pakistan's territorial integrity, political stability and economic viability. Some of the incidents reflective of Indo-US imperialistic designs unfolding in

Afghanistan are:

- The Indian factor focuses Pakistan's perception of Afghanistan and its policies there. From independence until 1992, India supported whatever government was in power in Kabul. The Pashtunistan issue offered India the possibility of trapping Pakistan between two fronts in the event of a clash along the Durand Line and along the Indo-Pakistan border.
- Things changed after 1992 when the internal fighting led to a split between Gulbuddin Hekmatyar and all other parties. India then supported whoever was opposed to Pakistan.
- After the fall of Kabul to the Taliban and execution of former Afghan president Najibullah, in September 1996, New Delhi continued to support President Burhanuddin Rabbani. It was the first time in the history of its relations with Afghanistan when India found itself supporting an

opposition group and not the Afghan government. India soon became a solid supporter of the Northern Alliance.

- India also exploited the anti-Taliban approach of Russia and Iran to forge closer relations with those countries and to develop its links with Central Asian States. As defined by Mr J. N. Dixit in his book, "*India, in co-operation with all like-minded countries, should resist the coercive propagation of any kind of religious, social, or ethnic extremism which can profoundly destabilize Afghanistan's Asian neighbours* ... An early solution to the Afghanistan crisis is critical for realizing the enormous opportunities for energy and economic co-operation in the Eurasian region"
- As a prelude to regain its lost influence in Afghanistan and counter Pakistan's support to the Taliban government, India established links with the Northern Alliance - non-Pashtun groups opposing Taliban regime and controlling part of northern Afghanistan. During this period, India provided all kind of support to the Northern Alliance and few of the glimpses of this support included:
  - Provided high-altitude warfare equipment worth $ 10 million to Northern Alliance through its Research and Analysis Wing (RAW).
  - Indian defence advisers provided technical advice to the Northern Alliance.
  - Established a hospital in Farkhor on the Afghan–Tajik border and Indian doctors provided medical assistance to the Alliance.
  - In the last seven years, India has promised $750 million in aid as reconstruction assistance to Afghanistan in the seven years since the Bonn conference, representing its second-biggest foreign aid commitment.
  - Farkhor, India's only military base outside its territory is offering New Delhi's armed forces unprecedented strategic reach. Afghanistan's membership of the South Asia Free Trade Agreement will strengthen its trade ties with India, which is now the largest regional donor to that country's reconstruction programme. At the

same time, India has succeeded in consolidating its presence. Farkhor, India's only military base outside its territory is thought to have been in a state of full operational readiness since last year, offering New Delhi's armed forces unprecedented strategic reach. Afghanistan's membership of the South Asia Free Trade Agreement will strengthen its trade ties with India, which is now the largest regional donor to that country's reconstruction program.

- o In a move to relieve Afghanistan of its dependence on Pakistan, India is focusing on rebuilding of transport and communication infrastructure that include: Kandahar- Iran highway, airports and power plants, and provides support to the health and education sectors. Afghan civil servants, diplomats, and police officials are being trained by India.
- o India increasing the number of its military personnel in Afghanistan on the pretext of providing security to the Border Roads Organization, indicating that the strength of Indian troops had reached almost a company size. Some of the U.S. officials have stated that they expect India to play its new role in Afghanistan.
- o India's announced US$450 million aid package on the eve of Afghan President Hamid Karzai's visit to New Delhi in August 2008, in addition to the US$ 750 million already pledged placing India amongst the top five donor countries.

Post 9/11 American game plans in Afghanistan brought pro-Indian forces in Kabul with unparalleled accumulation of power in the hands of Northern Alliance. The opening of Indian consulates in Afghanistan, in particular, became a bone of contention between the two countries. These Indian consulates are having less to do with humanitarian aid and more to do with India's top-secret intelligence agency, the Research and Analysis Wing. Pakistan has accused India consulates for setting up and monitoring networks of terrorist training camps located inside Afghanistan and operating in Balochistan and NWFP. Reportedly, Indian consulates in Southern Afghanistan have been supplying money as well as arms and ammunition to the militants that has added to the trouble and violence in the tribal belt.

India's return to the Afghan scene was bound to worry Pakistan. Pakistan's government officially expressed its "deep" concerns about the Indian government's activities along the Pakistan- Afghan border. Pakistan's allegations about India ranged from charges of printing false Pakistani currency to carrying out acts of sabotage and terrorism on Pakistani territory. The most worrisome acquisition came from the Balochistan Chief Minister that the Indian secret services were maintaining forty terrorist camps all over Baloch territory.

Foregoing in view, it has become evident that Indo US nexus revolves around their common desire for political and military hegemony, obsessive drive for control of oil and expansion of military bases around the region. In other words, both are imperialistic in their nature having the sole aim; attainment of economic aggrandizement. There is no reason to doubt that the US invasion of Afghanistan, in the wake of 9/11, was motivated by self-interest and not to end terrorism there, as was its stated objective. There is convincing evidence that the oil reserves in the Caspian Sea area were an important motivational factor for the US and India to gain control of Afghanistan on one hand and envelop Pakistan- the only nuclear power of the Muslim World on the other. It is reasonable to assume that if prevailing Indo- US imperialistic designs are allowed to continue then the last thing that Pakistan would like to see is an Indian presence on both of its eastern and western borders. The flow of massive aid under the guise of humanitarian relief, building of infrastructure, training of public sector human resources, are the indicators of the future prospects for large scale economico, political and military cooperation aiming at marginalizing Pakistan's future role in Afghanistan. The resultant vulnerability of Pakistan's Western border is becoming most serious security concern that terrifies Pakistan's security establishment, which is already short of the resources to meet even any conventional threat emanating from the East. Signing of Indo-Afghan preferential trade agreement and Indian generosity in waiving off tariff & other duties on certain types of dry fruits and precious stones from Afghanistan and duty free access to certain Indian items should be seen a substantial step of developing interdependence on private and public sectors.

In given geo- political and security environment Pakistan can't afford to allow any other regional or global player, in particular India, to gain a preponderance of influence in Afghanistan. Pakistan's interest is vital at a time when India's growing political, military, and economic ties with both Afghanistan and the United States lead many Pakistanis to believe their country is being marginalized. The annihilation of the Taliban after September 11, 2001, radically shifted the balance of power in Afghanistan in India's favour. Seeing political leadership of its own choice in Kabul, Indian consulates sprouted across Jalalabad, Kandahar, Herat, and Mazar-e-Sharif, besides the embassy in Kabul, India is in a position to pursue its own interests in Afghanistan. Instead of accommodating the Pakistan's concerns over the anti-Pakistan clandestine activities of Indian consulates in Kandahar and Jalalabad, India and the Karzai government are accusing Pakistan of harbouring terrorists and sponsoring cross-border infiltration to India and Afghanistan. The situation has come to the point that even Karazai is talking of hot pursuit operations in Pakistani territories. NATO/American Commandos have started conducting operation inside their one of the closest non NATO allies of war against Terror. Only in the months of October and November 2008 there have been more than 17 predators attacks in FATA and one on 17th of November in Bannu- a settled area of falling directly under the perview of Pakistan's territorial limits.

Americans expression of 'do more syndrome' and NATO / ISAF forces' persistent allegations that Taliban's insurgency is being fed and controlled from the sanctuaries inside the Pakistan's tribal areas seems to be a prelude to bring war from Afghanistan to Pakistan. Indian factor is also playing its role in aggravating the bitterness of bilateral relations and spoiling the environment of trust with a view to pursuing its own nefarious designs. If the state of affairs is allowed to move on similar direction then there are all the chances that relations between Kabul and Islamabad may reach to a point of no return.

Building up of such an anti-Pakistan scenario on Afghanistan's soil is more than alarming. It carries a very loud and clear challenge for Pakistan's security and Pak-Afghan relations. Pakistan can't afford to have another India on its western border. Nor it can allow a War against Terror (being fought in Afghanistan) to spread and spill over to Pakistan. In such deteriorating environment, therefore, Pakistan had to remain prepared for new situations on the Afghan side and be able to adapt accordingly. And the one long term solution rests on the defusing of ongoing cold war, establishing mutual trust and relations *based on mutual interests and brotherly sincerity*. There has to be a realization that any adversity faced by one could affect the other. It is thus, in the interest of both countries to have friendly and cordial relations marked with trust, and respect for sovereignty and territorial integrity of the other so as to promote peace, political stability, economic prosperity and socio-ethnic unity and cohesion in the region. If Afghanistan is passing through a phase of uncertainty because of decades of violence and civil war,

Pakistan is also facing a phase of instability because of extremism, militancy, political wrangling, socio-ethnic polarization, and range of other issues from bad governance, water and electricity crises to sectarian and ethnic discords. Therefore, normalization of Pak- Afghan relations is the only recipe to bring peace and stability in the two countries. Pakistan should be content with having an independent, integrated and friendly western neighbour. It could further be argued that, despite the present cold relationship between the two countries, other compulsions, especially those caused by economic and security issues are likely to draw them into a long-term, friendly relationship.

4

R&AW at War-Genesis of Secret Agencies

Espionage, euphemistically called the second oldest profession of the world finds a mention in the Indian Vedas, one of the most - if not the most - ancient of the human texts. References to espionage are also discernible in the ancient civilizations of Egypt, Babylon, Assyria, Greece and China. The Chinese sage Sun Tzu is considered by European scholars to be the first to study and analyse the whole question of espionage on scientific lines, and to set it down in a text book Ping Fa, The Art of War. This view is, however, not substantiated by cogent facts since there is ample proof of the greater antiquity and soundness of the system of Secret Services enunciated by the early Indians.

Varuna, one of the chief gods of the Vedic pantheon is considered to be a forerunner of Secret Services. Magha, one of the most erudite and lucid poets and pragmatic thinkers, unequivocally asserted that statecraft cannot exist without the assistance of espionage. He writes:-

'The statecraft in which even a single step is not taken in contravention of the science of dandaniti {(i.e. the law of danda (the rod)} which provides decent living (to the officers) and in which liberal grants are given in recognition of services rendered, does not shine to advantage without (the employment of) spies, just as the science of grammar does not shine without Papasa Bhasya (the introductory portion of Patanjali's Mahabhasya), though it is provided with Nyasa (a commentary of that name) which strictly follows the words of the Sutras (of Panini), a good

vrtti (explanatory work) and an excellent Bhasya (advance work of explanation, discussion and criticism)'.

Secret Agencies in ancient India were not conceived of as an instrument of oppression but as a tool of governance. Secret agents were considered as 'eyes of the king'.

Indian history illustrates that ancient Indians had gained great expertise in this secret art. The techniques and operational methods adopted by them were highly advanced, and can be usefully emulated today. From the spasas of Varuna, the fore-runners of the modern globe-trotting spies (the etymological affinity of the two terms is noticeable) to Chanakya's final manifestation of this art in the Arthasastra which is in fact a systematic codification of a wide variety of scattered information copiously found in the Epics, - the Mahabharata and the Ramayana - the Puranas and literary works of Bhasa, Kalidasa, Magha and Bana; and the Tamil Sangam literature, transcends unprecedented heights in this discipline.

The vision of the Arthashastra, is truly breath taking, its practical utility timeless and the clarity of its exposition unique. The techniques of manipulating public opinion and creating disinformation, propounded by Chanakya anticipated modern intelligence systems by several centuries. No wonder then that the nearly 2500 years old lessons in deceit, guile, hypocrisy, machination, and gore taught by that Master strategist, Chanakya alias Kautilya (literally meaning 'crooked') was adopted in toto by India and its chief intelligence agency, the Research and Analysis Wing (RAW).

While laying the foundation stone of RAW, India's late Prime Minister Mrs. Indira Gandhi approvingly quoted Louis F Hallis, when she said that its objectives should be the 'Ability to get what one wants by whatever means: eloquence, reasoned arguments, bluff, tirade, threat or coercion, as well as, by arousing pity, annoying others, or making them uneasy'.

RAW is basically a Secret Service established to perform clandestine operations based on the Chanakyan principles of deceit and guile. It has successfully destabilised neighbouring countries, disintegrated independent states and backed the most notorious guerrilla organizations to achieve its ends. If it is compared to other intelligence agencies of the region, it emerges as an aggressive, cold-blooded and ruthless institution, engaged in the most macabre deeds.

The organization and structure of RAW will be discussed in the second part of this paper. But to appreciate its working we must, first examine the origin and organization of India's ancient secret agencies.

Origin and Organization of Secret Agencies in Ancient India

The origin and development of Secret Agencies in ancient India is linked to the geopolitical conditions of the times when India was dotted with small states attempting to grab each other's territory and wealth. The art of espionage was thoroughly mastered, and almost all ancient Indian literary sources exhaustively dealt with this system. Spying came to be regarded as an indispensable feature and integral part of an efficient administration and of a sound foreign policy. It kept the rulers posted with the activities, afflictions, and operations of political adversaries: their disloyal and disgruntled elements, fifth columnists and foreign agents in their midst, also the strength and intentions of all foreign power. Espionage was considered to be as important an institution as diplomacy, and was sought to be governed by certain definite rules and usages. In Chanakya, the secret service department became a permanent feature of the state and was organised in the most 'uninhibited manner'.

While Chanakya presents a highly developed and complicated system of governance including an all-pervasive espionage system, references to it are found in pre-Mauryan literature, too. The Mahabharata refers to a mythological tradition on the origin of the dandaniti and the art of espionage, which was handed down from the past. It expounds 'Brahma, the creator, himself composed a work comprising 1,00,000 chapters relating to dharma (religion), artha (economy), kama (sexual desire) and moksa (spiritual salvation) - the four aspects of life.' Brahma's compilation, according to the Great Epic, included subjects of behaviour towards counsellors, of spies, the indication of princes, of secret agents possessed of diverse means, of envoys, and agents of other kinds, conciliation, fomenting discord, gifts and chastisement; deliberations including counsels for producing disunion; the three kinds of victory, first, that which served righteously, secondly, which was won by wealth, and, thirdly, the one obtained by deceitful ways; chastisement of two kinds, namely, open and secret; the disorder created in the hostile troops; inspiring the enemy with fear; the means of winning over persons residing in the enemy territory; and finally, the chastisement and destruction of those that are strong.'

No other civilization can claim such an antiquity for the techniques of war, diplomacy, intrigue and espionage and on such compulsive terms.

In short, Varuna and other deities of the Vedic pantheon heavily depended on their secret agents. Manu, Kamandaka, Yajnavalkya and Chanakya, besides the later digest writers, deliberated on the art of espionage, while Chanakya perfected the art and recommended the organisation of secret agencies in the most unabashed manner. Professor Ghoshal suggests that the Mauryas followed the Arthasastra tradition in four respects, i.e. precautions in recruiting spies, countrywide espionage, safeguards against false reports by secret agents and enlistment of the services of loose women.

Organization

The modest origin of secret agents in the form of Varuna's spasas brought about the imperative need for effective and vigorous espionage in an institutionalized form. The blue-print on espionage prepared by Chanakya has remained a model for successive generations. Various aspects of the organization of a secret agency as discussed in complete detail in the Arthasastra are briefly touched upon here.

Category of Agents. The Arthasastra mentions two wings of 'secret service', viz. 'samstha' and 'sancara'. The agents belonging to 'samstha' were stationed in the Establishment financed by the State, whereas the 'sancaras' moved from place to place depending on professional requirements. The spymasters of the two wings headed their respective cadre of agents, and controlled their operations. The members of one group were not aware of the existence of the other. This classification of Chanakya has been followed in India throughout the successive centuries.

Recruitment of Secret Agents. A study of Arthasastra, the Mahabharata, the Ramayana, the Manusmriti, Kamandaka and Sukra reveals that there was no fixed source of recruitment of secret agents. Modern intelligence services generally resort to three main sources of recruitment, the academic world, the armed services and the under-world. This was also the pattern followed in ancient India.

Training. After recruitment, the secret agents were put through a rigorous training in the techniques of adopting disguises, changing appearances, science of signalling, secret writing, detection and identification of criminals, manipulating public opinion and creating dissensions in the enemy ranks.

Control and Supervision. The complicated, comprehensive, all-pervasive and ubiquitous institution of spies in ancient India necessitated very close and personal supervision of the ruler or his most reliable officers. It must have been difficult for the king to personally handle the comprehensive and complicated department of intelligence.

According to the Arthasastra, the department of external affairs, which was covering military intelligence was managed by the king with the help of his foreign minister and the Commander-in-Chief. The agents detailed to cover the senior officers of the central government certainly reported to the king directly. In the far-flung areas of extensive kingdoms and in view of poor means of communication, the action specially in times of war had to be taken by men on the spot and not by the king who may be at a place far distant from the field of action. In foreign countries the spies were kept under the control and supervision of ambassadors who scrutinised their reports and directed intelligence operations. According to Chanakya, the institution of spies as an organization did not function under a unified command. The spies and secret agents worked under their respective heads of department, and also directly under the king.

Techniques of Espionage

Before discussing the working of RAW, it would be worthwhile to briefly examine some of the techniques of espionage employed by the ancient secret agencies of India.

Motivation and Recruitment of Sources. Motivation of persons to cater intelligence is directly proportionate to their weakness for sex and money, besides the burning desire of revenge or insatiable hunger for power. The Spymasters of ancient India exploited these weaknesses to their fullest advantage, and even the modern intelligence agencies heavily depend on these considerations. Chanakya advocated that the weak should be subjugated by means of conciliation and gifts, the strong by means of dissension and force.

Selection and Infiltration of Targets. Chanakya, in a very subtle manner and with an intimate knowledge of human psychology, selected his targets in foreign lands depending on their weaknesses and motivation. He advised secret agents to concentrate on targets:-

- Among those who are dissatisfied with the rulers or had been humiliated or exiled;
- Who have not been compensated for their expenditure;
- Those who have been deprived of their rightful inheritance to office;
- Whose women have been molested by force;
- Who were wrongly imprisoned;
- Whose property had been confiscated;
- Who are prone to blackmail due to some weakness.

Double-Agent Operation. A 'Double-Agent' is a spy who works for the opposition while pretending loyalty to those who employ him. this technique is an indispensable facet of agent-running and was extensively practised in ancient India. Chanakya suggested that secret agents should not refuse pay from the targets for working with them as their employees. This was to allay the misgivings on the part of the targets. 'Double-Agents' were used for creating dissensions and confusion among the confederates of the enemy. They floated false documents, got them seized from the possession of the enemy's army chiefs, and thus weakened the enemy. 'Double-

Agents' were used to winning over the confidence of their adopted masters by sacrificing a few exposed, treacherous, disaffected or inefficient spies.

Payment of Sources Encouragement of secret agents with money and honour was considered an imperative necessity. The sources were paid both in cash and kind, besides receiving extraordinary courtesies and favours. It was also recommended that secret agents not only be rewarded for the job done by them but, also, in the event of repeated mistakes, silent punishment-death-be awarded to them.

Communication of Intelligence Intelligence not properly and promptly conveyed and which cannot be acted upon loses its value and validity. Besides this, the Arthasastra, Mahabharata, Ramayana, Kamandaka and Kathasaritasagara all recommend the use of coded language and signals.

Interception of Mail Interception of messages, signals and letters by postal censorship; monitoring and tapping telephones; and breaking codes is the standard practice of modern intelligence agencies. In the ancient period, since intelligence was communicated through pre-determined signals and with the assistance of pigeons, secret agents must have made elaborate arrangements to intercept these messages.

Assessment of Information. The Arthasastra cautions against the placing of reliance on agents without proper corroboration. It is repeatedly emphasised that all aspects of a report must be gone through, including the source of information, the mode of its collection and the past performance of a source before it is accepted. Briefing and debriefing of secret agents was an elaborate exercise, and they were trained to be precise, accurate and truthful in reporting.

Working Under 'Cover'. The institution of espionage in ancient India, like modern times, required secret agents to work under some kind of 'cover' to preserve secrecy. Chanakya institutionalized the art of working under the most ingenious 'covers'. The most common disguises recommended by him were those of ascetic, mendicant, merchant, artisan, wandering minstrel, artiste, cook, barber and shampooer, bath and toilet attendant, deaf, dumb, eunuch and prostitute. Chanakya recommends the use of women as effective tools of espionage particularly those who were engaged in harlotry.

Counter-Intelligence. A counter-intelligence operation is directed at discovering the identities and methods of foreign spies and intelligence officers working for the opposition. One of the most important duties of the Secret Service in ancient India was to counteract the activities of such agents operating within the country. Chanakya recommends that secret agents should discover foreign spies by operating at the places of entertainment, conclaves of people, among beggars, in gardens and public places, and the houses of prominent citizens.

Disinformation and Dissension. Manipulation of public opinion is as important an object of the State today as it was in ancient India. It is used to create disharmony and distrust among the enemy's friends, ill-will among his allies, loss of confidence in their leadership and disruption by psychological means his capacity and will to fight. Chanakya had perfected the technique of disinformation and highly eulogised the use of dissension in enemy's ranks for winning a battle without any military action. His winning an extensive empire for his student Chandragupta Maurya without fighting any mentionable battle is awen, and one may be excused to add: admirationÑ, inspiring feat, unparalleled in history. The Sanskrit Classical drama Mudrakshasa has tried to depict it dramatically but, at best, has only partially succeeded.

Sabotage. The technique of sabotage, which the political strategists consider as the penultimate means to vanquish an adversary, had been greatly perfected in ancient India. Secret practices for sabotage were advocated by Chanakya to ensure victory. As a preface to sabotage, he suggests the creation of an atmosphere congenial to arousing terror, fear, demoralization, disappointment and loss of confidence among the enemy ranks. Prior to launching a full-scale assault on the enemy fort, Chanakya suggests implementation of secret measures to weaken its defences not only physically but in all respects. These include prevention of sowing the fields, destruction of the standing crops and cutting of the enemy's supply lines.

He also advises free and uninhibited use of poison in the articles used by the enemy. His detailed and scientifically valid knowledge of the subject has earned for him a place in Arabic medical literature, that knows him as Ibn Shanaq (son of Chanak). Some of the secret stratagems advocated by Chanakya include the use of smoke with properties seriously affecting the vision, and, arson or setting fires within the enemy fort.

The employment of Visakanyas (Poison-damsels). Secret Agencies in ancient India had perfected very ingenious techniques to subserve the interests of their monarchs. Besides using the nascent technological advancement available to them, they exploited human weakness for sex to achieve royal objectives. Visakanya is a unique feature of the Indian genius to poison the monarch. These venomous beauties can be classified, as follows:-

- A damsel whose body is saturated with gradual doses of poison, and who is likely to transmit poison from her body to another person coming in contact with her;
- A woman who treacherously captivates the heart of a person, and then mixes poison in his food or drink;
- A girl who is, one way or the other, so much poisoned or infected with disease that she is likely to convey her poison or disease to the person coming in contact with her. A woman suffering from Venereal disease or, in the latest situation one suffering from Aids is a Visakanya of this kind.

RAW AT WAR-II

The first part of this article briefly traced out the history of secret services in ancient India. Its chief progenitor was Chanakya, whose classic, the Arthasastra, not only provides a fairly graphic account of the activities of spies in the Mauryan and post-Mauryan polity but lays the foundation for the 'statecraft', guile and unscrupulous practices advocated by this master strategist.

He goes on to recommend, 'In the work of espionage, all methods are admissible snooping, lying, bribing, poisoning, using women's wiles and the assassin's knife. To a weak king menaced by strong neighbours, Chanakya's advice was to rely chiefly on spies and wage what he described as a 'battle of intrigues' (mantra yuddha) and 'secret wars' (kuta yuddha). The spies, in order to achieve their objective, were to practice all kinds of fraud, artifice incendiarism and robbery. Their objective was to demoralize the enemy's troops by circulating false news, and seduce the allegiance of his minister and commanders. The underlying idea seems to have been to keep the strong neighbour preoccupied with domestic troubles thus making it impossible for him to launch a foreign expedition. From the days of Chanakya, the rules of business of espionage have not changed, at least the basic principles remain as before. The development of science and technology has only given fresh impetus and tools to the art of spying.

Evolution of RAW

Origins in the Directorate of Intelligence Bureau, created by the Raj in November 1920 Ñ during the Khilafat and Swaraj movements Ñ out of the old Criminal Intelligence Department (CID). In 1933, sensing the political turmoil in the world which eventually led to the Second World War, the bureau's responsibilities were increased to include the collection of intelligence along India's borders. In 1947, after Independence, Sanjeevi Pillai took over as the first Indian Director. Having been depleted of trained manpower by the exit of the British and Muslims, Pillai tried to run the bureau along MI 5 lines. Although in 1949, Pillai organized a small foreign intelligence set-up, the inefficacy of it was proved by the Indian debacle in the Indo-China War of 1962, and the cry of 'not enough intelligence available', was taken up by the Indian Chief of Army Staff, General Chaudhry, after the 1965 Indo-Pak war.

It was towards the end of 1966 and the beginning of 1967 that the concept of a separate foreign intelligence agency began to take concrete shape. In 1968, after Indira Gandhi had taken over, it was decided that a full-fledged second security service was needed. R. N. Kao, then a deputy director of IB, submitted a blueprint for the new agency. Kao was appointed as the chief of India's first foreign intelligence agency named as 'the Research and Analysis Wing' or RAW.

RAW takes shape

Having started humbly as a Wing of the main Intelligence Bureau with 250 personnel and an annual budget of Rs 2 crore (by a rough estimate), in the early seventies, its annual budget had risen to Rs 30 crores while its personnel numbered several thousand. In 1971, Kao had persuaded the government to set up the Aviation Research Centre (ARC). The ARC's job was aerial reconnaissance. It replaced the Indian Air Force's old reconnaissance aircraft and by the mid-70s, RAW, through the ARC, had high quality aerial pictures of the installations along the Chinese and Pakistani borders. By 1976, Kao had been promoted to the rank of a fullfledged Secretary responsible for Security and reporting directly to the Prime Minister. His rise had raised RAW to become India's premier intelligence agency. RAW agents operated in virtually every major embassy and high commission.

RAW's objectives

The objectives of RAW according to Asoka Raina's famous book Inside RAW (Vikas Publishing House, New Delhi, 1981) have been:-

- To monitor the political and military developments in all the adjoining countries, which have, direct bearing on India's national security and in the formulation of its foreign policy.
- Secondly, RAW watched the development of international communism and the schism between the two communist giants, the Soviet Union and The Republic of China. For as in other countries both the powers had direct access to the Communist Parties in India.
- Thirdly, the supply of military hardware to Pakistan mostly from European countries, the USA and China, was of high priority.
- And last but not the least, the presence of a large ethnic Indian population in foreign countries, provided a powerful lobby. These countries could back a favourable policy in international councils, motivated by the ethnic Indian group.

The Organization

RAW has been organized on the lines of the CIA. The following chart (source: Inside RAW by Asoka Raina) signifies the organization of RAW and is self-explanatory.

Training of RAW Agents

Recruitment: Initially, induction in RAW relied primarily on trained intelligence officers who were recruited directly. These belonged to the external wing of IB. However, quite a few were taken from police and other services to fill the cadres of RAW owing to its sudden expansion. Later RAW began recruiting promising fresh graduates from the Universities directly. The criteria for selection are fairly stringent.

Phase - II: The fresh recruit's training continues and he is now posted in some remote outpost, attached to a Field Intelligence Bureau (FIB). His training here lasts for a period of six months to a year. He is given a first hand feeling of what it was to be out in the cold, in the danger area conducting clandestine operation. During night exercises, under conditions of absolute realism, he is taught infiltration and exfiltration.

He is instructed to avoid capture and if caught, how to face intensive interrogation; the art of reconnoiter, making contacts, and, the numerous skills of operating an intelligence mission. At the end of the field training, the new recruit is brought back to the School for final polishing.

Before his deployment in the field, he is given exhaustive training in the art of self-defence, an introduction to martial arts and the use of technical espionage devices. He is also drilled in various administrative disciplines so that he could take his place in the foreign missions without arousing suspicion. He is now ready to operate under the cover of an Embassy to gather information, set up his own network of informers, moles or operatives as the task may require.

Functions of RAW

The functions of RAW vary according to the target. Some functions for obtaining strategic intelligence are outlined below:-

Collection of Information: Emphasis is laid on obtaining information essential to Indian interests. Both overt and covert means are adopted.

Collection of Information : The vast myriad of data is sifted through, classified and filed. The modern computer network in the 13-storey bombproof building situated at Lodhi Road, New Delhi, is a great help.

Aggressive Intelligence: The primary mission of RAW includes aggressive intelligence which comprise espionage, psychological warfare, subversion, sabotage, terrorism and creating dissension, insurgency and, ultimately, insurrection to destabilize the target country.

Modus Operandi

Foreign Missions: Foreign Missions provide an ideal cover and RAW centres in a target country are generally located inside the Embassy premises.

Multinationals: RAW operatives find good covers in Multinational organizations. NGOs and Cultural programmes are also popular screens to shield RAW activities.

Media: International media centres can easily absorb RAW operatives and provide freedom of movement.

Collaboration with other agencies: RAW maintains active collaboration with other secret services to meet its ends in a particular target country. Its contacts with KGB of the former Soviet Union, KHAD, the erstwhile Afghan agency, Mossad, CIA and MI6 have been well-known. A common interest being Pakistan's Nuclear Programme.

Third Country Technique: RAW has been very active in obtaining information and operating through third countries like the Middle East, Afghanistan, UK, Hong Kong, Mayanmar and Singapore.

Spotting and Recruitment: RAW operatives are on the lookout for local recruits to serve their ends. Acting on the Chanakyan principles, they tend to exploit human weaknesses for wine, women and wealth, and, at times resort to blackmail. Separatist tendencies and ethnic or sectarian sensitivities are also well-known grounds for manipulation. Armed Forces personnel remain a primary target. Those journalists, intellectuals and politicians harbouring and preaching goodwill and better Indo-Pak relations also make suitable targets for inadvertent and unconscious recruitment by RAW agents.

MAJOR SUCCESSES OF RAW

Creation of Bangladesh: The Bangladesh operation, beginning with sowing seeds of dissension, leading to the Agartala Conspiracy, creation of Mukti Bahini and under its cover sneaking into East Pakistan for guerrilla operations to blow up bridges and other installations damaged the morale of Pakistani troops and India won the war even before the battle began, thanks to RAW as its agents had infiltrated every nook and corner of erstwhile East Pakistan. The paragraph entitled: 'RAW takes shape', in the initial part of this article, amply demonstrates the causal chain of events.

Plan to assassinate General Zia-ur-Rahman: According to the September 18-24, 1988 issue of the weekly Magazine Sunday (Calcutta), RAW was on the verge of assassinating Bangladesh's President General Zia-ur-Rahman (with Mrs Gandhi's approval) when the Congress government fell. RAW briefed the new Prime Minister Morarji Desai about it who was appalled at the idea and stopped the murder. General Zia continued to rule Bangladesh for many more years. He was assassinated after Indira Gandhi returned to power but RAW pleads innocence.

Poornima: Project Poornima was the name given India's Nuclear Programme. The task to keep it 'under tight wraps of security' was given to RAW. This was the first time that RAW was involved in a project inside India. The rest is history as India managed to surprise the world on 18 May, 1974 by detonating a 15-Kiloton plutonium device at Pokharan.

Kahuta's Blueprint: According to the September 18-24, 1988 issue of the weekly Indian Magazine Sunday, RAW agents claim that in early 1978, they were on the verge of obtaining the plans and blueprint for Kahuta nuclear plant that was built to counter the Pokharan atomic blast, but the then Indian Prime Minister

Morarji Desai not only refused to sanction the $ 10,000 demanded by the RAW agent, but informed Pakistan of the offer. According to the report, Pakistanis caught and eliminated the RAW mole.

It must be noted that the author of 'Ham Jang Nahin Hone Denge' held the external affairs portfolio at that time.

Sikkim: Encircled by Tibet, Nepal, Bhutan and West Bengal in the Eastern Himalayas, Sikkim presented a lucrative target to the Indians. It was ruled by a Maharaja. The Indian Government had recognized the title of Chogyal (Dharma Raja) for the Mahraja of Sikkim. After their kill in East Pakistan, in 1972, RAW was given the green signal to go ahead with the operation of installing a pro-Indian democratic government there. In less than three years, with the manipulation of RAW, Sikkim became the 22nd State of the Indian Union on April 26, 1975.

Maldives: To bring the smaller Independent States/countries in the Indian sphere of influence with the use of RAW, the case of Maldives makes an important example. In November 1988, the Eilam Peoples' Liberation Front comprising about 200 Tamil secessionists on the pay roll of RAW were tasked to stage the drama of an uprising on that peaceful island. At the request of the President of Maldives, Mr Mamoon Abdul Qayyum, Indian Armed Forces 'quelled' the insurgency engineered by themselves and thus tried to sneak into the administrative mechanism of that peace-loving country.

Operation Chanakya: This was the codename given to the RAW operation in Occupied Kashmir to create rifts among the various Kashmiri Mujahideen groups, suppress the uprising and bring the Kashmiris under total Indian subjugation. According to Tariq Ismail Sagar's book RAW, (Milli Book Depot, Lahore, 1997) in 1991, RAW operatives entered the Srinagar Valley in the guise of freedom fighters. They resorted to loot, rape and arson of Kashmiri Pundit families to give the popular non-communal uprising a bad name. Operation Chanakya gained momentum when Mossad provided its experienced Katsas to train RAW operatives. They did gain initial successes but when later actions of Operations Chanakya failed, RAW commenced an intensive propaganda to blame ISI.

Monitoring Pakistani Telecommunication: Raw operatives boast that at one time its monitoring complex had managed to break through Pakistani Telecommunications and were listening in to all telephonic conversations held by important Pakistani leaders.

SECURITY, SURVEILLANCE AND DATA SHARING: SCHEMES AND BODIES IN INDIA

Following the 2008 Mumbai terrorist attacks, India had implemented a wide range of data sharing and surveillance schemes. Though developed under different governments the purpose of these schemes has been to increase public safety and security by tackling crime and terrorism. As such, two data sharing schemes have been proposed - the National Intelligence Grid (NATGRID) and the Crime and Criminal Tracking Network & Systems (CCTNS), as well as several surveillance systems, such as the Lawful Intercept and Monitoring (LIM) system, the Network Traffic Analysis system (NETRA), state Internet Monitoring Systems and the Central Monitoring System (CMS). The various schemes and provides policy recommendations for their improvement, with regards to the protection of the right to privacy and other human rights.

National Intelligence Grid (NATGRID)

The National Intelligence Grid (NATGRID) is a proposed as an integrated intelligence grid that will link the databases of several departments and ministries of the Government of India in order to collect comprehensive patterns of intelligence that can be readily accessed by intelligence agencies. NATGRID is considered to be a data linking and mining project and the initial stage would have involved the "real-time linking" of data between various agencies. The Ministry of Home Affairs first proposed the creation of NATGRID following the Mumbai 2008 terrorist attacks and stated the following:

"Today, each database stands alone. It does not talk to another database. Nor can the 'owner' of one database access another database. As a result, crucial information that rests in one database is not available to another agency. In order to remedy the deficiency, the Central

Government has decided to set up NATGRID. Under NATGRID, 21 sets of databases will be networked to achieve quick, seamless and secure access to desired information for intelligence/enforcement agencies. This project is likely to be completed in 18 – 24 months from now."

In the aftermath of the Mumbai terrorist attacks, NATGRID was set up by the Government at an estimated cost of Rs. 4,000 – 5,000 crore to enable the monitoring of terrorist operations through existing banking, finance and transportation networks. NATGRID is an attached office of the Ministry of Home Affairs and has been conceived to develop a framework to enhance India's counter-terror capabilities. In order to achieve this, NATGRID engaged with the National Institute of Smart Government (NISG) to provide manpower. As such, NISG invited professionals from the fields of technology and management to work with NATGRID as consultants.

The Ministry of Home Affairs had sought over Rs. 3,400 crore for its high-tech intelligence network, NATGRID, which aims to collect sensitive information from databases of departments like the police, banks, tax and telecom to track any terror suspect and incident. The Cabinet Committee on Security has already approved NATGRID, which aims to bring together police and security agencies for a real-time exchange of data across the country.

The Ministry of Home Affairs had also announced that it will issue an executive order to give a legal framework to NATGRID that will give 11 security agencies real-time access to 21 citizen data sources to track terror activities. Such an executive order was needed since the various ministries and departments, otherwise called "provider agencies", would have needed a legal mandate to link and share their data sources in real-time through NATGRID with the 11 intelligence and investigative agencies, termed as user agencies. These citizen data sources include bank account details, telephone records, passport data and vehicle registration details, among other types of data.

Raghu Raman, the then CEO of NATGRID, had stated:

"In many ways it (NATGRID) has started. There are certain elements being helped out where it is required...[...]...NATGRID has been delayed

to make sure that the security protocols of the data sources it is using are very strong...[...]...The security (of NATGRID) has been kept at the highest level. As a matter of fact, I can technology-wise guarantee you that the way NATGRID will protect data will be far higher than the protection given to the data in its original location...[...]...NATGRID is a tool in background. It is assisting agencies. It is only a pointer, like a compass. It is like Google. When you search for anything on Google it points you to go here and go there...Likewise it (NATGRID) enables an officer to very quickly get a 360-degree view of a situation..."

It was further reported that NATGRID will utilize analytics to process the huge volumes of data generated from the 21 data sources so as to analyse events, match patterns and track suspects. Data mining appears to be at the core of NATGRID, which aims to create comprehensive patterns of intelligence by linking the 21 data sources and analysing them. To facilitate an early roll out, the Ministry of Home Affairs had allowed its databases, the National Population Register (NPR) and the Immigration, Visa, Foreigners Registration and Tracking System (IVFRT), to be linked to NATGRID.

Crime and Criminal Tracking Network & Systems (CCTNS)

Following the 2008 Mumbai terrorist attacks, the creation of the Crime and Criminal Tracking Network & Systems (CCTNS) was proposed. In particular, the Union Home Minister mentioned the role of the CCTNS during the IB Endowment lecture at Vigyan Bhawan, New Delhi on 23rd December 2009 in the following words:

"The police stations in the country are, today, virtually unconnected islands. Thanks to telephones and wireless, and especially thanks to mobile telephones, there is voice connectivity between the police station and senior police officers, but that is about all. There is no system of data storage, data sharing and accessing data. There is no system under which one police station can talk to another directly. There is no record of crimes or criminals that can be accessed by a Station House Officer, except the manual records relating to that police station. Realising the gross deficiency in connectivity, the Central government is implementing an ambitious scheme called "Crime and Criminal Tracking Network System (CCTNS)".

As such, the goals of the CCTNS are to facilitate the collection, storage, retrieval, analysis, transfer and sharing of data and information at the police stations and between the police stations and the State Headquarters and the Central Police Organisations. The Cabinet Committee on Economic Affairs approved the CCTNS in 2009 within the outlay of Rs. 2,000 crore in the 11th Five Year Plan. This project was initiated by the Ministry of Home Affairs and implemented by the National Crime Records Bureau.

The CCTNS was formally launched in early January 2013 in New Delhi. This project aims to create a comprehensive and integrated system for effective policing and sharing data of crimes and criminals among 14,000 police stations across all the 35 states and Union Territories of India. The CCTNS is part of the process of modernising the police force and was introduced under the national e-governance scheme. In its first phase in Tamil Nadu in February 2012, the CCTNS was introduced in Thiruvallur, Ariyalur, Sivaganga and Coimbatore, where the First Information Reports and details of the cases have been computerised and stored at the State Informatics Centre.

It is estimated that Rs. 2,000 crore have been allocated for the CCTNS, which connects more than 21,000 locations. Under the CCTNS project, approximately 14,000 police stations throughout India are being automated and connected, excluding 6,000 police offices which are high in the police hierarchy. The objectives of the CCTNS project are the following:

- Increase transparency by automating the function of police stations
- Improve the delivery of citizen-centric services through the effective usage of ICT
- Provide the Investigating Officers of the Civil Police with tools, technology and information to facilitate the investigation of crime and detection of criminals
- Improve the function of the police in various other areas, such as Law and Order, Traffic Management, etc.
- Facilitate the interaction and sharing of information among police stations, districts, State/UT headquarters and other police agencies

- Assist Senior Police Officers in the better management of the Police Force
- Keep track of the progress of cases (including those in Court)
- Reduce the manual and redundant keeping of records.

Home Secretary R.K. Singh stated that the CCTNS will provide a comprehensive database of crimes and criminals, which will enable law enforcement agencies in tracking down criminals moving from one place to another. Mr. Singh also stated that the CCTNS will increase transparency in police administration, since individuals will be able to launch complaints online and to view the status of their reports. Moreover, Mr. Singh stated:

"This will be a wide database. It will help in arresting criminals and investigating any case. This will be a big milestone."

Additionally, the Minister of State for Home R.P.N. Singh stated that the CCTNS will create a nation-wide environment for real-time sharing of crime and criminal information. Referring to the gang-rape of a girl in Delhi, Singh said:

"We could not protect this one daughter of India but now we have to protect the over a billion men and women for whom we are responsible. This is the greatest service we can do for our country."

Data Sharing Centres and Bodies

- The National Cyber Coordination Centre: The Central Government is currently in the process of approving a new security body that would be responsible for cyber intelligence and cyber security. According to news items, the body will come under the National Information Board and would be a multi- agency body under the Department of Electronics and IT. The NCCC is currently a Rs. 950 crore project with the objective of streamlining coordination between intelligence agencies and to screen all forms of meta data. The NCCC will also monitor internet traffic within the country and coming in and out of the country at the international gateways for cyber threats. Mandates that are currently beyond the scope of India's CERT-IN.
- The Forensics Science Laboratories: Under the Information

Technology Act Forensic Science Laboratories are 'Examiners of Electronic Evidence' for the purpose of providing expert opinion on digital evidence. Divisions within Forensic Science Laboratories include: physics, chemistry, biology, serology, ballistics, documents, finger prints, forensic psychology, photo, computer forensic science & scientific aids divisions with laboratories for computer forensics and DNA profiling which are ISO/IEC 17025 compliant. Forensic Science Laboratories are under the administrative control of the CBI and answer to the Ministry of Home Affairs. Experts from the CFSL can also give expert opinion, testify, and provide evidence in a court of law.

- New Delhi Police – Centre for analysing social media: As of June 2014 the New Delhi Police are reported to be in the process of establishing a centre to monitor social media content for the purpose of understanding the 'mood' of the public and to identify potential threats or worrisome content. The centre is supposed to run on its own dedicated server with software approved by the government. In news items, officials have noted that, though not as complex, the centre is meant to be like the monitoring centre set up by the London police after riots that took place in 2011.
- The National Counter Terrorism Centre (NCTC): In 2012 the NCTC was proposed as a centralized body under the Unlawful Activities (Prevention) Act, 1967, for the purpose of addressing and deploying counter terrorism measures of the Union and state governments. Though the NCTC was supported by the Central Government, many State Governments opposed its establishment citing concerns around lack of consensus amongst states and effectiveness of the centre. The Home Ministry justified the need for a centralized counter terrorism centre that specifically had jurisdiction over state governments because of the lack of action by states, a lack of professionalism, and the use of state forces for political purposes. It was proposed to locate the NCTC under the umbrella of the Intelligence Bureau,

with the Director of the NCTC being the Additional Director of the IB. The stated purpose of the NCTC was to analyse and maintain relevant intelligence and develop and direct responses to the Union and State government in the face of terror threats. Additionally, the NCTC was to maintain a data base of terrorists and their associates, friends, families, supporters, and all other information pertaining to terrorists. In an order titled "The National Counter Terrorism Centre (Organisation, Functions, Powers, and Duties Order, 2010" it was highlighted that the NCTC should not replicate the efforts of other agencies in the country, and instead should 'work through' them. To enable this, the order recommended that NCTC staff should be drawn from RAW, JIC, NTRO, DIA, DGMI, DAI, CEIB, CBDT, CBEC etc. The Order also noted that Officers in the 'Operations' division will have the power to search and arrest as per section 43A of the Unlawful Activities (Prevention) Act, 1967, the NCTC will also have the power to set up Inter-State Intelligence Support Teams and to use the services of the National Security Guard and other special forces, and seek information such as documents, reports, transcripts, and cyber information from other agencies. A Standing Council to ensure that the NCTC in the single and effective point of control and coordination for counter terrorism measures.

- Safe City Project and Fusion Data Centres: In 2013 the Ministry of Home Affairs, PM Division published guidelines for the development of mega policing projects. It is envisioned that Delhi, Kolkata, Mumbai, Chennia, Hyderabad, Bangalore, and Ahemadabad would implement the Mega City Policing projects. Among other aspects, the guidelines provide instructions for the establishment of Fusion Cenres/Data Centres. According to the guidelines: "*The Fusion/Data Centre would be playing a very crucial role in prevention and detection as also investigation of crime or security related challenges. It will, however be necessary to have upto date and comprehensive databases from various fields, for example, Vehicle registration numbers, Unique*

ID numbers of the citizens, residential addresses, Pan card details, crime related details. The accessibility of these databases by the Fusion Centres will have to be ensured by defining MoU or Law Enforcement Agreements or State Legislations to enable the State to have access to the private data on individuals without any encroachment on the privacy rights of the individuals."

In 2010, 66.92 crores were dedicated to revamping special branches/intelligence agencies. This included GIS mapping, integrated documentation systems and integrated data centres, voice loggers, IED Jammers, VHF Mobile Jammers. These funds are sanctioned by the High Powered Committee under the MHA.

Lawful Intercept & Monitoring (LIM) Systems

In September 2013 it was reported that the Indian Government was running Lawful Intercept and Monitoring (LIM) systems over the last years, widely in secret. Following the Mumbai 2008 terrorist attacks, the Centre for Development of Telematics (C-DOT) deployed the LIM systems for the monitoring of Internet traffic, emails, web browsing, Skype and any other Internet activity of users in India.

In particular, mobile operators in India have deployed their own LIM systems to monitor communications running through their networks, which allow for the "lawful interception" of calls by government agencies. Such "lawful interception" is carried out under Section 5(2) of the Indian Telegraph Act, 1885, read with Rule 419(A). In the case of Internet traffic, the LIM systems are deployed by the Government of India at the international gateways of large Internet Service Providers (ISPs). As such, the functioning of the LIM systems is beyond the control of these ISPs and these surveillance systems are completely controlled by the Government.

Lawful interception by mobile operators using LIM systems appears to entail targeted The In 2013 the Government of India proposed Standard Operating Procedures (SOPs) for phone-tapping in the country. According to news items reporting on these guidelines:

"The purpose of the Standard Operating Procedures (SOPs) is to lay minimum required guidelines for lawful interception and monitoring

process across all telecom service providers (TSPs) to ensure systematic and tamper-proof monitoring of target numbers and have uniformity on critical issues of interception and monitoring which should be followed scrupulously."

All requests for interception and monitoring of voice, SMS, GPRS, VAS, MMS, video calls or VoIP can be made under the Indian Telegraph Act, 1885. These Standard Operating Procedures provide guidelines for all interception and monitoring of telecommunications, which is carried out under the Indian Telegraph Act, 1885, or under the Information Technology (Amendment) Act, 2008. As such, mobile operators in India which use LIM systems for the lawful interception of their communications may have to comply with the Standard Operating Procedures issued by the Government.

In the case of Internet traffic though, the Government's monitoring systems appear to have the capability to carry out mass surveillance, since they are installed between the ISPs Internet Edge Router (PE) and the core network and have an "always live" link to the entire traffic. As such, LIM systems appear to have broad surveillance capabilities with access to all Internet activity, which is not limited to IPs, email addresses, URLs or webmails, but which expand to a broad search across all Internet traffic using "keywords" and "keyphrases".

LIM systems are available to nine security agencies, including the Intelligence Bureau (IB), the Research and Analysis Wing (RAW) and the Ministry of Home Affairs (MHA). Other agencies which are authorised for lawful interception include the Central Board of Direct Taxes (CBDT), the Central Bureau of Investigation (CBI), the Directorate of Revenue Intelligence (DRI) and the Narcotics Control Bureau (NCB).

In early 2012 the Government of India issued Standard Operating Procedures (SOPs) for lawful interception and monitoring. The Standard Operating Procedures provide guidelines to security agencies based on which the lawful interception and monitoring of communications should be carried out. These guidelines state, among other things, that the interception of communications should not exceed 180 days and that orders for interception should be issued in emergency situations. It remains unclear, though, if the LIM systems used by the Government at the international gateways of ISPs are in compliance with the Standard Operating Procedures.

Additionally, it was reported in July 2013 that BlackBerry granted the Indian Government access to its messaging services, which include BlackBerry Messenger (BBM) and BlackBerry Internet Service (BIS) email. BlackBerry though emphasized that the Government of India will not have access to the BlackBerry Enterprise Server (BES). Through the lawful interception system for BlackBerry services, the Indian authorities will be able to track email and email attachments sent over the consumer-version of BlackBerry Internet Service (BIS), to see when chats sent over BlackBerry Messenger (BBM) were delivered and read and to monitor which websites were visited. BlackBerry has issued a statement confirming its cooperation with the Indian Government and has stated the following:

"The lawful access capability now available to BlackBerry's carrier partners meets the standard required by the Government of India for all consumer messaging services offered in the Indian marketplace."

Network Traffic Analysis (NETRA) System

In 2013 it was reported by the media that the Indian Government was soon launch a Network Traffic Analysis (NETRA) system, which will possibly be capable of real-time detection of suspicious "keywords" and "keyphrases" in social media, emails, blogs, tweets, instant messaging services, and in other types of Internet content. It has also been reported that the Ministry of Home Affairs is finalising the NETRA system, which will also likely be capable of capturing any dubious voice traffic through online communications. This system is possibly going to be carried out with the purpose of tackling crime and terrorism in India.

The NETRA system has been developed by the Centre for Artificial Intelligence and Robotics (CAIR), a lab under the Defence Research and Development Organisation (DRDO). The deployment strategy of NETRA was recently discussed between an inter-ministerial group comprising of officials of the Cabinet Secretariat,

Home Ministry, DRDO, CAIR, Intelligence Bureau, Centre for Development of Telematics (C-DOT) and Computer Emergency Response Team (CERT-In). Along with the discussion on NETRA's deployment strategy, this inter- ministerial group also discussed a strategy on how to deal with computer security incidents, track system vulnerabilities and promote effective IT security practices across India. As quoted in news items, a government official stated:

"When NETRA is operationalised, security agencies will get a big handle on monitoring activities of dubious people and organisations which use the Internet to carry out nefarious designs."

Central Monitoring System (CMS)

In 2009, following the Mumbai 2008 terrorist attacks, the Government of India envisioned the creation of a Central Monitoring System (CMS) which would centralise the interception of communications data and enable access to it by law enforcement agencies. As such, the Central Monitoring System started off as a project run by the Centre for Communications Security Research and Monitoring (CCSRM), along with the Telecom Testing and Security Certification (TTSC) project.

The Central Monitoring System (CMS), which was largely covered by the media in 2013, was actually approved by the Cabinet Committee on Security (CCS) on 16th June 2011 and the pilot project was completed by 30th September 2011. Ever since, the CMS has been operated by India's Telecom Enforcement Resource and Monitoring (TERM) cells, and has been implemented by the Centre for Development of Telematics (C-DOT), which is an Indian Government owned telecommunications technology development centre. The CMS has been implemented in three phases, each one taking about 13-14 months. Government funding of the CMS has reached at least Rs. 450 crore (around USD 72 million).

Prior to the CMS, all service providers in India were required to have Lawful Interception Systems installed at their premises in order to carry out targeted surveillance of individuals by monitoring communications running through their networks. As per amendments to service providers licenses, all Telecom Service

Providers (TSPs) in India are required to integrate Interception Store & Forward (ISF) servers with their pre-existing Lawful Interception Systems. Once ISF servers are installed in the premises of TSPs in India and integrated with Lawful Interception Systems (LIM), they are then connected to the Regional Monitoring Centres (RMC) of the CMS. Each Regional Monitoring Centre (RMC) in India is connected to the Central Monitoring System (CMS). In short, the CMS involves the collection and storage of data intercepted by TSPs in central and regional databases.

In other words, all data intercepted by TSPs is automatically transmitted to Regional Monitoring Centres, and subsequently automatically transmitted to the Central Monitoring System. This means that the CMS authority will have centralized access to intercepted data. This is due to the fact that, unlike in the case of the current lawful interception regime where the nodal officers of TSPs are notified about interception requests, the CMS allows for data to be automatically transmitted to its data centre, without the involvement of TSPs.

The interface testing of TSPs and their Lawful Interception Systems has already been completed and, as of June 2013, 70 ISF servers have been purchased for six License Service Areas and are being integrated with the Lawful Interception Systems of TSPs. The Centre for Development of Telematics has already fully installed and integrated two ISF servers in the premises of two of India's largest service providers: MTNL and Tata Communications Limited. In Delhi, ISF servers which connect with the CMS have been installed for all TSPs and testing has been completed. In Haryana, three ISF servers have already been installed in the premises of TSPs and the rest of currently being installed. In Chennai, five ISF servers have been installed so far, while in Karnataka, ISF servers are currently being integrated with the Lawful Interception Systems of the TSPs in the region.

The Centre for Development of Telematics plans to integrate ISF servers which connect with the CMS in the premises of service providers in the following regions:

- Delhi
- Maharashtra

- Kolkata
- Uttar Pradesh (West)
- Andhra Pradesh
- Uttar Pradesh (East)
- Kerala
- Gujarat
- Madhya Pradesh
- Punjab
- Haryana

In order to require Telecom Service Providers (TSPs) to intercept all telecommunications in India as part of the CMS, clause 41.10 of the Unified Access Services (UAS) License Agreement was amended in June 201360. In particular, the amended clause includes the following:

"But, in case of Centralized Monitoring System (CMS), Licensee shall provide the connectivity up to the nearest point of presence of MPLS (Multi Protocol Label Switching) network of the CMS at its own cost in the form of dark fibre with redundancy. If dark fibre connectivity is not readily available, the connectivity may be extended in the form of 10 Mbps bandwidth upgradeable up to 45 Mbps or higher as conveyed by the Government, till such time the dark fibre connectivity is established. However, LICENSEE shall endeavor to establish connectivity by dark optical fibre at the earliest. From the point of presence of MPLS network of CMS onwards traffic will be handled by the Government at its own cost."

With regards to the UAS License Agreement that TSPs are required to comply with, amended clause 41.10 specifies certain details about how the CMS functions.

In particular, the amended clause mandates that TSPs in India will provide connectivity up to the nearest point of presence of MPLS (Multi Protocol Label Switching) network of the CMS at their own cost and in the form of dark optical fibre.

From the MPLS network of the CMS onwards, traffic will be handled by the Government at its own cost. It is noteworthy that a Memorandum of Understanding (MoU) for MPLS connectivity has been signed with one of India's largest ISPs/TSPs: BSNL. In fact, Rs. 4.8 crore have been given to BSNL for interconnecting 81 CMS locations of the following License Service Areas:

- Delhi
- Mumbai
- Haryana
- Rajasthan
- Kolkata
- Karnataka
- Chennai
- Punjab

Clause 41.10 of the UAS License Agreement also mandates that the hardware and software required for monitoring calls will be engineered, provided, installed and maintained by the TSPs at their own cost. Moreover, this clause mandates that TSPs are required to monitor *at least 30 simultaneous calls* for each of the nine designated law enforcement agencies. In addition to monitored calls, clause 41.10 of the UAS License Agreement also requires service providers to make the following records available to Indian law enforcement agencies:

- Called/calling party mobile/PSTN numbers
- Time/date and duration of interception
- Location of target subscribers (Cell ID & GPS)
- Data records for failed call attempts
- CDR (Call Data Records) of Roaming Subscriber
- Forwarded telephone numbers by target subscriber

Furthermore, draft Rule 419B under Section 5(2) of the Indian Telegraph Act, 1885, allows for the disclosure of "message related information" / Call Data Records (CDR) to Indian authorities.

Call Data Records, otherwise known as Call Detail Records, contain metadata (data about data) that describe a telecommunication transaction, but not the content of that transaction.

In other words, Call Data Records include data such as the phone numbers of the calling and called parties, the duration of the call, the time and date of the call, and other such information, while excluding the content of what was said during such calls. According to draft Rule 419B, directions for the disclosure of Call Data Records can only be issued on a national level through orders by the Secretary to the Government of India in the Ministry of Home Affairs, while on the state level, orders can only be issued by the Secretary to the State Government in charge of the Home Department.

5

Operation Blue Star: A Recap

Sword-wielding clashes in India's Golden Temple today marked the 30th anniversary of Operation Blue Star, a small recap of the violent yet successful effort of Prime Minister Indira Gandhi to rid the temple of militarized squatters. Few were seriously injured in today's incident.

Operation Blue Star was a six-day Indian military operation, ordered by Prime Minister Indira Gandhi in June 1984, with the intent of establishing control over the Sikh religion's most sacred temple in Amritsar, the Golden Temple. Many died on both sides, but the controversial operation was successful in its desired outcome. Leading up to the assault, buildings within the Harmandir Sahib (Golden Temple) complex had become the residence of Jarnail Singh Bhindranwale and his entourage. Bhindranwale was a leader of the Sikh religious group, Damdami Taksal, and he believed that Gandhi's policies were strongly anti-Punjab. The north Indian state of Punjab is predominantly Sikh. In all, the Indian government reports that 492 were killed, although others claim the number is closer to 5,000. Of the Indian army, 83 died and 220 were injured.

Harcharan Singh Longowal, President of the Akali Dal, a Sikh-centric political party that believes religion and politics go hand in hand, extended an invitation to Jarnail Singh Bhindranwale to take residence inside the Golden Temple complex. Such a refuge held appeal, as Bhindranwale was in danger of being arrested for threats he made against some Indian nationalist organizations.

Over the objection of the head priest of the Golden Temple, Jarnail Singh and his armed followers moved into the holy Akal Takhat within the Golden Temple complex. Bhindranwale used his political connections to overrule the priest.

The group armed themselves with self-loading rifles and fortified the temple with heavy machine-guns. In their book *Amritsar: Mrs. Gandhi's Last Battle,* Mark Tully and Satish Jacob recap the lead-in to the execution of Operation Blue Star by noting that shopkeepers and neighbors who lived in the areas surrounding the temple knew each of the invaders by name and so the police would certainly have known them as well. Arrests were not made, however. "By this time," they wrote, "Bhindranwale and his men were above the law." The operation began on June 3 with the imposition of a 36-hour curfew around Punjab. Public communication and travel services were suspended. The military portion of the operation is infamous for its brutality, with troops from the Indian Army having used tanks, heavy artillery, helicopters, armored vehicles and even chemical weapons. Some argue that excessive deaths could have been avoided with the use of blockade tactics.

Jarnail Singh Bhindranwale did not survive the battle. Nor did Indira Gandhi, as Operation Blue Star is acknowledged as the main reason for her murder. Five months after the operation, Gandhi's Sikh bodyguards, Satwant Singh and Beant Singh, ambushed and killed her.

Recently declassified documents from the United Kingdom (UK) provide a more contemporary recap of Operation Blue Star. The records reveal that a series of meetings took place between India's Research and Analysis Wing (RAW) and the UK's Secret Intelligence Service, known as MI6. The meetings took place to formulate a plan to remove those holed up in the Golden Temple complex while minimizing civilian casualties.

THE UNTOLD STORY BEFORE OPERATION BLUESTAR

It was a blistering April afternoon in 1984. A white Ambassador car drove into the driveway of a modest Lutyens Delhi bungalow,

1 Safdarjung Road, Prime Minister Indira Gandhi's residence. A tall bespectacled man got out. He was known only as DGS or director general security, a key official in the Research and Analysis Wing (RAW) who controlled a small air force and two covert paramilitary units, the Special Frontier Force and the Special Services Bureau. Three years earlier, DGS had raised another unit, called the Special Group or sg, for clandestine counter-terrorist missions in Punjab and Assam. For the past two months, SG personnel, all drawn from the Army, had been training in secret at a base near Delhi for a critical mission.

DGS was ushered into the living room where a pensive Mrs Gandhi sat with a salt-and-pepper-haired gentleman wearing thick black glasses-Rameshwar Nath Kao, 66, the reclusive spymaster who had built the external intelligence agency, RAW, in 1968 and used it to train Mukti Bahini guerrillas during the Bangladesh war in 1971. He had returned to government as Mrs Gandhi's senior aide in 1981 and was now her de facto national security adviser. More important, he was a key adviser on the Punjab problem. For over two years now, India's most prosperous state had been engulfed by communal violence. A radical group of Sikhs led by a fiery religious preacher Jarnail Singh Bhindranwale, 37, had declared war against the state. His motley group of armed supporters had, by 1984, murdered over 100 civilians and security personnel. The radical militant leader had then been ensconced near the Golden Temple since 1981 with his heavily armed followers, shielded by his proximity to Sikhism's holiest shrine.

DGS briefed Mrs Gandhi on a surgical mission that fell short of a military strike to evict the rebels. Operation Sundown, he explained, was a 'snatch and grab' job: Heliborne commandos would enter the Guru Nanak Niwas guesthouse near the Golden Temple and abduct the militant leader. The operation was so named because it was timed for past midnight when Bhindranwale and his guards would least expect it.

SG operatives had earlier infiltrated the Golden Temple, disguised as pilgrims and journalists, to study its layout. Then, for several weeks, over 200 SG commandos had rehearsed the operation on a wood and Hessian cloth mock-up of the two-storeyed resthouse at their base in Sarsawa in Uttar Pradesh. Commandos would rope down from two Mi-4 transport helicopters onto the guest house and make a beeline for Bhindranwale. Once they captured him, he would be spirited away by a ground assault team which would drive in. There was a possibility of a firefight with the militant leader's bodyguards and civilians who could rush in to protect him.

Mrs Gandhi's listened to the details impassively. She had just one question. "How many casualties?" Twenty per cent of the commando force and both helicopters, dgs replied. Mrs Gandhi grimaced. She wanted to know how many civilians would die. The RAW official did not have an answer. No one did. That was it. Mrs Gandhi said no and Operation Sundown died before the first helicopter could take off.

Just two months later, Mrs Gandhi ordered the Army to flush militants out of the temple.

Eighty-three armymen and 492 civilians died in Operation Bluestar, the single bloodiest confrontation in independent India's history of civil strife. Machine guns, light artillery, rockets and, eventually, battle tanks were used to overwhelm Bhindranwale and his mini army and the Akal Takht, the highest seat of temporal authority of the Sikhs, was reduced to a smoking ruin. In the maelstrom of Bluestar, Sundown and its extensive preparations got buried in RAW's secret archives.

Three decades later, Operation Sundown resurfaced in an unexpected location-London. On January 13, the United Kingdom was shocked by declassified letters dating to February 1984 that revealed that Margaret Thatcher's government had helped India on "a plan to remove Sikh extremists from the Golden Temple". This plan, according to a top-secret letter from the principal private secretary of then British foreign secretary Geoffrey Howe to the then home secretary Leon Brittan, was drawn up by an officer of the Special Air Services (SAS), UK's elite commando force. The letter, written four months before Bluestar, sparked fears of a backlash from the UK's Sikh community, prompting Prime Minister David Cameron to order an inquiry into the findings.

FESTERING WOUND

Operation Bluestar still touches a raw nerve in India and abroad. On September 30, 2012, four Sikh youths attempted to murder retired Lt-Gen Kuldip Singh Brar on London's Oxford Street. Brar, who led Bluestar, and a frequent visitor to London, survived. Two of his attackers were handed down a 14-year sentence in December last year. The new revelations about a possible British role in the build-up to Bluestar have already inflamed passions. "This obviously raises huge questions over the role of the British government at the time," Labour MP Tom Watson told bbc on January 13. Watson's constituency, West Bromwich East, has many Sikh constituents. New Delhi has so far not responded to the revelations. Brar calls reports of sas involvement in Bluestar "utter nonsense".

Retired RAW officials and former members of its secret military wing, however, tell a different story. The sas assistance was not for Bluestar, a pure army assault, they told india today. It was to vet Operation Sundown, a commando raid. As revealed by B. Raman, former head of raw's counter-terrorism division, in his 2007 book The Kaoboys of R&AW, two MI-5 intelligence liaison officials at the British high commission had scouted the Golden Temple complex in December 1983. They briefed a senior sas officer sent by the UK to Delhi who deemed the special operation feasible. The sas expertise was sought by Mrs Gandhi's spy chief R.N. Kao who had a personal equation with several foreign intelligence chiefs.

Though Sundown was aborted, some of the commandos who had trained for it spearheaded a near-suicidal frontal assault on the heavily fortified Akal Takht during Bluestar and stayed till the last militant was flushed out of the temple three days later. This is one reason those officers, long since retired, refuse to be identified. "My anonymity is my only protection," says one of the officers who lives in a metro.

If Kao was unhappy with Mrs Gandhi's rejection of Sundown, he didn't show it. In fact, his thinking was in line with her extreme caution. Weeks earlier, RAW station chiefs in foreign capitals, particularly those with large Sikh expatriate populations, had warned Kao of the adverse fallout of a military operation to flush out the militants. Kao had personally led the parleys with overseas Sikh separatists to persuade Bhindranwale to vacate the Golden Temple. "They promised him a lot," says a former RAW chief who is close to Kao, "but delivered nothing." "Another possible reason for the commando operation being called off was the influence of a 'soft group' within the Congress headed by Rajiv Gandhi which favoured a negotiated settlement with Bhindranwale," says Mandeep Singh Bajwa, a Chandigarh-based analyst.

In January 1984, the government had instituted secret talks with Bhindranwale at the behest of Rajiv. But within four months, hardliners on both sides prevailed. In late April 1984, Satish Jacob of bbc's Delhi bureau saw trucks carrying construction material into the temple. He also saw a slim, fair man of medium height in a white salwar kameez and sporting a flowing beard. Major General Shabeg Singh was a war hero who had trained Mukti Bahini fighters in 1971 but was stripped of his rank and court-martialled on charges of corruption just before he was to retire in 1976. Now, as the military adviser of Bhindranwale, he oversaw conversion of the five-storeyed Akal Takht into a fortress. "We're doing it for the community," the soft-spoken former general told Jacob.

INDIRA GANDHI GIVES THE GO-AHEAD

By May 1984, Punjab teetered on the brink. The daylight murder of dig A.S. Atwal inside the Golden Temple in April 1983 had paralysed Punjab Police into inaction. And the thousands of paramilitary personnel sent by Delhi after it dismissed the state government in October 1983 had failed to prevent the state's descent into chaos. On May 11, 1984, Bhindranwale rejected the final settlement offered by Mrs Gandhi's think tank led by Narasimha Rao to the Akali Dal. Soon after, Army chief General Arun Kumar Vaidya became a frequent visitor to Mrs Gandhi's office. Her personal secretary and confidant R.K. Dhawan was present at one of those half-hour meetings. "Gen Vaidya assured her there would be no casualties and there would be no damage to the Golden Temple," Dhawan told India Today. On June 2, talks with the Akalis collapsed.

As Mark Tully and Satish Jacob wrote in their 1985 book Amritsar: Mrs Gandhi's Last Battle, "Mrs Gandhi was not a decisive woman, she was very reluctant to act, and she only fought back when she was firmly pinned against the ropes." The Army was her last resort. She green-lit Operation Bluestar. Dhawan says two "extra-constitutional authorities" in Rajiv Gandhi's inner circle, who would later become key figures in his Cabinet, were responsible for her change of mind. "They told her the military option was the only solution," he says. The mantle fell on the Western Army commander, the flamboyant Lt-Gen Krishnaswamy Sundarji. He had briefly considered a plan to starve out the defenders but junked it fearing an uprising in the countryside.

BLUESTAR BLOODBATH

Shortly after 10.30 p.m. on June 5, 1984, 20 men in black dungarees stealthily entered the Golden Temple. They wore night-vision goggles, M-1 steel helmets, bulletproof vests and carried a mix of MP-5 submachine guns and AK-47 assault rifles. The men of sg's 56th Commando Company were then the only force in India trained for room intervention, the specialised art of fighting in confined spaces. Each commando was a sharpshooter, diver and parachutist and could do 40-km speed marches. Some of them wore gas masks and carried stubby gas guns meant to launch CX gas canisters, a more potent tear gas. Three months before this night, the commandos had stayed around the temple and rehearsed for Operation Sundown. Some of them still sported the beards they had grown for their undercover work as volunteers in the Golden Temple's langar. When the plan was called off, they returned to their base in Sarsawa. They had flown into Amritsar the previous day at the request of Lt-Gen Sundarji.

The three battalions that Lt-Gen Brar's 9th Infantry Division sent into the Golden Temple that night were trained to fight a conventional combat on the plains of Punjab and in the deserts of Rajasthan. They would overwhelm the enemy by sheer force of numbers. The commandos, who spearheaded the assault, made use of stealth, speed and surprise to achieve results. Soon after arriving, one of the sg officers had briefed Lt-Gen Ranjit Singh Dayal, Sundarji's chief of staff, on a plan to capture the Akal Takht by blowing off its rear wall. General Dayal, a paratrooper who had captured the Haji Pir pass in an unconventional operation in the 1965 war, immediately overruled it. "There must be no damage to the Akal Takht," he said. The commandos were to capture the sacred building by using gas to flush out the militants, he said.

The Army had clearly underestimated the defences. As soon as they entered the temple, a sniper shot the unit's radio operator clean through his helmet. The rest took cover in the long gallery of pillars that led to the Akal Takht. Light machine guns and carbines crackled from behind impregnable walls of the temple, their multiple gun flashes blinding the commandos' night-vision devices, forcing them to take them off. The commandos and infantry soldiers cautiously advanced, sheltering behind rows of pillars. Those who tried to advance towards the Akal Takht were cut down on the marble parikrama. An armoured personnel carrier bringing in troops was immobilised by a rocket-propelled grenade. "Shabeg knew the Army's Achilles heel," says an SG colonel. "He knew we couldn't fight in built-up areas."

Post-midnight, remnants of the sg unit and the Army's 1 Para huddled near a fountain at the base of the Akal Takht. The area between the Akal Takht and the Darshani Deori that led to the Golden Temple had turned into a killing zone, covered by Shabeg's light machine guns. Attempts by the para-commandos to storm the defences were repeatedly beaten back. They lost at least 17 men, their black dungaree-clad bodies lying prone on white marble. Commandos who tried to fire the CX gas canisters discovered that the Akal Takht's windows had been bricked up. The only openings were horizontal slots out of which machine guns poured deadly fire. The commandos neutralised two of the machine gun nests by dropping grenades into them but the Akal Takht was impregnable. Then, around 7.30 a.m. on June 5, three Vickers-Vijayanta tanks were deployed. They fired 105 mm shells and knocked down the walls of the Akal Takht. Commandos and infantrymen then moved in to mop up the defenders, tossing gas and lobbing grenades inside the building.

The temple premises resembled a medieval battlefield, one sg trooper recalls. Bloodied and blackened bodies lay scattered around the white temple parikrama. In the basement of the blackened, still-smoking ruin of the Akal Takht, the commandos found the body of Shabeg. The Army recovered 51 light machine guns, 31 of which had been concentrated around the Akal Takht. "Normally, an army unit (of around 800 soldiers) would deploy this quantum of firepower to cover an area of about eight km," Lt-Gen Brar recounted in his book Operation Blue Star: The True Story. Shabeg, he believed, wanted to hold out until daylight in the hope that there would be a popular uprising among the people when they get to know of the army action. The former war hero had extracted a bloody price on an army he felt had wronged him.

'Oh my God,' she said.

Around 6 a.m. on June 6, 1984, the phone rang in R.K. Dhawan's Golf Links home. Minister of State for Defence K.P. Singh Deo wanted Dhawan to convey an urgent message to Mrs Gandhi. The operation was a success, he said, but there were heavy casualties-both armymen and civilians. Mrs Gandhi's first reaction was anguish. "Oh my God, she told Dhawan. "They told me there would be no casualties."

It took the Army two more days to clear Bhindranwale's men from the temple's labyrinthine corridors. The commanding officer of the sg contingent, a lieutenant-colonel, was seriously wounded by a sniper as he escorted President Zail Singh around the temple on June 8.

Operation Bluestar inflamed Sikh sentiments and triggered a mutiny in certain Indian Army units. It also led to the death of Mrs Gandhi: Her two Sikh bodyguards gunned her down on October 31 that year. The communal holocaust in which over 8,000 Sikhs were murdered by mobs around the country-including 3,000 in Delhi-fanned another decade of insurgency in Punjab. In the aftermath of Mrs Gandhi's assassination, sg commandos, several of whom had seen action at the Golden Temple, were rushed to 7 Race Course Road to guard Rajiv Gandhi and his family round-the-clock for a year. They had plenty of time to wonder if history would have turned out differently had they been given the chance to carry out Operation Sundown.

RAW CHIEF CONSULTED MI6 IN BUILD-UP TO OPERATION BLUESTAR

Former Research and Analysis Wing chief Girish Saxena initiated a series of meetings with the United Kingdom's Secret Intelligence Service, commonly known as MI6, in the build-up to Operation Blue Star, highly-placed intelligence sources have told *The Hindu*.

The intelligence-sharing meetings, the sources said, were authorised by Prime Minister Indira Gandhi and included at least one visit by a mid-ranking officer of the élite Special Air Service commando unit to frame an assault plan which would minimise civilian casualties.

The sources were responding to revelations that India and the U.K. cooperated on Operation Bluestar, which have led to a snowballing controversy in both countries.

Mr. Saxena, who served as chief of RAW from 1983 to 1986, and then as security adviser to Prime Minister Rajiv Gandhi and Governor of Jammu and Kashmir, now lives in retirement in New Delhi. He remained unavailable for comment despite repeated efforts by *The Hindu*.

However, another RAW chief familiar with the period, Amarjit Singh Dulat, said the consultations may have formed part of regular India-U.K. consultations on Khalistan terrorism."

"In those days," said former RAW chief Amarjit Singh Dulat, "there was very close cooperation with the U.K. on the Khalistan issue. Key leads emanated from MI6 monitoring of Khalistan leaders based in the United Kingdom." "I do not recall any specific cooperation on Bluestar, though — and I think it is probably stretching the evidence to suggest that the United Kingdom had any role to play in the actual execution of the operation itself."

Declassified Revelations

Earlier this week, declassified United Kingdom government documents, first posted online by the Stop Deportations blog, stopdeportations.wordpress.com, revealed that India had consulted the United Kingdom on its decision to storm the Golden Temple in 1984. In a February 23, 1984 letter, B.J.P. Fall, private secretary to British Foreign Secretary Geoffrey Howe, wrote that "Indian authorities recently sought British advice over a plan to remove Sikh extremists from the Golden Temple in Amritsar." "The Foreign Secretary decided to respond favourably to the Indian request and, with the Prime Minister's agreement, an SAD [SAS] officer has visited India and drawn up a plan which has been approved by Mrs. Gandhi."

"The Foreign Secretary believes that the Indian Government may put the plan into operation shortly," the letter states.

F.E.R. Butler, at Prime Minister Margaret Thatcher's office, the documents reveal, wrote to the Defence Ministry and Cabinet Office on February 6, 1983, conveying her instructions to the Foreign Secretary to proceed with the SAS adviser's request.

Limited Consultations

RAW sources said the consultations were limited to seeking expert opinion on whether revanchist Sikh preacher Jarnail Singh Bhindranwale could be removed from the Golden Temple without killing pilgrims thronging the faith's most venerated institution. Bhindranwale, under pressure from a rival pro-Khalistan group, the Babbar Khalsa, had fled rooms on the periphery of the complex, taking up residence in the Akal Takht, the sanctum sanctorum.

Prime Minister Gandhi had contemplated military action against Bhindranwale since at least April, 1983, when a hit-squad he dispatched killed senior police officer A.S. Atwal. She however held back, fearing large-scale civilian killings. However, violence continued to escalate. K.P.S. Gill, Punjab's former police chief, has said that Bhindrawale's hit-squads killed 298 people between January 1, 1984 and June 3, 1984.

The SAS plan, the sources said, was rejected because Mr. Saxena was unconvinced it would work. Prime Minister Gandhi eventually handed charge of the operation to the Indian Army.

"The only plans we had were drawn up on the fly," said Brigadier Israr Khan, who led the attack under the command of Lieutenant-General Kuldip Singh Brar. "Major Jasbir Singh Raina, one of my officers, infiltrated the temple dressed as a pilgrim, scouting out hardened defences inside the temple on June 2, just one day before operations to clear the complex began."

Later, Brigadier Khan said, his troops broke open the shutters on stores near the Golden Temple, taking photographs and posters meant for pilgrims in order to develop crude operations maps.

A BRITISH ROLE IN 1984

Thirty years on from the horrific events of 1984 that took place across Punjab and India, the true story behind Operations Bluestar, Woodrose and the Delhi Genocide remains untold. It is a sensitive topic for both Punjabis and Sikhs alike of all generations, wherever they might be in the World today, and any news or media attention is jumped upon instantly for the insights that it may provide. In that regard, newly released records at the National Archives in London which prove that the British Government was involved in planning the military assault on Darbar Sahib have spread rapidly throughout social media this morning.

The documents in question are part of a series of letters depicting UK-Indian relations that were released a fortnight ago. They consist of correspondence between members of the Cabinet and their senior staff – such items are usually released to the public 30 years after their creation – and images of the two particular documents of interest were published on the Stop Deportations website along with a summation of their importance. The Member of Parliament (MP) for West Bromwich East, Tom Watson shared his concerns about the information contained in the documents and has stated that he, *"is writing to the Foreign Secretary about this matter and will raise it in the House of Commons,"* expecting a full explanation.

The correspondence between Private Secretaries to the Home Secretary and Foreign Secretary in the early months of 1984 acknowledge that an SAS advisor had travelled in secret to India to offer advice and assist in drawing up a plan to invade the Darbar Sahib. These are not new revelations; British involvement (as well as that of Russian intelligence) has been suspected by a number of writers dating back to as early as the latter months of 1984 itself, but this is the first irrefutable evidence of such collusion to be presented. The questions it raises are numerous particularly for the Sikh Diaspora in the United Kingdom who should no doubt now be demanding answers from our own Government and Parliamentarian representatives as to how and why they deemed interference in Punjab-State affairs a worthwhile activity. However, of greater interest should be what actions the British Government took to monitor and control the "*domestic implications*" that they foresaw following an assault on Darbar Sahib. It is again no secret that a number of prominent Sikhs in the United Kingdom were acting in private and/or third party interests in the years that followed 1984, all of which was intended to halt political activism and progress within the Sikh Diaspora; indeed some of them continue to enjoy positions of influence today – perhaps they will be sleeping uneasily tonight knowing that it is only a matter of time before their own incendiary purposes are revealed.

The build-up to what eventually took place in June of 1984 had begun years earlier, decades even, and so the advice of any British Special Forces coming early in 1984 is limited in scope. The full-scale model of the Darbar Sahib that had been built in the Chakrata-Mussoorie range, as well as the mobilisation of troops into key towns and cities for the all-too-often unmentioned Operation Woodrose had been planned for well in advance, as had processes to ensure a media blackout and total curfew on travel. Nevertheless, evidence that shows there was collusion of some sort between the British and Indian Governments heralds a new dawn for better understanding the battle for Amritsar and the wider events of 1984. Activists and researchers (including myself) will be buoyant in the knowledge that the truth of what took place and why will find its way to the public's ear, some way, some how. Thirty years may have passed, but the Truth is still out there.

GANDHI TOLD THATCHER ON OPERATION BLUE STAR

Former Prime Minister Indira Gandhi wrote a personal letter to her British counterpart Margaret Thatcher soon after the 1984 Operation Bluestar in an attempt to justify her decision to send army to flush out militants from the Golden Temple, the holiest Sikh shrine.

The letter, dated June 14, 1984, was made public for the first time on Tuesday as part of a British government inquiry into the role played by the UK in the lead up to the Indian army operation on Golden Temple in Amritsar to remove militants.

"It is never easy to undertake security action involving a place of worship... but this place, so sacred to the people of the Sikh faith, had been converted by terrorists into a base of operations," wrote Gandhi just days after the operation that left more than 1,000 people dead.

Also Read: UK admits 'purely advisory' role in Operation Blue Star

"We did know that arms were being collected there. But only after last week's action did we realise how vast and sophisticated these weapons were... For months a reign of terror was unleashed from the temple complex, holding all Punjab to ransom. We had no choice but to send an army unit which exercised the utmost restraint, using a minimum of force," she added.

The former Indian prime minister also shared her regrets over the fallout of the military action with Thatcher, one of her close political allies.

"Many in the Sikh community have been shaken by this traumatic event. The process of healing and conciliation will take time but we shall persevere," she wrote.

The letter is among five additional documents released with the inquiry report by UK Cabinet Secretary Jeremy Heywood which would not normally have been published.

Among them is a note dated February 23, 1984, that sets out how an eight-day visit by a British military expert had helped draw out a "realistic and workable plan" to root out extremists from the Golden Temple as the Indians were fairly unprepared for action and were applying a "sledgehammer to crack a nut" principle to the whole operation.

British Prime Minister David Cameron had ordered the inquiry after documents released under the 30-year declassification rule here implied British SAS commanders had advised the Indian government as it drew up plans for a military operation on Golden

Temple in February 1984. "We have taken this step because the whole investigation has been based on a commitment to the maximum possible transparency," Britain's foreign secretary William Hague told parliament in London on Tuesday as part of a statement on probe.

"We want to be as open as possible with the British public, in so far as that does not undermine the principle upheld by successive British governments of not revealing any information relating to Intelligence or Special Forces," Hague added in reference to certain names and sentences blanked out in the documents.

Describing the loss of life as part of Operation Bluestar an "utter tragedy", he revealed that the nature of the UK's assistance was "purely advisory, limited and provided to the Indian government at an early stage in their planning".

"It is also consistent with an exchange of letters between Mrs Gandhi and Mrs Thatcher on 14th and 29th June 1984 discussing the operation, which made no reference to any UK assistance," he said.

Labour's Douglas Alexander, the shadow foreign secretary, called on the government to publish the second letter as well as all other related material. Hague, however, stressed that no further documents will be made public, adding: "The investigation did not find any evidence in the files or from officials of the provision of UK military advice being linked to potential defence or helicopter sales, or to any other policy or commercial issue.

"There is no evidence that the UK, at any level, attempted to use the fact that military advice had been given on request to advance any commercial objective."

The cabinet secretary's inquiry report also points out that the fact that the UK provided some operational advice at the request of the Indian intelligence coordinator had already been put in the public domain in 2007 through a book by Bahukutumbi Raman, a former member of India's Intelligence Research and Analysis Wing.

"The UK government did send one military officer to provide military advice on Indian contingency plans for an operation at

Sri Harmandir Sahib. This military advice was a one-off. It was not sustained. There was no other UK military assistance, such as training or equipment, to the Indians with Operation Blue Star," the Heywood report states.

"The UK government did not link the provision of this military advice to defence sales. The decision to help was taken in response to a request for advice from a country with which the UK had — and has — a close relationship. The military advice from the UK officer had limited impact in practice.

"The actual operation implemented by the Indian army differed significantly from the approach suggested by the UK military officer," it concludes.

6

R&AW Involvement in East Pakistan Secession

A sensational American report has confirmed the Research and Analysis Wing (RAW), India's most powerful intelligence agency, was directly involved in the secession of East Pakistan into Bangladesh, and is currently engaged in similar activities. RAW has a long history of activity in Bangladesh supporting both secular forces and the area's Hindu minority, masterminding the break up of Pakistan in 1971, says the report made available to the News Intelligence Network (NIN) The report has been prepared by the innocent sounding Federation of American Scientists (FAS), a group which is however engaged in analysis and advocacy on science, technology and public policy concerning global security, especially about countries which have nuclear capability.

It is a privately funded non-profit policy organisation, whose Board of Sponsors includes 55 American Nobel laureates. FAS was originally founded as the Federation of Atomic Scientists in 1945 by members of the Manhattan Project, who produced the first atomic bomb. RAW is extensively engaged in disinformation campaigns, espionage, sabotage and terrorism against Pakistan and other neighbouring countries, reveals the sensational secret report. It also gives details of the truly alarming involvement of RAW in terrorist activities in Pakistan. The report reveals the involvement of RAW in Bangladesh dating from the 1960s, when it promoted dissatisfaction against Pakistan in the then East Pakistan, including funding Mujibur Rahman's general election in

1970 and providing training and arming to the Mukti Bahini. The report claims an estimated 35,000 RAW agents have entered Pakistan at various times between 1983-99, with 12,000 having worked in the past or working presently in Sindh, 10,000 in Punjab 8,000 in North West Frontier Province and 5,000 in Balochistan. "As many as 40 terrorist camps are currently operating at Rajasthan, East Punjab, [occupied] Kashmir, Uttar Pradesh and other parts of India and are run by RAW's Special Service Bureau [SSB]," the report reveals. The report further confirms that throughout the Afghan War, RAW was responsible for the planning and execution of terrorist activities in Pakistan to deter Islamabad from supporting the Afghan liberation movement against India's ally, the Soviet Union.

"The assistance provided to RAW by the KGB enabled RAW to arrange terrorist attacks in Pakistani cities throughout the Afghan War," the report says. "The defeat of the Soviet Union in Afghanistan did not end the role of RAW in Pakistan, as it established training camps in East Punjab, [occupied] Kashmir, Uttar Pradesh and Rajasthan where agents are trained for terrorist activities," it reveals.

It further says that RAW has become "an effective instrument of India's national power, and has assumed a significant role in formulating India's domestic and foreign policies." RAW, according to the report, has enjoyed the backing of successive Indian governments in these efforts. Working directly under the Prime Minister, the structure rank, pay and perks of the Research and Analysis Wing are kept secret from parliament.

"Current policy debates in India have generally failed to focus on the relative priority given by RAW to activities directed against India's neighbours versus attention to domestic affairs to safeguard India's security and territorial integrity," the report says. It points out that RAW has had limited success in dealing with separatist movements in Manipur and Tripura in the northeast, Tamil Nadu in the south and Punjab and Kashmir in the northwestern part of the country.

RAW, it adds, has failed to neutralise freedom fighters in Kashmir and similar indigenous movements in Kerala, Karnataka and other places, along with economic and industrial espionage activities in New Delhi and Bombay. Giving a background of the intelligence agency, the American report says RAW was set up in 1968 "specifically targeted on Pakistan".

Pakistan, the report says, has accused RAW of sponsoring sabotage in its Punjab province, where it has been supporting the Seraiki movement, "providing financial support to promote its activities in Pakistan and organising an International Seraiki Conference in Delhi in November December 1993". It adds: "RAW has an extensive network of agents and anti-government elements within Pakistan, including dissident elements from various sectarian and ethnic groups of Sindh and Punjab."

According to it, India is funding the current upsurge of terrorism in Pakistan "and has been behind the sectarian violence between Shias and Sunnis, which has resulted in thousands of deaths in the last few years." Terrorist activities in Pakistan attributed to the clandestine activities of RAW in the report include:

A car bomb explosion in the Saddar area of Peshawar on 21 December 1995, which caused the death of 37 persons and injured over 50 others.

An explosion at Shaukat Khanum Hospital on 14 April 1996, claiming the lives of seven persons and injuries to over 34 others.

A bus traveling from Lahore to Sahiwal was blown up at Bhai Pheru on 28 April 1996, causing the deaths of 44 persons on the spot and injuring 30 others.

An explosion in a bus near the Sheikhupura Hospital killed nine persons and injured 29 others on 08 May 1996.

An explosion near Alam Chowk, Gujranwala on 10 June 1996 which killed three persons and injured 11 others.

A bomb exploded on a bus on GT Road near Kharian on 10 June 1996, killing 2 persons and injuring 10 others.

On 27 June 1996, an explosion opposite Madrassah Faizul Islam, Faizabad, Rawalpindi, killed 5 persons and injured over 50 others.

A bomb explosion in the Faisalabad Railway Station passenger lounge on 8 July 1996 killed 3 persons and injured 20 others.

Another startling claim made by the American report is that it was RAW that was behind the hijacking of an Indian airliner to Lahore in 1971, "attributed to the Kashmiris, to give a terrorist dimension to the Kashmiri national movement".

The report continues: "During the course of its investigation the Jain Commission received testimony on the official Indian support to the various Sri Lankan Tamil armed groups in Tamil Nadu," the report reveals. From 1981, RAW and the Intelligence Bureau, according to the report, established a network of as many as 30 training bases for these groups in India. Centres were also established at the high-security military installation of Chakrata, near Dehra Dun, and in the Ramakrishna Puram area of New Delhi.

The report says that RAW and the Ministry of External Affairs are provided Rs. 250 million annually as "discretionary grants" for foreign influence operations. "These funds have supported organisations fighting Sikh and Kashmiri separatists in the UK, Canada and the US," it says.

It further reveals: "An Extensive network of Indian operatives is controlled by the Indian Embassy in Washington, DC whose covert activities include the infiltration of US long distance telephone carriers by Indian operatives, with access to all kinds of information, to blackmail relatives of US residents living in India". Citing an example, it says that in 1996, an Indian diplomat was implicated in a scandal over illegal funding of political candidates in the US. Under US law foreign nationals are prohibited from contributing to federal elections.

The US District Court in Baltimore sentenced Lalit H. Gadhia, a naturalised US citizen of Indian origin, to three months imprisonment. Gadhia had confessed that he worked as a conduit between the Indian Embassy and various Indian-American organisations for funnelling campaign contributions to influence US lawmakers. Over US $46,000 from the Indian Embassy was distributed among 20 Congressional candidates. The source of the cash used by Gadhia was Devendra Singh, a RAW official assigned to the Indian Embassy in Washington, the report says. It adds that illicit campaign money received in 1995 went to Democratic candidates including US Senators Charles S Robb (D-VA), Paul S. Sarbanes (D-MD) and US Representatives Benjamin L Cardin (D-MD) and Steny H. Hoyer (D-MD) – (May 24, 1998).

INDIAN SECRET AGENCY RAW BEHIND SECESSION OF EAST PAKISTAN

As commonly believed in Pakistan, it has now been confirmed that India played a pro-active role in causing discontent in former East Pakistan, resulting in its cessation from rest of the country. Here are the details:

In May, 1999 the US State department, in its annual report on terrorism, spared three lengthy paragraphs for Pakistan (as a victim of terrorism and sectarian strife). It is learnt that the US authorities strongly believe that RAW and some other Indian intelligence agencies have been the only source of terrorism in Pakistan.

It is learnt that experts are of the firm view that RAW, India's external intelligence agency, is not the only secret agency of India, assigned the duties to carry out subversive activities in Pakistan but in fact several other Indian agencies have also been given similar assignments.

According to The Daily Mail findings, a Joint Intelligence Committee (JIC) at Delhi assigned terrorist and sabotage duties to the Intelligence Bureau, RAW, Military Intelligence, Naval Intelligence, Air Intelligence, Special Frontier Force, Joint Cipher Bureau etc. All these agencies have been actively executing plans of terrorism formulated by the succeeding governments in many countries of the region, particularly Pakistan. RAW during Partition and Thereafter RAW has a long history of activity in Bangladesh, supporting both secular forces and the area's Hindu minority.

The involvement of RAW in East Pakistan is said to date from the 1960s, when RAW promoted dissatisfaction against Pakistan in East Pakistan, including FUNDING Mujibur Rahmanh's general election in 1970 and providing training and arming the Mukti Bahini. Indian intelligence agencies, were involved in East Pakistan now, Bangladesh, beginning, in the early 1960's.

Its operatives were in touch with Sheikh Mujib for quite some time. Sheikh Mujib went to Agartala in 1965. The famous Agartala case was unearthed in 1967.In fact, the main purpose of raising R.A.W. in 1968 was to organize covert operations in Bangladesh.

As early as 1968, R.A.W. was given a green light to begin mobilizing all its resources for the impending surgical intervention in erstwhile East Pakistan.When in July 1971 General Manekshaw told Prime Minister Indira Gandhi that the army would not be ready until December to intervene in Bangladesh, she quickly turned to R.A.W. for help.

R.A.W. was ready. Its officers used Bengali refugees to set up the guerilla force Mukti Bahini. Using, this outfit as a cover, the Indian military sneaked deep into Bangladesh. The story of Mukti Bahini and R.A.W.'s role in its creation and training is now well known. R.A.W. never concealed its Bangladesh operations.

The creation of Bangladesh was masterminded by R.A.W. in complicity with the K.G.B under the covert clauses of the Indo-Soviet Treaty of Friendship and Cooperation (adopted as the 25-Year Indo-angladesh Treaty of Friendship and Cooperation in 1972).

R.A.W. retained a keen interest in Bangladesh even after its independence. R.A.W. was involved in training of Chakma tribes and Shanti Bahini, who carried out subversive activities in Bangladesh.

It also unleashed a well-organized plan of psychological warfare, created polarization among the armed forces, propagated false allegations of the use of Bangladesh territory by Pakistan's Inter-Services Intelligence agency, created dissension among the political parties and religious sects, controlled the media, denied the use of river waters, and propped up a host of disputes in order to keep Bangladesh under constant political and socio-economic pressure.

International RAW Foreign Missions provide an ideal cover and RAW centres in a target country are generally located inside the Embassy premises.

The RAW and the Ministry of External Affairs are provided Rs 25 crore annually as "discretionary grants" for foreign influence operations. An extensive network of Indian operatives is controlled by the Indian Embassy in Washington DC. The Indian embassy's covert activities are reported to include the infiltration of US long distance telephone carriers by Indian operatives, with access to all kinds of information, to reverse blackmail of relatives of US residents living in India. In 1996 an Indian diplomat was implicated in a scandal over illegal FUNDING of political candidates in the US.

Under US law foreign nationals are prohibited from contributing to federal elections. The US District Court in Baltimore sentenced Lalit H Gadhia, a naturalised US citizen of Indian origin, to three months imprisonment.

Gadhia had confessed that he worked as a conduit between the Indian Embassy and various Indian-American organizations for funneling campaign contributions to influence US lawmakers.

Over $46,000 from the Indian Embassy was distributed among 20 Congressional candidates. The source of the cash used by Gadhia was Devendra Singh, a RAW official assigned to the Indian Embassy in Washington.

RAW-MOSSAD-CONNECTION

Janes information group, the world's foremost source on intelligence information, reported in July 2001 that the Indian spy agency RAW and the Israeli spy agency Mossad have create" four new agencies to infiltrate Pakistan to target important religious and military personalities, journalists, judges, lawyers and bureaucrats.

In addition, bombs would be exploded in trains, railway stations, bridges, bus stations, cinemas, HOTELSand mosques of rival Islamic sects to incite sectarianism. Pakistani intelligence agencies also said that RAW had constituted a plan to lure Pakistani men between 20 and 30 years of age to visit India so they could be entrapped in cases of fake CURRENCY and subversion' and then be coerced to spy for India.

This was high point of cementing an unholy alliance which began much earlier and which continues to tighten its noose around the neck of Pakistan, Iran, Afghanistan and Central Asia.

It appears that RAW and Mossad-either singly or jointly, either covertly or overtly-have been making efforts to penetrate sensitive circles of top echelon in Pakistan. What is clear right now in RAW-Mossad connection is that Indian RAW and Israeli Mossad are collaborating extensively to curb the freedom movement of Kashmir and destabilize Pakistan.

Pakistani intelligence agencies also said that RAW had constituted a plan to lure Pakistani men between 20 and 30 years of age to visit India so that they could be entrapped "In cases of fake currency and subversion and then be coerced to spy for India."

It appears that RAW and Mossad - either singly or jointly, either covertly or overtly - have been making efforts to penetrate sensitive circles of top echelon in Pakistan.

Aziz writes:"Top secret details of Indian Home Minister LK Advani's visit to Israel in June 2000, show that the deals he has struck with the Israelis would make India and Israel partners in threatening the

Muslim world with diabolic conspiracies to fragment and cripple it as a political force in the world. The details of his meetings with Israel's rulers, particularly the heads of the Israeli Home Ministry and its intelligence agencies, Mossad and Sabak, reveal that the arrangements he has made for joint Indo-Israel espionage operations in key areas of the Muslim world would make the Indian embassies in these Muslim countries the eyes and ears of the worldwide cloak-and-dagger Israeli spy network.

"Under the euphemism of 'counter-terrorism,' India is allowing Israel to establish a huge spy establishment in India which will, inter alia, unearth and monitor 'Islamic fundamentalist' individuals and groups for elimination by extra judicial process or by cold-blooded murder and kidnapping.

"The Indian side showed a keen interest in learning from Israeli security experts how they had run the slice of Lebanon which Israel ruled for 18 years and gave up recently. Some information about the Israeli torture and investigation methods was gathered by the Indian side from the Israelis with regard to dealing with Arab dissidents within Israel and in the Palestinian Authority region.

"The Indians gave the Israelis a long shopping list of spying, torture and surveillance equipment such as electronic fencing of sensitive sites, laser systems, short-range rockets, eagle-eyed long distance snipers, observation blimps, giant shields, night vision device, unmanned aircraft of the MALAT wing of the Israeli Aircraft Industries Limited, special protective dress and gear for security personnel, cross border snooping devices and gadgets, training and deployment of spies and the special gear for them, use of computers and Internet for espionage and disinformation, code-breaking, tailing of enemy agents and their elimination, nuclear espionage, purloining state secrets of hostile countries and pooling them for the good of India and Israel and their mutual friends.

"The Israelis were interested in having access to the secret reports of Indian undercover RAW diplomats from certain Muslim countries of special interest to Israel (especially Pakistan, Libya and Iran). India is apparently willing to grant access to Israeli agents to the Indian Home Ministry's Central Intelligence Processing Unit (CIPU) in New Delhi. This was set up under Advani's direction with Israeli and US help. A handpicked RAW officer, trusted by Advani's, heads this unit. Israel wants full access to its information data. The Indian government has already allowed access to it by American intelligence agencies now working with the Indian government on so-called anti-terrorist assignments.

Tarek Fatah, a Turkish scholar settled in Canada, wrote: "Britain's authoritative and respected defense publication, Jane's Terrorism & Security Monitor, reports that Israel and India have formed a military relationship and that Israeli intelligence is active in Occupied Kashmir.

"Israel has several teams now in Kashmir training Indian counter-insurgency forces to fight the dozen separatist guerrilla groups operating in the Indian-controlled sector of the disputed state.

Ed Blanche writes in Janes' Security on 14 August 2001:

"Israeli intelligence agencies have been intensifying their relations with India's security apparatus and are now understood to be heavily involved in helping New Delhi combat Islamic militants in the disputed province of Kashmir, India's only Muslim-majority state which lies at the core of the conflict with neighbouring Pakistan. "Israel It has several teams now in Kashmir training Indian counter-insurgency forces to fight the dozen separatist guerrilla groups operating in the Indian-controlled sector of the disputed state.

"The exact extent of the involvement in Kashmir by Israel s intelligence agencies is far from clear, but it fits into Israel's increasing focus on events in Central Asia, and as far field as Indonesia, the world's most populous Muslim state, to counteract Islamic fundamentalism, which it perceives as a major threat.

We have been reading the name MOSSAD.Mossad and its role in destroying Muslims around the world and especially in South East Asia with the help of India RAW wraps, in a fascinating plot, full of intrigue and betrayal.

It is said that it is the joint venture of the trigone that is the core point of consideration. Mossad, RAW and Israeli Russian Ukrainian drug mafia have been performing these functions as coalition partner previously.

Summary

In summary, R.A.W. over the years has admirably fulfilled its tasks of destabilizing target states through the unbridled export of terrorism.

It goes to its credit that it has accomplished its assigned objectives due to the endemic weakness in the state apparatus of these nations and the failures of their leaders.

The Daily Mail has credibly cited and as written by Isha Khan, Dhaka, Bangladesh September 12, 2007.

"Highly informed sources revealed that the US, the French and the British counter terrorism specialists, who were constantly keeping a very vigilant eye on the affairs of the Indian intelligence agencies, particularly Research and Analysis Wing (RAW), very strongly believe that while the Indian Government and its political leadership has constantly been claiming to be the champion of the cause of anti-terrorist campaigns, its own intelligence agencies have been causing first degree terrorist activities not only in the neighbouring countries but even beyond the regional ambits, making India a Numero Uno state, sponsoring organized terrorism in different parts of the world mainly targeting Pakistan, either covertly orovert.

It is learnt that the investigators are convince on killing of the French Naval engineers, in Karachi as an activity carried out by a very cunning enemy of Pakistan who desires to strongly harm Pakistan's foreign collaborated Defence projects and its further enhancements in this field.

They are of the view that the attack might have been planned by the Indians when they started their new Naval ventures with Russian and Israeli collaboration, which includes the assembling of a powerful electro accelerating machine i.e. Kilo-Ampere Liner Injector(KALI) etc.

It is learnt that after September 11 incident RAW is mainly using ex-KHAD operators to carry out subversive activities in different parts of the world particularly Pakistan. The intelligence officials of the above mentioned countries are of the firm view that even if the terrorists behind incident are of different origins, they are surely having a full backing of a highly organized agency who prepared a fool-proof plan for them.

The Daily Mail findings indicate that there is a great resentment and disliking for RAW among the International Intelligence community as RAW operates in a Mafia style, each time overstepping the limits of Intelligence operations.

The RAW has not only indulged in cross border terrorism, it has also played a very significant role in creating and FUNDING militant and terrorist political and under cover extremist religious parties within India and other countries of the region. It plays a key role not only in the national politics but also tries to have an impact on the political life of other regional countries.

According to the Daily Mail findings, RAW is the godfather of some hostile and terrorist political and fundamentalist parties of India including the Hindu Dharma Raksha Samiti (HDRS), Bajrang Dal (BD) Rashtria Sawayamsevak Sankh (RSS) Shiv Sena (SS) etc.

RAW not only played a vital role in establishing and organizing these parties but it constantly financing and patronizing them with full strength.The agency uses these parties not only to carve out a role for itself in the internal politics but to divert the international focus from its terrorist activities.

AN INDIAN PLOT TO BREAK UP PAKISTAN IN 1971?

The sweeping victory of Sheikh Mujib-ur-Rehman's Awami League in the 1970 Pakistani elections was warmly received in India. The Bengalis of East Pakistan had always favoured a more cooperative approach in relations with India. New Delhi hoped for a progressive improvement in bilateral relations with a new democratic Pakistan, in which the eastern wing had its rightful representation. However, some observers questioned the possibility of bridging the vast political divide between the two wings of Pakistan. They felt that the eastern wing was likely to secede.

Secession, Objectives

In December, High Commissioner B.K. Acharya expressed a view that was widely accepted in New Delhi. He recognised the possibility of secession but argued that majority control of the Central Pakistan Government by the East Pakistanis offered the only hope of achieving India's policy objectives towards Pakistan and overcoming the stonewall resistance of West Pakistan against better ties. Moreover, a secessionist East Bengal might demand integration with West Bengal and a United Bengal and might pass under the control of pro-Chinese Marxists. Such developments would further complicate India's defence and strategic problems. Foreign Secretary T.N. Kaul agreed that India should do nothing to encourage the separation of East Pakistan from West Pakistan but he added that it did not lie in India's hands to stop it. Much would depend on the rulers of Pakistan and the realisation by West Pakistan of the need to come to an equitable arrangement with East Pakistan.

Indian officials reviewed the situation in early January. MEA Secretary S.K. Banerjee and Acharya observed that the question of a secessionist movement would arise only if the eastern wing failed to secure its six-point autonomy demand through constitutional means. Acharya observed that Zulfiqar Ali Bhutto, the leader of the Pakistan Peoples' Party, might accept the autonomy demand if he himself could be all-powerful in the western wing, or if each wing was allowed to go its own way. However, a basic point of disagreement was in regard to powers of taxation. The army would not accept an arrangement under which it would have to depend upon subventions from the provinces for its FUNDING.

R.N. Kao, the head of India's Research & Analysis Wing (RAW), said that he had received information that Mujib himself considered secession to be a definite possibility and was preparing for such an eventuality. Kao's assessment was that Mujib's hands were tied. He would either have to adopt an unyielding stand on the six-point demand or be swept aside by popular opinion. He would go through the motions of seeking implementation of the demand through constitutional means but a secessionist movement was a definite possibility. In this case, India could expect appeals for assistance in a variety of fields, including arms, MONEY and military training. He urged that India should position itself to offer the assistance that might be requested.

What The Records Show

The records show that New Delhi had no prior intention of dismembering Pakistan. However, events moved rapidly in East Pakistan. At the end of January 1971, RAW confirmed that the Awami League leadership was not very optimistic about the outcome of the negotiations on a new constitution and was preparing to launch a mass movement for an independent Bangladesh if the talks proved abortive. In early March, Tajuddin Ahmad met secretly with Deputy High Commissioner K.C. Sen Gupta, on Mujib's instructions, to explore whether India would provide political asylum and other assistance in the event of a liberation war. After consulting Delhi, Sen Gupta gave a response that was insufficiently specific to satisfy Sheikh Mujib. In mid-March, the latter repeated his appeal for assistance at this critical hour for his country, which was left with no alternative but to fight for independence.

India was not taken by surprise by the Pakistani crackdown on the Bengalis on March 25. She was not prepared, however, for the savagery of the onslaught. This drew impassioned condemnation from all sections of the Indian public. It also resulted in a refugee influx on a totally unexpected and unprecedented scale.

Though border inhabitants offered unstinting hospitality to the victims of the barbaric crackdown, it became evident that economic and political stability in the border provinces would be in danger unless conditions were created for the return of the millions of refugees to their homeland.

The Plan

By the beginning of April, India's political aims had crystallised. New Delhi entertained deep apprehensions concerning a long-drawn guerrilla war in East Pakistan. It feared that a freedom struggle initially led by the moderate Awami League might eventually be taken over by pro-Chinese extremists if it dragged on for years. Thus the freedom fighters had to be assisted to bring the hostilities to the earliest possible conclusion and open military intervention might be required in the final stage.

Second, conditions had to be created to enable the return of the refugees to their homes as early as possible. In the absence of a political settlement between the Awami League leadership and Islamabad, the refugees would return only to an independent Bangladesh.

These cerebral reasons were powerfully reinforced by the moral outrage caused by Pakistan army atrocities and the strong public support for intervention on behalf of the victims. After March 25, Indian public opinion was unanimous in demanding that the government should extend full assistance to the Bangladesh freedom struggle.

At the beginning of the year, India had hoped for a united Pakistan in which the eastern wing exercised a degree of influence proportionate to its population. The prospect of secession was viewed with some misgiving. It soon became evident, however, that secession was a very real possibility as the dominant forces in Pakistan were not prepared to accept the six-point programme. The brutal crackdown of March 25 sealed the fate of a united Pakistan. The emergence of an independent Bangladesh was inevitable after the massacre. Public sympathy for the people of Bangladesh and India's national interests demanded that full cooperation be extended to the freedom struggle in order to ensure its speedy success.

THE ISI REACHES EAST

Anatomy of a Conspiracy

The geo-strategy of a region normally hinges - at least in one primal sense - on its proximity or susceptibility to alienation. The susceptibility to alienation, in this context, implies proximity to 'outer lands', which, although not overtly hostile, possess a measure of, or potential for, sustained outward subversion.

If this thesis is to count as even minimally true, then the Northeastern States of India expressly qualify as a region of immense strategic importance. As a result, the security considerations of the Northeast, threatened by way of the strategic encirclement it is heir to, cannot be glossed over.

If the geography of the region mandates its strategic encirclement, history provides the reasons for its fortification. Until 1826 and the Treaty of Yandabo concluded between the Burmese and the British, whereby, on 24 February 1826, the King of Burma 'renounced all claims' upon, and agreed to 'abstain from all future interference with the principality of Assam and its dependencies', the region, at least in a strict political sense, was itself something of an 'outland'. However, British policy in the region (after its annexation) was an all-encompassing attribute and its geo-strategy took into account the policies of the encircling nations. Independent India's policies towards the bordering nations, unfortunately, and at least during the early years, were rather impressionistic and did not seek to consolidate the position inherited from the British. Indeed, India engaged reluctantly in a war with Chinain 1962 over territorial disputes in the region. And although recent years have witnessed lesser sabre rattles, an amicable solution to certain disputes continues to elude these two countries.

'The little wars' of the Northeast have also found (active) covert support by neighbouring countries, including Pakistan and China. In addition, Myanmarese fringe outfits (primarily the Kachins) have deepened existing historical-cultural ties further by supporting local movements by offering training, safe havens and outward routes. As a matter of detail, the Myanmarese connection in the separatist campaigns of the region predates almost all other such external aid.

According to at leas one theory, India's intervention in, and contribution to the formation of,Bangladesh - erstwhile East Pakistan - was motivated by a desire to thwart a Sino-Pakistani pincer formation which was thought to be gaining in ground in the late 1960s. Discounting the convenient theory of simply an Indo-Pakistani rivalry, which brought about the dismemberment of Pakistan, a noted South Asia watcher and journalist writes:

A close look at the map of the subcontinent and the growing Sino-Pakistani nexus in the late 1960s would surely convince anyone with a sense of geopolitics and military strategy that in the event of a total war between India on the one hand and China and Pakistan on the other, a determined Chinese drive through Assam or North Bengal could link up with Pakistani forces in East Pakistan and cut off the Northeast. Two decades after the break up of Pakistan into two countries and the relative stability achieved by the Indian politico-military effort in the Northeast, Pakistani talk (notably from Z.A. Bhutto) of entrusting the security of East Pakistan to the 'China factor' might, in retrospect, seems to have been without substance. But to an Indian decision maker in New Delhi in the late 1960s, besieged as he was with growing overtly pro-Chinese left radicalism in West Bengal; virulent guerrilla movements in Nagaland, Mizoram, Manipur and Tripura; language riots in Assam; and a number of ethnic insurrections on the doorstep in North Burma, many directly backed by China, Bhutto's threat raised India's worst fears of a Chinese sweep through the region, an eventual link-up with Pakistani forces in East Pakistan, and the secession of the entire Northeast Indian states .

Quoting a senior Research & Analysis Wing (RAW) source, the author goes on to state that the late P.N. Banerji, the then Chief of RAW's Eastern division, in a briefing to RAW Field Officers at Calcutta in August 1971 had insisted that a fear of the Northeast being cut off was primarily the reason for the Indian enthusiasm for supporting the Bengali liberation struggle in 1971 .

But three decades of independent statehood for Bangladesh and pre-liberation Indian concern as detailed above - while achieving the absence of a proactive Pakistani state in India's Eastern fringes - have not prevented radical pro-Pakistani Islamic elements from emerging in that country and providing aid and sustenance to separatist groups waging a war against India. The reasons for this, as a former Foreign Secretary states, are that:

...a metamorphosis in the social and political scene of Bangladesh had occurred, first because of Mujib's own lack of conviction about transforming his country into a genuine secular-democracy and, second, because he had consciously allowed reinduction of pro-Pakistani and anti-liberation elements into Bangladesh's politics, civil services and armed forces. He adopted such a strategy in order to reduce the influence of political leaders and armed forces personnel who were actively involved in the freedom struggle.

My assessment is that he hoped to ensure supreme power for himself by counter-balancing and playing of these two groups against each other in the domestic political processes. With the passage of time, Bangladesh became an Islamic republic. It must not be forgotten that the first step in the direction was taken by Mujib himself who attended the OIC (Organisation of Islamic Countries) Summit conference in Lahore in 1974. Whosoever came to power in Bangladesh had to fulfil two stipulations for surviving in power: first, that he or she should maintain a certain amount of distance from India and second, the person should confirm the Islamic identity of Bangladesh .

Pakistan's renewed interest in the Northeast, therefore, received a boost as a result of Bangladesh's acts of affirmation. Pakistan's Inter Services Intelligence's (ISI) 're-entry into the game' became possible either because of direct support of the Bangladesh authorities or through the Bangladesh Field Intelligence or other agencies on the old-tie net.

The roles of Bhutan and Nepal in 'the little wars' have largely been those of accessories. The two Himalayan nations have provided safe havens to separatist groups from the Northeast, as also transit facilities. The United Liberation Front of Asom (ULFA) and the National Democratic Front of Bodoland (NDFB) have their headquarters in Bhutan, and although latest reports suggests that the Royal Bhutan Army is planning a clamp down on the Assamese rebels , many an anti-India agency has reportedly set up operations and bases in these countries. Recent reports have also spoken of a Nepal-based ISI operation through which counterfeit CURRENCY, in connivance with some local agents, is being pumped into Assam. Such reports notwithstanding, the Nepalese Ambassador to India, B.B.Thapa, during the course of a press conference in Guwahati, said that his country has never allowed anti-India activities to grow on its soil and that vigilance has been stepped up along the border.

To be fair to the separatist groups of the region, however, it must be added these foreign interventions are far from an adequate explanation of militancy, and that a situation of discontentment and upheaval was already prevalent in the region when foreign support was sought or provided. Samir Kumar Das, in his political analysis of the ULFA thus provides a strong critique of the 'foreign hand' theory:

It is sometimes believed that the ULFA movement is the handiwork of some neighbouring foreign powers like China, Bangladesh and Burma. The Government of India reportedly possesses 'impeccable evidences' that can decisively prove the involvement of the foreign hand. The erstwhile Assam movement is taken to be part of a greater CIA sponsored project of Operation Brahmaputra with the sole objective of curbing Soviet influence in India and in South East Asia via India. The ULFA movement is allegedly masterminded by Bangladesh and Burma. The theory of the 'foreign hand' suffers from a number of limitations, two of which deserves mention at this point.

First, to say that the movement is sponsored and masterminded by foreign powers might imply that it has no internal basis. It thus glosses over the economic, political and cultural variables that are taken into consideration here. However, there is no denying the fact that the foreign powers might have taken advantage of large-scale unrest, violence and breakdown of law and order, particularly in Assam and in the Northeast, in general. The foreign powers usually fish in already troubled waters. Secondly, it is true that the foreign powers might have a hand in keeping the disturbances alive and destabilising the region with an eye to carve out a separate state (sometimes, named, United States of Bengal) and thereby inflicting a dismemberment on India to avenge that of Pakistan in 1971. But there is no independent source to verify their role in aiding and abetting unrest and 'insurgencies', political turmoil and subversion, whether by financing these activities or by supplying sophisticated arms and training to hard-core rebels. Hence, their latent motives in most cases, remain unknown and we have nothing to do but to rely helplessly on the assertions and counter-assertions of the respective governments.

Nevertheless, while it is not a matter of debate that long years of neglect and subversion have led the region to the present state of affairs and the rise of militancy, the aid which most separatist movements have been receiving from foreign powers cannot be discounted.

As a matter of analysis and case study, this paper examines the role of Pakistan's Inter Services Intelligence in Assam. A cursory look at the agency in question is, perhaps, in order in this context.

Founded in 1948 by a British army officer, Major General R. Cawthome, then Deputy Chief of Army Staff of Pakistan, the role of the Directorate of Inter Services Intelligence (ISI) was expanded by President Ayub Khan in order to safeguard Pakistan's national interests, monitor opposition politicians and sustain military rule in Pakistan.

The ISI is tasked with the collection of foreign and domestic intelligence; co-ordination of intelligence functions of the three armed services; surveillance of its cadre, foreigners, the media, politically active segments of Pakistani society, diplomats of other countries accredited to Pakistan as also of Pakistani diplomats abroad; the interception and monitoring of communications; and the execution of covert offensive operations. Staffed by hundreds of civilian and military officers, and thousands of other employees, the ISI has its headquarters in Islamabad. The Agency reportedly employs a total of about 10,000 officers and staff members, a number which does not include informants and other assets. It is reportedly organised into between six and eight divisions.

The division of the Joint Intelligence Bureau which is responsible for political intelligence consists of three sections, one of which is devoted to operations against India. The Joint Intelligence/North is responsible for operations in Jammu and Kashmir (J&K) including propaganda, infiltration, exfiltration and other clandestine operations. The Joint Signal Intelligence Bureau operates a chain of signals to militants operating in Kashmir.

The ISI is of paramount importance at the joint services level. Its importance stems from the fact that it is in complete charge of all covert operations outside Pakistan. Democratic governments of the past have had only very loose control over the Agency. The Agency also reportedly supplies weaponry, advice, training and other forms of assistance to separatist groups in the Indian Punjab and Kashmir, as also to the ones waging a war against the Indian state in the Northeast.

The 1965 Indo-Pak War provoked a major crisis of intelligence in Pakistan. The War revealed the inefficiency of the intelligence agencies, which had, until then, been committed primarily to domestic investigative work. Ayub Khan set up a committee headed by Yahya Khan (who was later to succeed him) to examine the working of the agencies.

The ISI has been deeply involved in domestic politics and has kept track of the opponents of various incumbent regimes. Before 1958 and the imposition of Martial Law, the ISI reported to the Commander-in-Chief of the Army. When Martial Law was promulgated in 1958, all intelligence agencies fell under the direct control of the President and Chief Martial Law Administrator.

It was the late President Zia-ul-Haq who initiated the present pattern of the ISI's interventions in India after the failure of 'Operation Gibraltar' in 1988. 'Operation Topac', a realistic representation of the Pakistani strategy, envisaged a three-part action plan for the 'liberation' of Kashmir. Phase I of this strategy envisaged a low-level insurgency in J&K, a subversion of all major state, administrative, FINANCIAL and political institutions, mass mobilisation on religious issues, the training of subversive elements and the development of means to cut off lines of communication between Jammu and Kashmir, and within Kashmir and Ladakh. The road upto Kargil and the road over Khardungla were to receive 'special attention'. The Phase also envisaged collaboration with the then very active Sikh extremists in neighbouring Punjab. The primary Phase II objective was to "Exert maximum pressure on the Siachen, Kargil and Rajouri-Punch sectors to force the Indian Army to deploy reserve formations outside the main Kashmir Valley." This was to be backed up by a campaign of co-ordinated attacks against a wide range of military and infrastructure targets, including airfields, the Banihal Tunnel and the Kargil-Leh highway. Infiltration by 'Afghan Mujahideen' was integral to this stage. Phase III conceived of the liberation of the Kashmir Valley and the establishment of an "*independent* Islamic State".

According to a report compiled by the Joint Intelligence Committee (JIC) of India in 1995, the ISI spent roughly Rs. 24 million every month to sponsor its activities in J&K. Although all militant groups receive arms and training from Pakistan, the pro-Pakistan groups - who advocate the merger of Kashmir with Pakistan - are reported to be favoured by the ISI. At least six major militant organisations, and several smaller ones, are presently operating in J&K. Their strengths are variously estimated at between 5,000 and 10,000. They are roughly divided between those who seek *azaadi* (independence) and those who support accession to Pakistan. The oldest militant organisation, the Jammu and Kashmir Liberation Front (JKLF), had spearheaded the movement for an independent Kashmir. The JKLF has, however, fallen from the ISI's grace, and is now largely an overground political organisation with secessionist aims. Its thunder has been stolen by the powerful pro-Pakistani group, the Hizbul-Mujaheddeen. The other major groups are Harakat-ul Ansar (which absorbed the Afghan veterans of the Harkat-ul-Mujahideen and the Harkat-ul-jihad-ul-Islami), a group which reportedly has a large number of non-Kashmiris in it; the Al Umar; the Al Barq; the Muslim Janbaz Force; and the Lashkar-e-Toiba (LeT), which is also made up largely of Mujahideen from Afghanistan and Pakistan, and includes a suicide cadre, the*fidayeen*. An emerging group is the Jaish-e-Mohammad-Mujahideen-e-Tanzeem, established by Maulana Masood Azhar, who was released by the Indian Government after the hijack of the Kathmandu-Delhi Indian Airlines Flight IC 814 to Kandahar in Afghanistan. Several thousand fighters from Afghanistan and other Muslim countries (estimated variously at strengths upto 5,000 men) have also joined some of the militant groups or have formed their own *tanzeems* (groups).

Recent evidence suggests that the ISI is now executing a much wider strategy of encirclement, exploiting every potential area of conflict, and the extensive, sensitive and poorly managed land borders all along the East and Northeast of India. It is under this larger programme that the ISI now operates training camps near the border in Bangladesh where separatist groups of the Northeast, collectively known as the 'United Liberation Front of Seven Sisters', are trained in terrorist activities. These groups include the National Socialist Council of Nagaland (NSCN), People's Liberation Army (PLA), the United Liberation Front of Asom (ULFA) and the Northeast Student's Organisation (NESO).

The situation in Assam is of special significance in this context, primarily because of the demography of the State, and of the historical movement of populations. Long years of a tryst with separatism and a continuous stream of illegal immigration from Bangladesh accords the State a unique place in the examination of the ISI's activities in the Northeast. The State has a sizeable Muslim population and has, in fact, had two Muslim Chief Executives in the past. The demographic mosaic also includes a tribal population as well as a smattering of people from other parts of India, mainly from Bengal, Bihar and Rajasthan. A tea workers community, largely comprising *Santhal* tribals, transferred into the region by the British in the nineteenth century in order to quell a Central Indian rebellion, has also become an inalienable part of the Assamese soil. In this scenario, there has been a mushroom growth of separatist groups in the State whose search for newer, elusive identities occasioned an outward look for external assistance. The most significant groups operating in the State include the United Liberation Front of Asom (ULFA) and the National Democratic Front of Bodoland (NDFB), though there are a myriad of others, swearing allegiance to almost every identifiable ethnic sub-group. There has, moreover, been a recent and sudden proliferation of Muslim militant organisations in the State.

The ULFA, which had initially looked to the Myanmarese fringe outfits for help and an outward conduit, came under some pressure during the early nineties. As B.G. Verghese mentioned in his seminal work on the Northeast, pressures in Myanmar led the ULFA a couple of years later to establish contacts with the ISI and the Afghan Mujahideen in Pakistan, and still later with the Bangladesh Field Intelligence in Dhaka, and less successfully with the Liberation Tigers of Tamil Eelam (LTTE). Indeed, the Assam Assembly was told in March 1994 that some 200 ULFA militants had reportedly received training with the help of Pakistan's ISI, many of them in Afghanistan, over the preceding two years. It is interesting to note that a newspaper report attributes a statement by the present Assam Chief Minister, Prafulla Kumar Mahanta, where he accused his predecessor, the late Hiteswar Saikia, of inaction even after being informed about ISI activities way back in 1994. A senior officer of the Barak Valley district administration had reportedly informed the then Chief Secretary, H.N. Das, through a letter about a group comprising the ISI, the Hijbulla Mujahid of Iran, ULFA and other Islamic fundamentalist groups planning to carry out violence, particularly in Hindu villages.

The first comprehensive report on the subject was placed before the Assam State Assembly on April 6, 2000 by Chief Minister Prafulla Kumar Mahanta, after almost a year-long engagement with the ISI's activities throughout the State. The Report followed the penetration and eventual dismantling of one of the Pakistani intelligence Agency's network in the State. On August 7, 1999, the Assam Police achieved a major breakthrough and arrested two officers of the ISI as well as two other agents of the same Agency from A HOTEL in Guwahati. The police also arrested twenty seven other persons belonging to different Islamic militant groups. The four ISI operatives arrested were identified as Mohammad Fasih Ullah Hussaini alias Mamid Mehmood alias Khalid Mehmood of Hyderabad (Sind), Pakistan' Mohammad Javed Waqar alias Mohammad Mustaffa alias Mohammad Mehraj alias Abdul Rahman of Karachi, Pakistan; Maulana Hafiz Mohammad Akram Mallik alias Muzaffar Hussain alias Atabullah alias Bhaijan alias Abdul Awal of Mukam Shahwali village of Jammu and Kashmir; and Kari Salim Ahmad alias Abdul Aziz alias Sadat of Mehilki village of Muzaffarnagar, Uttar Pradesh.

The Chief Minister's Report to the State Assembly - while seeking to establish the scale, nature and degree of the ISI threat - was mainly a glossary of the events which had occurred in the period following the August arrests of 31 persons. In the interregnum, according to the Report, the State police had exposed the *modus operandi* of the foreign Agency. The 16-page Report (which included photographs and profiles of the main accused) identified the activities of the ISI mainly in the following areas:

1. Promoting indiscriminate violence in the State by providing active support to local militant outfits.
2. Creating new militant outfits along ethnic and communal lines by instigating ethnic and religious groups.
3. Supply of explosives and sophisticated arms to various terrorist groups.
4. Causing sabotage of OIL pipelines and other installations, communication lines, railways and roads.
5. Promoting fundamentalism and militancy among local Muslim youths by misleading them in the name of *Jehad*.
6. Promoting communal tension between Hindu and Muslim citizens by way of false and highly inflammatory propaganda.

The Report goes on to state that the Assam Police has adequate evidence in its possession to show that the top ULFA leadership is in close touch with certain officials of the Pakistani High Commission in Dhaka. ULFA leaders have also been travelling to Pakistan regularly, and Pakistani agencies have already imparted arms training to hundreds of ULFA cadres. According to the Report, the confessional statements of many ULFA leaders, including its Vice Chairman, Pradip Gogoi, have revealed that the Pakistani officials in their High Commission at Dhaka make arrangements for their passports under various fake identities.

The Chief Minister's Report further speaks of the ISI being involved in the provision of different passports for the ULFA Commander-in-Chief, Paresh Barua. Providing a facsimile of Paresh Barua's passport, the report also reveals that the ULFA leader has been travelling to Karachi under the name of Kamaruddin Zaman Khan. The ULFA-ISI nexus had, in fact, begun way back in the early nineties. An enumeration of a list of some of the early events and meetings which had taken place between the two is perhaps necessary at this juncture.

- In the month of November 1990, ULFA decides to send Munin Nabis and Partha Pratim Bora alias Jabed to Bangladesh to contact the ISI at Dhaka, to arrange the supply of arms and ammunition. They were instructed to set up a base camp in Bangladesh.
- Munin Nabis sets up a base camp in Dhaka in 1990 with the help of a certain Colonel (Retired) Faruque of the Bangladesh Freedom Party and Gani Shapan of the Jatiya Party. Nabis rents a house at Mogbazar in Dhaka.
- Munin Nabis assumes the name 'Iqbal' and contacts Samsul Siddique, the Second Secretary in the Pakistan High Commission at Dhaka. Contacts with the ISI are established through Siddique.
- Munin Nabis visits Pakistan to negotiate with a terrorist group headed by Mustafa Ali Jubardo to negotiate training for ULFA cadres on payment.
- The Vice Chairman of ULFA, Pradip Gogoi visits Dhaka in January 1991 and contacts an ISI officer called Haque

and signs an agreement for the training to ULFA cadres. He also meets another ISI officer, Jalal, there.

- After the agreement with the ISI, Munin Nabis calls a group of ULFA members for training in Pakistan in April 1991. Pradip Gogoi accompanies a six-member group to Islamabad for training with the ISI.
- Hari Mohan Roy alias Rustar Choudhury of ULFA, along with ten other ULFA cadres, undergoes training in camps organised by the ISI in Pakistan in 1993. Hari Mohan Roy obtains a passport under the name of Jamul Akhtar son of Akhtar Hussain of Bangladesh .

The ISI had also organised training for ULFA cadres in association with the Directorate General of Field Intelligence of Bangladesh, at a camp located 35 kilometres west of the Karnaphulli Hydro-electric project in the Chittagong Hill Tracts in 1993.

The training was supervised by Brigadier Joimullah Khan Choudhury. The ISI had reportedly also imparted specialised training to 48 ULFA cadres in Pakistan Occupied Kashmir (PoK) along with Muslim United Liberation Front of Assam (MULFA) cadres. There is also evidence to suggest that the ISI is activating the border areas in Nepal for relocation of some separatist groups. ULFA and the NDFB have reportedly already set up camps in Jhapa, Tapegunj and Panchthar in eastern Nepal.

The Pakistani misadventure in Kargil brought the ULFA-ISI nexus into the open. According to the army operating in Assam, the ULFA was involved in the passing of information of troop movements to and from Assam to the ISI. The ULFA was also allegedly pressured by the ISI to make anti-Indian statements - primarily supporting the liberation of Kashmir. Informed intelligence sources also spoke of the Muslim Liberation Tigers of Assam (MULTA) meeting the ISI backed *Sipah-e-Sahiba* at the Hathajari Jamait Ul Ulum Ali *Madarsa* in Chittagong. The *Sipah-e-Sahiba,* whose links with the Taliban are well known, was represented by a Didar Bakth .

The ULFA has, of course, in a statement to the Press, denied any links with the ISI.

There has been a great deal of activity in the days following the foiling of 'Mission Assam'. Newer insights into the ISI threat are now available. The refrain that is heard the most relates to the ISI blueprint to form an Islamic State in the Northeast, and there are widespread reports of Muslim social institutions such as *madarsas* (religious schools and seminaries), and in certain cases, mosques, aiding the cause of the ISI.

The present situation is one of continued confrontation. The Barak Valley of Assam has reportedly emerged as a hotbed for anti-India activities by the ISI. The arrest of Bilal alias Nanoo Mian, the ISI courier implicated in the Indian Airlines hijacking episode, has further revealed the extent to which the Pakistani intelligence Agency has spread its tentacles. Interrogation of the courier revealed that he had helped 40 Muslim youth from Assam to cross over to Bangladesh for training under the *Harkat-Ul-Mujahideen*. The immediate emphasis of the ISI, it would appear, is of breaking into the Assamese Muslim psyche. However, reports have suggested that it has not been very successful in its efforts in this direction. Indeed, many an Assamese Muslim intellectual has condemned the activities of the ISI.

There are, nevertheless, critical danger signals, the most important being the success of Pakistan's strategy of encirclement. In Bangladesh an Islamic resurgence is reportedly taking place, and a number of extremist groups are now operating openly in that country. The Harkat-ul-Jihad-al-Islami (HuJI), led by Shawkat Osman alias Sheikh Farid, was established in 1992, and is estimated to have a strength of about 15,000. The HuJI maintains six camps in the hilly areas of Chittagong, where the cadres are imparted arms training. Several hundred recruits have also been trained in Afghanistan. The cadres are recruited mainly from among students of various *madarsas* and style themselves as the 'Bangladeshi Taliban'. HuJI activists regularly cross over into several Indian States and maintain contact with 'sources' there. Reports indicate that the ISI has an open hand in the activities of the HuJI. The ISI has intensified subversive activities in Bangladesh since the Awami League came to power in June 1996. A party called the Freedom Party, formed by the convicted killers of Sheikh Mujibur Rahman, has also raised the slogan "*Amra hobo Taliban,Bangla hobe Afghan*" (We will be the Taliban; Bangladesh will be Afghanistan) and it seems that this sloganeering has been carried into rural Bangladesh. The Bangladesh Jamaat-e-Islami and its students' wing, the Islamic Chattra Shibir, have also escalated their activities, and recently killed five pro-Government students of the Bangladesh Chattra League (BCL). The BCL is the student wing of the ruling Awami League, and the Prime Minister, Sheikh Hasina Wajed, condemned the *Razakars* for having "crossed the limit." The Jamaat is currently led by Golam Azam, who is widely held responsible for the activities of the *Razakars* whom he led, and who collaborated with Pakistan's Army in the genocide in Bangladesh during the 1971 War that resulted in the country's independence. After the War, Golam Azam fled to Pakistan, but was allowed to return to Bangladesh during the predecessor regime of Prime Minister Begum Khalida Zia. The present Home Minister, Mohammad Nasim, at a condolence meeting for the murdered students stated, "I am deeply shocked that the defeated forces of Golam Azam, who led a genocide throughout the liberation war of Bangladesh in 1971, are now again craving for blood to take revenge." The Jamaat has close and continuous links with Pakistan.

There is now also incontrovertible evidence of the ISI's increasing success in consolidating its hold in Nepal, and in engineering critical demographic changes along the Indo-Nepal border. There has been an 'alarming' increase in Islamic institutions (*madarsas* and mosques) on both sides of the Indo-Nepal border, including the no-man's land that lies between. A study conducted by the Nepalese Government has revealed that about 225 *madarsas* have come up in the border districts during the past few years. An Indian intelligence report lists as many of 26 active Islamic organisations in Nepal, and identifies as many as 66 *madarsas* on the Indo-Nepal border that are known to be linked with and backed by the ISI.

With India's tenuous land link with the Northeast along the Chiken's Neck located between Nepal and Bangladesh, these demographic shifts and subversive activities clearly have a critical and sinister significance. Moreover, with an active ISI network at work in Dhaka, there appears to be no foreseeable end to the assistance extended to separatist groups in the Northeast (primarily Assam). Moreover, recent developments in Bhutan will probably see at least one faction of the ULFA returning to Bangladesh. And for all its denials, it is quite clear that the separatist group is controlled by the ISI. An invigorated ULFA presence in Bangladesh could, consequently, significantly further an ISI agenda of abetment to and facilitation of the continuing illegal immigration into, and destabilisation of, India's troubled Northeast.

INDIA'S EXPERIENCE AND NEED FOR ACTION AGAINST PAKISTAN

Intelligence organisations the world over require means of getting information using covert methods. While it is possible for nations to get information, at times active measures become necessary to achieve certain foreign policy objectives. For this purpose, intelligence organisations undertake covert action, which involve intervention in a variety of clandestine ways in the internal affairs of other nations. Such operations, often called covert or special missions, involve carrying out clandestine missions, ranging from pro-insurgency, insurgency, sabotage and deception to, political assassination and political subversion. Missions often encompass the whole spectrum of activity from para-military to military operations, at times even the overthrow of governments.

Covert action (CA) is separate from covert intelligence gathering. The difference is that the latter involves clandestine gathering of information in enemy territory using human or technical means, by activity that the enemy is not aware of. Covert action is employed to influence politics and events in another country without revealing one's involvement or at least while maintaining plausible deniability.

Covert action is an important tool for policy makers seeking an alternative between the application of large-scale military force and sitting quiet when confronted by a foreign policy challenge or when opportunities arise to further national interests and goals. For this purpose, intelligence agencies have separate units or organisations to undertake special missions. In a way, covert political action is an extension of foreign policy. If properly coordinated and controlled, such action can have results out of proportion to the inputs. For instance, India's support to the Mukti Bahini preceding the Bangladesh war gave it an advantage in terms of information flow and in aiding the advance of Indian troops during actual military operations after 3 December 1971. It also provided the base for the creation of Bangladesh.

Nations undertake covert operations based on their peace and wartime needs. The former USSR and US carried out such missions during the Cold War to fulfil their goals. Both the superpowers have organisations specialising in such activity, which pursue pro-insurgency, political assassination and subversion to suit their national interests. The Sandinista experience, the Iran-Contra affair, and the Bay of Pigs operations come to mind when discussing such type of missions. In the US, the period from the 40s to 60s saw a strong consensus concerning the need for covert action. Opposition to covert action began during the Congressional investigations in the mid-1970. Since then classic covert action has reduced considerably and congressional oversight ensures the CIA does not act on its own.

CA can be broadly found to be in five forms; Propaganda; Political action; Para-military assistance; coup d' etat and, secret intelligence support. Perhaps the most telling comment on CA was made by a former chief of the CIA, Admiral Stansfield Turner who says "Only do covertly that which if it is exposed will cause you little political harm." To this end it is important that covert action be carried out with the aim that it has certain plausible deniability.

It may well be argued that democratic states should not exercise the CA option. But instruments of statecraft, whether covert or overt can be used to achieve objectives that are vital for national security. In this sense, nations can find the way to blend strategic interest and democratic norms to protect vital interests. In India's case, foreign policy has the long-term vision of living in peace with its neighbours and does not seek relations to be held hostage on singular issues as it is with Pakistan. Which is why India's world vision is expansive and seeks to foster cooperation rather than confrontation. Within this paradigm it is necessary to view relations with Pakistan.

It is argued in this analysis that India's experience suggests undertaking covert action has not always been to fulfil foreign policy goals or to serve vital national interests. Secondly, it is perceived that inadequate covert action has been undertaken against Pakistan, enough to dissuade it from engaging in a proxy war with India. This is an essential part of the politics of persuasion that India must engage in, if it is to realise a meaningful dialogue with Pakistan.

The reason why covert action by India in other countries has not been so effective is because more often than not clear directives are not forthcoming for the objectives with which covert action is to be undertaken. Also due to the autonomous nature of agencies engaged in such activity, and changing political equations it is not possible to sustain covert action.

In a few cases, there has been links between foreign policy and operations undertaken to further national security goals, like in the creation of Bangladesh in 1971. This paper studies the role of Indian intelligence in utilising this asset to further national goals. Its links to foreign policy and the national executive are also examined. The Indian experience in undertaking covert action has been mixed; this is due to the varying politico-military objectives and level of coordination with institutions that determine policy.

This paper is divided into two parts. The first section narrates the Indian experience of covert operations in various parts of the South Asian region. It also provides inputs on some missions undertaken by other agencies.

Part two outlines a strategy for India in engaging in covert action against Pakistan. It is suggested here that India must undertake active and passive covert operations against Pakistan with the objective of breaking the stronghold of the army, bureaucracy and Inter-Services Intelligence (ISI) on Pakistani society. There is a belief that covert action against Pakistan could lead to the break-up of an already anarchic state, but Indian aims must be focused on breaking the stranglehold of the army, ISI and bureaucracy in Pakistan. This could have two effects. By playing the Pak game in their own backyard, it would keep them occupied and perhaps take attention away from India.

Alternatively, it could force them to re-think strategies, vis-à-vis the region, including Afghanistan and create circumstances for a new diplomatic initiative with India. There is always the worst-case situation where a special forces strike by India on mujahid training camps across the LoC could lead to a war, but this eventuality India must be prepared for.

INDIA'S EXPERIENCE OF COVERT ACTION

Intelligence agencies have undertaken covert operations, independently and in cooperation with agencies of other countries. The Intelligence Bureau (IB), Research and Analysis Wing (R&AW) and Military Intelligence (MI) have undertaken operations covertly with certain objectives. These have been low grade and little has been achieved. In the present context, the focus is on operations conducted by India's external intelligence agency, R&AW, termed as RAW for this paper.

India, in the late 50s and 60s with the help of the CIA aided the Tibetan rebellion, providing training facilities in India. The 1962 border war with China led to the establishment of several organisations that are today under the Cabinet Secretariat, the Special Frontier Force (Establishment 22 at Chakrata) and Special Services Bureau. Additionally, a group was raised with the objective of carrying out aerial reconnaissance of China and Tibet, the Aviation Research Centre (ARC). One source suggests that at Charbatia in December 1964 a U-2 aircraft was deployed for operations over Tibet. The Tibet operation continued till the early 60s when the CIA, withdrew its operations on Indian soil and moved to Nepal.

The Tibetan rebellion against the Chinese forces and Indian help straddled an era of post-colonial assertion of non-alignment as the major plank of foreign policy, and yet Jawaharlal Nehru chose to engage in covert action as a foreign policy tool knowing fully well, that India could do little for Tibet. He was keen to have friendly relations with China, but he still believed, like the British did, that a Tibet with an identity was important for sub-continental India. The question may well ask if this policy did not contradict the policy of non-alignment? Possibly yes, but in Nehru's mind, the best way of dealing with the Chinese was diplomatic, and towards this end he was even willing to sponsor China's candidature to the UN. The help given to the Tibetans was probably a small cog in the larger worldview and helping the US in this was a part of geo-politics of the time. This did of course have the adverse effect of changing Chinese perceptions about India. All this is of course based on the scanty evidence that is available in different sources but this is important to suggest directions of discourse in order to dilate on the foreign policy angle to covert operations.

Then in the late sixties, the need for an organisation tasked with gathering external intelligence led to the formation of RAW, and the Directorate General of Security was transferred from IB to RAW. As the Bangladesh crisis arose, RAW was given the task of gathering intelligence and undertaking covert missions, including pro-insurgency. This is the most successful operation till date, publicly written about, carried out, involving the training of the Mukti Bahini of East Pakistan and their role in helping the Indian military intervention.

The operation involved getting the freedom fighters in East Pakistan (now Bangladesh) together and training and arming them. This was essentially a Research and Analysis Wing (R&AW) operation, with the Indian army providing the training infrastructure. The Mukti Bahini was formed in January 1971 and for the next ten months people who came across the border were selected for training. By September-November 1971, these forces were infiltrated into East Pakistan for covert missions, including sabotage of lines of communication and command and control centres.

When war did officially break out on 3 December, the Mukti Bahini was ready, (just like the French resistance in 1944, when Operation Overlord the invasion at Normandy began). The Mukti Bahini helped Indian troops find their way, harassed Pak troops and generally made itself a nuisance. Naval Mukti Bahini divers planted mines in the harbours around Bangladesh and sunk many merchant and warships, playing a crucial role in blockading the ports. Another facet of covert action was witnessed in the trans-border attacks carried out by the Special Frontier Force (SFF) in the Chittagong Hill Tracts. Thus a combination of para-military action in the form of the Mukti Bahini and direct covert action using special forces, complimented the main military action in the 1971 Bangladesh war. The benefits accruing from coordinated covert action allowed implementation of foreign policy to secure national interests namely liberation of East Pakistan and creation of Bangladesh.

Subsequently measures taken to integrate Sikkim into the Indian Union by the RAW proved crucial. One authority states that RAW performed the task of counter-intelligence in Sikkim preventing foreign agencies from getting a foothold in the sensitive Himalayan kingdom and allowing it to accede to India. But soon after the successful mounting of Bangladesh and Sikkim operation, leading to the latter's integration as a state in the Indian union, came the Sri Lanka operation. This pro-insurgency operation launched by Mrs Gandhi during her second term in office, meant to train Tamil separatists followed the same lines of the 1971 case. Equipping and training of insurgents from across the Palk Straits took place on Indian soil, in the state of Tamil Nadu and in places as far as, Chakrata and Dehradun. With the active support of the state and central government, Indian intelligence agencies took up the task with gusto. But what was missing was the broad institutional oversight so essential for tying up the loose ends. Foreign policy makers and defence planners were scarcely aware of what was happening as political masters changed and priorities shifted.

Former foreign secretary JN Dixit covertly has identified the reasons for India getting involved in Sri Lanka. He says Mrs Gandhi was aware that all political parties in Tamil Nadu were sympathetic to the aspirations of Sri Lanka Tamils. Therefore extending support to Sri Lanka Tamil parties and Tamil militant groups from 1980 onwards was a natural corollary. There was also the security factor, Sri Lanka getting Israeli and US military personnel to train its own army and para-military. And there was the VoA station in Trincomalee. India perceived this to be an opening for US strategic presence in South Asia. These factors created the conditions for Indian covert intervention in Sri Lanka. The main point was that Mrs Gandhi did not like J Jayawardhane, for his policies and thus began Operation Sri Lanka.

Secrecy is undoubtedly called for in operations of this sort. But as the Iran-Contra affair in America showed, in the Sri Lanka operations also one part of the government did not know what the other was doing. In the Indian case, while RAW knew what it was doing politically, neither it nor the government was unable to fathom the potential for trouble that was generated by this operation. This was because the mission sought to achieve too much at one time. The number of groups being trained were one too many and difficult to control. No accountability existed and eventually not enough attention was paid to the risks of losing control over the insurgents. Thus by the time Mrs Indira Gandhi was killed in 1984, and Rajiv became prime minister the priorities changed and so did policy towards Sri Lanka.

In politico-military terms, covert action eventually proved to be of little use when the Indian Peace Keeping Force (IPKF) went into Sri Lanka in 1987. For the simple reason that intelligence on the insurgents trained by India was not forthcoming. Additionally, the intelligence agencies continued to covertly continue political dealings with the insurgents to suit their ends, even during the IPKF's stay in Sri Lanka. This undermined the foreign policy goal of sending a peacekeeping force to restore peace in Sri Lanka. The problem was that too many prime ministers were involved in the Sri Lanka episode, resulting in several conflicting decisions. Also involvement of state leaders like MG Ramachandran created more complications for command and control.

Intelligence agencies have been involved in various covert acts, both within India and in the surrounding region. Intelligence agencies often make alliances and then forget to inform their cousins resulting in confusion. In February 1998, the Armed Forces intercepted ships at sea off the Andamans killing six people and arresting 73 others. This was essentially a "sting" operation carried out by MI in collaboration with their Burmese counterparts. But the result was a big hue and cry.

In April, the leader of the National Unity Party of Arakans (NUPA) wrote to the Defence Minister that the men abroad the ship were in fact Arakanese revolutionaries who were cooperating with the Indians. He wrote, "The Indian military intelligence had okayed our voyage and that is why we entered Indian territorial waters to avoid the Burmese Navy." The issue is whether it was a case of military intelligence not giving the information to its forces in the field in time or it was a case of giving up its people. Maung wrote, "We were cooperating with each other. The Indians asked us for help to track down gunrunners carrying weapons to Northeast India and we helped them. So it came as a shock to us that our ship, about which the Indians were given full information, should be attacked." The point here is that at one level India is willing to help the pro-democracy movement in Burma, but due to the insurgents buying arms from South-East Asia and this having a direct influence on the insurgent movement in India's north-east it becomes necessary for the army to curb such activity. The dichotomy in policy towards the region is a reflection of the lack of understanding how to secure vital interests in the north-east.

It needs recalling that in the 80s, RAW supported tribal and ethnic factions fighting the SLORC in Myanmar. One of the factions supported by India was the Kachin Independence Army. The Kachins, known more accurately as Jingphaws or Marus, account for some 3 per cent of Myanmar's ethnic population. They inhabit the north-east of the country and have the reputation for resorting to arms to assert what they believe are their rights.

A senior officer in RAW deputed to Bangkok in the 80s, made contact with Burmese underground leaders in the hope of gaining some information. Then this officer decided that the KIA could be beneficially used to channelise information. And RAW could aid them with money and arms. Having made contact, the idea was to get members of KIA into India for training and contact creation. After the controlling officer returned from Bangkok, infiltration of KIA cadres was started. They came as students, youths touring India and helpers, sent for training to Chakrata and other locations in north and north-east. Arms and other material began to filter through to camps in North Myanmar and this reached its peak in 1991-92. Arunachal Pradesh and Mizoram provided exfiltration sites, while some material went via Bangkok. This was the post election period when Aung Sang Suu Kyi had won but was not allowed to take power by SLORC. All this was stopped by Prime Minister Narasimha Rao, as part of his "Look East" policy.

Looking back, one may well ask what purpose did this operation serve? What national interests or foreign policy goals did it serve? Keeping in mind the dimension of policy in the 80s, that of coercive diplomacy there is little doubt that the Government thought it fit to aid all rebels across the borders, wherever it suited us. But on many an occasion it backfired, as it did in Sri Lanka.

There is one other aspect of covert action that requires highlighting in the present study. Nation-states also engage in action within the territorial confines of the country for politico-military aims, such as pro-insurgency or counter-insurgency or counter-terrorism. Since the institutional framework for covert action exists in most countries in the South Asian region, indulging in domestic covert action is a continuing tool for governments. In India for instance, it was suggested that SSB was used to raise and train the Bodos in the late 80s in an effort to counter other groups in the region. Their employment to fulfil political goals has affected their organisation and performance and impinges on their role, which is really to engage in "stay-behind" operations.

It has been often suggested that RAW should function as efficiently as Pakistan's ISI. In fact both India and Pakistan accuse each other of encouraging subversion through their intelligence agencies. ISI's activities in India get greater media coverage than RAW's activities in Pakistan. The latter seems to lack the intensity of operations in Pakistan to counter or duplicate ISI's activities in India.

The ISI has been involved in covert action in various parts of India since the 80s. The main focus has been on Punjab and Jammu & Kashmir. Infiltration of arms and drugs into India, along with men to stoke insurgencies has been common. For Jammu & Kashmir, the ISI has a special cell to fuel the insurgency. It has been responsible for the setting up and maintenance of training camps in POK and Pakistan, the provision of arms and equipment, infiltration and exfiltration of both recruits and trained militants into the Valley. The entire plan to infiltrate Kashmir and launch a covert low-intensity war there has been described in the part fact, part fictionalised Operation Topac in 1989. The Pak strategy has followed the lines suggested in this analysis.

Op Topac visualised a three-phased strategy in Kashmir. First, fuelling of a low-level insurgency in the Valley. Next, attacks on military and infiltration of mujahids and other special forces for strikes and attacks on soft targets. And then finally, to liberate Kashmir.

The Kashmir operation was an offshoot of the US-Pakistan fight against Soviet Union. The CIA backed the Mujahadeen, via the ISI. The latter siphoned off money and weapons meant for Afghanistan to stoke the insurgency in Kashmir. But infiltration into the Valley has been taking place on a low key since the early eighties, first of Kashmiris who were alienated from India and currently of Pak mercenaries, including criminals and foreign soldiers of fortune from Afghanistan and further afield. This occurred through training camps in POK and Pakistan proper.

The enormous powers enjoyed by ISI were brought to the notice of Robert Gates in May 1990 on a visit to India and Pakistan. Benazir Bhutto apparently expressed her helplessness to Gates, in controlling the training camps run by ISI in POK and Afghanistan used for anti-India operations. Even accounting for an element of exaggeration, the illustration speaks much for the ISI's independence. Being a military controlled organisation, covert operations are tightly controlled. A more recent statement by Benazir Bhutto portrays an intelligence operation that has run amok and that one wields enormous power within Pakistan.

The Indian case is slightly different in terms of the methods of control. In theory there are levels of civilian control, but in practice agencies like RAW function in their own spheres of influence. If proper command and control had been established with clear political objectives the Sri Lanka operations would have been better tasked. All covert operations, both domestic and foreign require political clearance, but covert intelligence activity can be decided upon by the chief of RAW. Here too, the authority of the Prime Minister is needed if the intelligence gathering is done in a friendly country. The chain of command in the case of RAW is Special Services Bureau/Special Frontier Force through to the Directorate General of Security and Secretary (R), in the Cabinet Secretariat, who reports to the Prime Minister.

Most intelligence organisations the world over have a department or section for active measures. Recruitment and training is often based on special operations lines involving, parachuting, electronics, weapons and languages. Area orientation and mobility along with, light but powerful weaponry for fire fighting is essential for covert operations teams. The use of covert action to support national foreign and security policy has been commonplace amongst intelligence agencies round the world. Their success or failure has often depended on the command and control, and the level of involvement of political controllers. India's experience shows that results have often been positive when proper attention was paid to proper control and coordination. When this has not been possible misuse of covert assets has taken place. This combined with the duplication of covert efforts has reduced the impact of such action on national security.

COVERT OPERATIONS AGAINST PAKISTAN

India has limited experience of covert operations against its western neighbour. Clandestine electronic intelligence gathering and aerial reconnaissance gives it some part of the picture. Additionally, it has gained experience in exfiltrating agents into POK into the training camps and this has helped in keeping tabs on activity in the POK region. But India's ability to influence events in Pakistan itself is limited. Small-scale moral and material support does go out to ethnic groups in Pakistan and some effort is made to infiltrate 'spies' by Military Intelligence in the border regions. But the larger picture is still dependent on Technical/electronic intelligence and even here capability to tap landlines in Pakistan is limited. Human intelligence from within Pakistan is much less than required. It is however suggested by one source on the Internet that RAW has over 35,000 agents in Pakistan.

Therefore, plans have to be made to covertly gather intelligence from inside Pakistan to help in foreign policy objective of breaking the monopoly of the ISI and army over Pakistan. India has to have a plan of action to destabilise Pakistan, its economy and society, to the extent that it gives us leverage in foreign policy terms. It must however, be clear that it is not in India's interests to have a disintegrated Pakistan. The aim is to break the stranglehold of the intelligence agencies, the bureaucracy and the military in Pakistan.

The proposed strategy is to undertake covert passive and active measures against Pakistan including, *psy. ops,* disinformation, strikes in rear areas, border raids and so on. The last may include strikes by special forces against training camps in POK and Northern Areas. Such operations require a clear national will and motivation. They also require sustained funding from the political leadership and it requires highly trained and motivated manpower to execute this task. *The objectives of such operations are to first, penetrate Pakistani society and its institutions of power. Obtaining intelligence from within the establishments of power is the main aim. Associated with this is the second, long-term aim of breaking the stranglehold of the main power brokers in Pakistan.*

For the above mission, there is a need to create, to start with two sets of teams. First, a plans section and second, an operations section. The first will draw up the plans and stages for operations against Pakistan. Also recruiting agents for the task and training them should be completed in about six months. Planning from conception to actual operations should take 8-12 months, depending on the resources and manpower available. Once this is achieved the operations begin.

The operation can be politically cleared by RAW and then a separate section can be raised under the Director RAW, drawing the best talent from within and other agencies including the army, all volunteers of course. Known as Plans Directorate (PD), this will mastermind the operation. Personnel for Strike Directorate (SD) should be picked from SSB, Army para-commandos and NSG. For the agents and sleepers recruitment has to be from outside. The need to know principle has to be strictly followed. Accountability should be from Prime Minister, National Security Advisor, to Director RAW and to PD head.

The entire operation can be divided into three phases. First phase is penetration and setting up of networks. Second phase is to begin operations in rear areas. Strikes against soft targets in Sind, Baluchistan and Northern Areas. These will make the enemy react and make them sensitive.

The main aim is to infiltrate and subvert Pak institutions, the police, communication network and other important organisations. To this end, it makes sense to penetrate Pakistan from two sides, from outside the sub-continent and from POK. Then, in the next stage, focus moves to organising and training subversive elements. These groups would target communication and logistic lines inside POK. Threatening the Mangla dam or Kahuta for instance, would be a major psychological factor. Third phase is hitting hard targets. First, to carry out disinformation campaign carried out by agent provocateurs and others.

A few expendable agents are used to plant false information on police and intelligence agencies. At this stage, the strike teams begin hitting hard targets like economic centres, financial markets (like Karachi), ports and the like. Military installations like ammunition dumps, communication centres, airfields can be targeted in case a war breaks out. Otherwise the aim is to penetrate and gather intelligence with the intention of breaking the stranglehold of the military over Pakistan society.

The mission entails sending two teams of men (and women) into Pakistan for two separate missions. This first team will consist of sleepers, and agent provocateurs, and the second team will be the strike force. The sleepers and agents will consist of network builders and specialists who will recruit local people for both disinformation and strikes in the rear areas of Pakistan. The agent provocateurs will be placed such that they can engage in disinformation and activate sources within who can be expendable when required. The second team is for strikes against key targets of economic and military importance.

Both teams will have to be infiltrated on the basis of genuine documents and placements in Pakistan. Identities can range from middle level social workers, journalists and political workers. Crucially, the persons selected for this job will have to be extensively trained for operations in living off the land in Pakistan. One may at this stage refer to the operation conducted by the Israeli Mossad in Syria aimed at the KHAD party. The agent was an Israeli but was trained to behave and live like a Muslim. Therefore it should not be difficult to train an Indian, Hindu or Muslim to live in Pakistan. The key lies in creating excellent and plausible identities. Training has to be rigorous and thorough. Training will also be common initially and then separate and compartmentalised for the two teams - one, sleepers and agent provocateurs and two, demolition teams that will serve as strike teams in the rear.

While both teams need training in explosives, weapons and communications, each has a specific role, which calls for intensive training. For the sleeper the aim is to penetrate Pakistani society and build a local network for further infiltration. The important thing is therefore for these members to be 'Islamised.' For the strike teams it is going further afield, into Sind, Baluchistan and Northern Areas. This means differing identities and covers; identities are important. The first team has to consist of "Pakistani nationals." Punjabi or Sindhis, who are from abroad, can be targeted. Some thought can be given to recruiting people from the Asian community in UK. Some members can be selected from Uzbekistan or Turkmenistan. For those coming in from the west, penetration point is obviously the United Kingdom, USA or Europe. Even the Middle East can be used. In other words, the potential areas for recruitment are large and this needs to be analysed carefully.

The strike teams could penetrate from Afghanistan or Tajikistan. The NWFP is full of Afghan refugees and the Northern Areas have Turks, Tajiks and Uzbeks. Finding these persons who are reliable and capable is going to be the tough part, but not impossible.

Another option is to exfiltrate these teams from Indian soil. Therefore, the strike teams could penetrate from northern Kashmir.

The northern areas of Jammu & Kashmir bordering Gilgit and Baltistan, mainly Kargil is a Shia dominated region, this could also serve as a recruiting base.

There are also traditional routes that could be used for exfiltration into POK. Additionally, India can find local recruits from amongst the Turks and Tajiks in these regions who could act as couriers and informants. Similarly, in POK the Gujjars and Bakkarwals can be recruited for the same purpose. Seasonal migrants and sheepherders come from the Northern Areas, Chitral and Koistan areas. They can also be recruited. The aim of penetrating the strike teams is to get them to strike in the rear areas of Pakistan. The entire infiltration process of both teams, will take at least one year. Then it is a slow task of making inroads into Pak society.

So it is clear that mission objectives of both teams are different and require different infiltration and exfiltration routes. As suggested above, the first team cannot jump off from India; the second might, given the right circumstances. The sleepers and agent provocateurs are always in danger of exposure. Thus their exfiltration will depend on their own resources and on the overall command and control of the mission. If mission control did want to abandon the task, then alternative exfilitration routes will require to be planned. The strike teams consisting of individuals, usually two to four must have routes of escape, and this is possible in those areas bordering India. It is thought best, diplomatically, at some stage to use Tajikistan as the exfilitration route for those employed in the Northern Areas and surrounding regions. Those in Baluchistan, Sind and NWFP will have to use Afghanistan or get to the Arabian Sea for exfiltration.

The first team should consist of 10-20 persons, both men and women who will be sent to Islamabad, Karachi, Rawalpindi and Lahore. The second team, consisting of only men will go to towns in Sind, Baluchistan and NWFP, as also the areas of Gilgit and Chitral. Numbers will depend on how much rear area attack is envisaged, perhaps initial numbers may be 8-10 in groups of two, to each region. The entire operation has to be planned keeping in mind that the initial period of infiltration and consolidation should be about four-six months. And then once the strike teams have got into place, situations can be created.

The aim of the first team is to settle in Pakistan, infiltrate society, make inroads and build networks for information gathering and find niches in high places. The agent provocateurs will be expendable and need to be locally recruited, though for the sake of authenticity, one or two sleepers need to be expendable also. Key areas of penetration are the bureaucracy, the army, ISI, elite middle class and media. After a lull of a year, information should be leaked, through available means of the existence of these agent provocateurs, who will have in their possession, propaganda material, disinformation material and generally stories that lull Pakistani intelligence into a sense of complacency that they have achieved a coup. Further, as the Russians so successfully did with the CIA and MI-6, the agent provocateurs should talk of moles and other sleepers in the Pak military and intelligence establishment to create internal dissension.

Once this leads to internal turmoil, it is time to activate the strike teams who will launch rear area attacks on installations of economic and military value. This will lead to further conspiracy theories being floated, leading to political uncertainty. The risk that this entails is that it will weaken the democratic process and possibly lead to military rule in Pakistan, but that is a contingency that India has to prepare for. The aim of strikes is to create a situation where the establishment is caught in an over-reach situation. The rear areas, which are under the administrative control of Pakistan, but given its tribal and ethnic composition are quite independent, can be suitably engaged by India for its own purposes. Strikes will mean deploying more police and para-military troops to these regions and will stretch the Pak establishment.

Surprise and timing are an important element in these missions and those in the strike formations should be constantly on the move, working from small towns, crowded market places and religious places. Rear area operations are to succeed by strikes in a few important cities and installations of economic value such as oil fields and tankers. Karachi city and its port is an example. Period of operations will depend on the nature of Pakistani response; if they do according to plan then teams can be exfiltrated. If they need to be in for some more time, then further deception plans need to be put into operation.

The duration of operations in most cases is stretchable. The first phase may take anything between one and three years, while the second phase will be carried out in synchronised fashion for a month or two in one place and then move on to another target. After a respite of a few months it will be time to carry out operations again. The long-term objective is to build information networks in Pakistan that will provide a human intelligence source for India and additionally it will help us make inroads into the military establishment and bureaucracy.

Along with the strike missions carried out by the second team, plans may be made to carry out heliborne operations and SF strikes in the border regions against militant training camps and other suitable targets. Forces for this are already available in the form of the National Security Guards and Indian Army para-commandos. These can be configured and trained for operations in a near-war like situation or simultaneously with the covert strike missions outlined above. All this of course requires a national security policy that seeks to engage and contain Pakistan in foreign policy terms.

To aid this process and to improve intelligence gathering on Pakistan the above covert action plan is commended to the Indian decision-maker and political leadership. The Indian diplomatic and security response to Pakistan sponsored terrorism has often been to fight fires within after the incidents have taken place. Additionally, there is a dialogue track, which seeks to engage Pakistan in a meaningful bilateral exchange. But little thought is given to the possibility of engaging in covert operations on a scale suggested above and its usefulness as a tool of diplomacy. The intention as stated above is not to help the disintegration of Pakistan but to engage Pakistan in a battle in which the key players, the army, ISI and bureaucracy will get embroiled to an extent that it creates conditions for, first Pakistan's disengagement from the sub-continent and second, may help the process of bilateral dialogue.

IMPERIAL EYE ON PAKISTAN

As the purported assassination of Osama bin Laden has placed the focus on Pakistan, it is vital to assess the changing role of Pakistan in broad geostrategic terms, and in particular, of the changing American strategy toward Pakistan. The recently reported assassination was a propaganda ploy aimed at targeting Pakistan. To understand this, it is necessary to examine how America has, in recent years, altered its strategy in Pakistan in the direction of destabilization. In short, Pakistan is an American target. The reason: Pakistan's growing military and strategic ties to China, America's primary global strategic rival. In the 'Great Game' for global hegemony, any country that impedes America's world primacy even one as historically significant to America as Pakistan – may be sacrificed upon the altar of war.

Part 1 of 'Pakistan in Pieces' examines the changing views of the American strategic community – particularly the military and intelligence circles – towards Pakistan. In particular, there is a general acknowledgement that Pakistan will very likely continue to be destabilized and ultimately collapse. What is not mentioned in these assessments, however, is the role of the military and intelligence communities in making this a reality; a veritable self-fulfilling prophecy. This part also examines the active on the ground changes in American strategy in Pakistan, with increasing military incursions into the country.

Imperial Eye on Pakistan

In December of 2000, the CIA released a report of global trends to the year 2015, which stated that by 2015, "Pakistan will be more fractious, isolated, and dependent on international financial assistance." Further, it was predicted, Pakistan:

Will not recover easily from decades of political and economic mismanagement, divisive politics, lawlessness, corruption and ethnic friction. Nascent democratic reforms will produce little change in the face of opposition from an entrenched political elite and radical Islamic parties. Further domestic decline would benefit Islamic political activists, who may significantly increase their role in national politics and alter the makeup and cohesion of the military – once Pakistan's most capable institution. In a climate of continuing domestic turmoil, the central government's control probably will be reduced to the Punjabi heartland and the economic hub of Karachi.

The report further analyzed the trends developing in relation to the Pakistan-India standoff in the region:

The threat of major conflict between India and Pakistan will overshadow all other regional issues during the next 15 years. Continued turmoil in Afghanistan and Pakistan will spill over into Kashmir and other areas of the subcontinent, prompting Indian leaders to take more aggressive preemptive and retaliatory actions. India's conventional military advantage over Pakistan will widen as a result of New Delhi's superior economic position.

In 2005, the Times of India reported on a US National Intelligence Council report, written in conjunction with the CIA, which predicted a "Yugoslavia-like fate" for Pakistan, saying that, "by year 2015 Pakistan would be a failed state, ripe with civil war, bloodshed, inter-provincial rivalries and a struggle for control of its nuclear weapons and complete Talibanisation."

In November of 2008, the US National Intelligence Council released a report, "Global Trends 2025," in which they outlined major trends in the world by the year 2025. When it came to Pakistan, the report stated that, "Ongoing low-intensity clashes between India and Pakistan continue to raise the specter that such events could escalate to a broader conflict between those nuclear powers." It stated that Pakistan "will be at risk of state failure." In examining potential failed states, the report stated that:

outh bulges, deeply rooted conflicts, and limited economic prospects are likely to keep Palestine, Yemen, Afghanistan, Pakistan, and others in the high-risk category. Spillover from turmoil in these states and potentially others increases the chance that moves elsewhere in the region toward greater prosperity and political stability will be rocky.

The report referred to Pakistan as a "wildcard" and stated that if it is "unable to hold together until 2025, a broader coalescence of Pashtun tribes is likely to emerge and act together to erase the

Durand Line [separating Pakistan from Afghanistan], maximizing Pashtun space at the expense of Punjabis in Pakistan and Tajiks and others in Afghanistan."

In January of 2009, a Pentagon report analyzing geopolitical trends of significance to the US military over the next 25 years, reported that Pakistan could face a "rapid and sudden" collapse. It stated that, "Some forms of collapse in Pakistan would carry with it the likelihood of a sustained violent and bloody civil and sectarian war, an even bigger haven for violent extremists, and the question of what would happen to its nuclear weapons," and as such, "that 'perfect storm' of uncertainty alone might require the engagement of U.S. and coalition forces into a situation of immense complexity and danger."

A top adviser to former President George Bush and current President Obama warned in April of 2009, that Pakistan could collapse within months, and that, "We have to face the fact that if Pakistan collapses it will dwarf anything we have seen so far in whatever we're calling the war on terror now." The adviser and consultant, David Kilcullen, explained that this would be unlike the conflicts in Afghanistan and Iraq, which each had a population of over 30 million, whereas "Pakistan has million people and 100 nuclear weapons, an army which is bigger than the American army, and the headquarters of al-Qaeda sitting in two-thirds of the country which the Government does not control."

Target: Pakistan

Going back to the later years of the Bush administration, it is apparent that the US strategy in Pakistan was already changing in seeing it increasingly as a target for military operations as opposed to simply a conduit. In August of 2007, newly uncovered documents revealed that the US military "gave elite units broad authority" in 2004, "to pursue suspected terrorists into Pakistan, with no mention of telling the Pakistanis in advance."

In November of 2007, an op-ed in the New York Times stated categorically that, "the United States simply could not stand by as a nuclear-armed Pakistan descended into the abyss," and that, "we need to think — now — about our feasible military options in Pakistan, should it really come to that." The authors, Frederick Kagan and Michael O'Hanlon are both well-known strategists and scholars at the American Enterprise Institute and Brookings Institution, two of the most prominent and influential think tanks in the United States. While stating that Pakistan's leaders are still primarily moderate and friendly to the US, "Americans felt similarly about the shah's regime in Iran until it was too late," referring to the outbreak of the Iranian Revolution in 1979. They warn:

> The most likely possible dangers are these: a complete collapse of Pakistani government rule that allows an extreme Islamist movement to fill the vacuum; a total loss of federal control over outlying provinces, which splinter along ethnic and tribal lines; or a struggle within the Pakistani military in which the minority sympathetic to the Taliban and Al Qaeda try to establish Pakistan as a state sponsor of terrorism.

They state that the military solutions are "daunting" as Pakistan is a nation of 187 million people, roughly five times the size of Iraq. They wrote that, "estimates suggest that a force of more than a million troops would be required for a country of this size," which led them to conclude, "Thus, if we have any hope of success, we would have to act before a complete government collapse, and we would need the cooperation of moderate Pakistani forces." They suggested one plan would be to deploy Special Forces "with the limited goal of preventing Pakistan's nuclear materials and warheads from getting into the wrong hand." However, they admit that, "even pro-American Pakistanis would be unlikely to cooperate." Another option, they contend:

> would involve supporting the core of the Pakistani armed forces as they sought to hold the country together in the face of an ineffective government, seceding border regions and Al Qaeda and Taliban assassination attempts against the leadership. This would require a sizable combat force — not only from the United States, but ideally also other Western powers and moderate Muslim nations.

The authors concluded, saying that any state decline in Pakistan would likely be gradual, therefore allowing the US to have time to respond, and placed an emphasis on securing Pakistan's nuclear arsenal and combating militants. They finished the article with the warning: "Pakistan may be the next big test."

In December of 2007, the Asia Times Online ran a story about the US plan to rid Pakistan of President Musharraf, and that the US and the West, more broadly, had begun a strategy aimed at toppling Pakistan's military. As part of this, the US launched a media campaign aimed at demonizing Pakistan's military establishment. At this time, Benazir Bhutto was criticizing the ISI, suggesting they needed a dramatic restructuring, and at the same time, reports were appearing in the US media blaming the ISI for funding and providing assistance to Al-Qaeda and the Taliban. While much of this is documented, the fact that it suddenly emerged as talking points with several western officials and in the media does suggest a turn-around against a long-time ally.

Both Democratic and Republican politicians were making statements that Pakistan represented a greater threat than Iran, and then-Senator (now Vice President) Joseph Biden suggested that the United States needed to put soldiers on the ground in Pakistan in cooperation with the "international community." Biden said that, "We should be in there," and "we should be supplying tens of millions of dollars to build new schools to compete with the madrassas. We should be in there building democratic institutions. We should be in there, and get the rest of the world in there, giving some structure to the emergence of, hopefully, the reemergence of a democratic process."

In American policy-strategy circles, officials openly began discussing the possibility of Pakistan breaking up into smaller states, and increasing discussion that Musharraf was going to be "removed," which obviously happened. As the Asia Times stated:

Another worrying thing is how US officials are publicly signaling to the Pakistanis that Bhutto has their backing as the next leader of the country. Such signals from Washington are not only a kiss of death for any public leader in Pakistan, but the Americans also know that their actions are inviting potential assassins to target Bhutto.

If she is killed in this way, there won't be enough time to find the real culprit, but what's certain is that unprecedented international pressure will be placed on Islamabad while everyone will use their local assets to create maximum internal chaos in the country.

Of course, this subsequently happened in Pakistan. As the author of the article pointed out with startlingly accurate foresight, "Getting Bhutto killed can generate the kind of pressure that could result in permanently putting the Pakistani military on a back foot, giving Washington enough room to push for installing a new pliant leadership in Islamabad." He observed that, "the US is very serious this time. They cannot let Pakistan get out of their hands."

Thus, it would appear that the new US strategic aim in Pakistan was focused on removing the Pakistani military from power, implying the need to replace Musharraf, and replace him with a new, compliant civilian leadership. This would have the effect of fracturing the Pakistani elite, threatening the Army's influence within Pakistani politics, and undertaking more direct control of Pakistan's government.

As if on cue, in late December it was reported that, "US special forces snatch squads are on standby to seize or disable Pakistan's nuclear arsenal in the event of a collapse of government authority or the outbreak of civil war following the assassination of Benazir Bhutto."

The New York Times ran an article in early January 2008, which reported that, "President Bush's senior national security advisers are debating whether to expand the authority of the Central Intelligence Agency and the military to conduct far more aggressive covert operations in the tribal areas of Pakistan." The article stated that the new strategy was purportedly in response to increased reports of Al-Qaeda and Taliban activity within Pakistan, which "are intensifying efforts there to destabilize the Pakistani government." Bush's National Security team supposedly organized this effort in response to Bhutto's assassination 10 days previously.

Officials involved in the strategy discussions said that some "options would probably involve the C.I.A. working with the military's Special Operations forces," and one official said, "After years of focusing on Afghanistan, we think the extremists now see a chance for the big prize — creating chaos in Pakistan itself." Of pivotal importance to the strategy, as the Times reported: "Critics said more direct American military action would be ineffective, anger the Pakistani Army and increase support for the militants." Perhaps this is not simply a "side-effect" of the proposed strategy, but in fact, part of the strategy.

As one prominent Pakistani political and military analyst pointed out, raids into Pakistan would expand anger and "prompt a powerful popular backlash" against the Pakistani government, losing popular support. However, as I previously stated, this might be the intention, as this would ultimately make the government more dependent upon the United States, and thus, more subservient.

On September 3, 2008, it was reported that a commando raid by US Special Forces was launched in Pakistan, which killed between 15 and 20 people, including women and children. The Special Forces were accompanied by five U.S. helicopters for the duration of the operation.

In February of 2009, it was reported that, "More than 70 United States military advisers and technical specialists are secretly working in Pakistan to help its armed forces battle Al Qaeda and the Taliban in the country's lawless tribal areas." So not only are U.S. Special Forces invading Pakistani territory; but now US military advisers are secretly advising the Pakistani Army on its own operations, and the advisers are themselves primary made up of Special Forces soldiers. They provide the Pakistani Army "with intelligence and advising on combat tactics," and make up a secret command run by US Central Command and Special Operations Command (presumably JSOC – Joint Special Operations Command).

In May of 2009, it was reported that, "the U.S. is sending Special Forces teams into one of Pakistan's most violent regions as part of a push to accelerate the training of the Pakistani military and make it a more effective ally in the fight against insurgents there." The Special Forces were deploying to two training camps in the province of Baluchistan, and "will focus on training Pakistan's Frontier Corps, a paramilitary force responsible for battling the

Taliban and al Qaeda fighters." Further, the project "is a joint effort with the U.K.," which helps "fund the training, although it is unclear if British military personnel would take part in the initiative. British officials have been pushing for such an effort for several years."

In December of 2009 it was revealed that, "American special forces have conducted multiple clandestine raids into Pakistan's tribal areas as part of a secret war in the border region where Washington is pressing to expand its drone assassination programme," which was revealed by a former NATO officer. He said these incursions had occurred between 2003 and 2008, indicating they go even further back than US military documents stipulate. The source further revealed that, "the Pakistanis were kept entirely in the dark about it. It was one of those things we wouldn't confirm officially with them." Further, as the source noted, British "SAS soldiers have been active in the province" of Bolochistan in 2002 and 2003 and "possibly beyond."

The "Balkanization" of Pakistan: Blaming the Pakistanis

Selig S. Harrison is a director of the Asia Program at the Center for International Policy, senior scholar of the Woodrow Wilson International Center for Scholars, former senior associate of the Carnegie Endowment for International Peace, and former journalist and correspondent. "His reputation for giving 'early warning' of foreign policy crises was well established during his career as a foreign correspondent. In his study of foreign reporting, Between Two Worlds, John Hohenberg, former secretary of the Pulitzer Prize Board, cited Harrison's prediction of the 1965 Indo-Pakistan war eighteen months before it happened." Further, "More than a year before the Russians invaded Afghanistan, Harrison warned of this possibility in one of his frequent contributions to the influential journal Foreign Policy."

On February 1, 2008, Selig Harrison threw his renowned "predictive" abilities on Pakistan in an op-ed for the New York Times in the run-up to the Pakistani elections. He started by stating that, "Whatever the outcome of the Pakistani elections, now scheduled for Feb. 18, the existing multiethnic Pakistani state is not likely to survive for long unless it is radically restructured."

Harrison then went on to explain that Pakistan would likely break up along ethnic lines; with the Pashtuns, concentrated in the northwestern tribal areas, the Sindhis in the southeast uniting with the Baluch tribesmen in the southwest, with the Punjab "rump state" of Pakistan.

The Pashtuns in the north, "would join with their ethnic brethren across the Afghan border (some 40 million of them combined) to form an independent 'Pashtunistan'," and the Sindhis "numbering 23 million, would unite with the six million Baluch tribesmen in the southwest to establish a federation along the Arabian Sea from India to Iran," presumably named Baluchistan; while the rump state of Pakistan would remain Punjabi dominated and in control of the nuclear weapons. Selig Harrison explained that prior to partition from India, which led to the creation of the Pakistani state in 1947, Pashtun, Sindhi and Baluch ethnicities had "resist Punjabi domination for centuries," and suddenly:

they found themselves subjected to Punjabi-dominated military regimes that have appropriated many of the natural resources in the minority provinces – particularly the natural gas deposits in the Baluch areas – and siphoned off much of the Indus River's waters as they flow through the Punjab.

The resulting Punjabi-Pashtun animosity helps explain why the United States is failing to get effective Pakistani cooperation in fighting terrorists. The Pashtuns living along the Afghan border are happy to give sanctuary from Punjabi forces to the Taliban, which is composed primarily of fellow Pashtuns, and to its Qaeda friends.

Pashtun civilian casualties resulting from Pakistani and American air strikes on both sides of the border are breeding a potent underground Pashtun nationalist movement. Its initial objective is to unite all Pashtuns in Pakistan, now divided among political jurisdictions, into a unified province. In time, however, its leaders envisage full nationhood.

... The Baluch people, for their part, have been waging intermittent insurgencies since their forced incorporation into Pakistan in 1947. In the current warfare Pakistani forces are widely reported to be deploying American-supplied aircraft and intelligence equipment that was intended for use in Afghan border areas. Their victims are forging military links with Sindhi nationalist groups that have been galvanized into action by the death of Benazir Bhutto, a Sindhi hero as was her father, Zulfikar Ali Bhutto.

This passage is very revealing of the processes and perceptions surrounding "Balkanization" and "destabilization." What I mean by this, is that historically and presently, imperial powers would often use ethnic groups against each other in a strategy of divide and conquer, in order "to keep the barbarians from coming together" and dominate the region.

Zbigniew Brzezinski wrote in his 1997 book, "The Grand Chessboard," that, "Geopolitics has moved from the regional to the global dimension, with preponderance over the entire Eurasian continent serving as the central basis for global primacy." Brzezinski then gave a masterful explanation of the American global strategy, which placed it into a firm imperialistic context:

To put it in a terminology that hearkens back to the more brutal age of ancient empires, the three grand imperatives of imperial geostrategy are to prevent collusion and maintain security dependence among the vassals, to keep tributaries pliant and protected, and to keep the barbarians from coming together.

While imperial powers manipulate, and historically, even create the ethnic groups within regions and nations, the West portrays conflict in such regions as being the product of these "ethnic" or "tribal" rivalries. This perception of the East (Asia and the Middle East) as well as Africa is referred to as Orientalism or Eurocentrism: meaning it generally portrays the East (and/or Africa) as "the Other": inherently different and often barbaric. This prejudiced perspective is prevalent in Western academic, media, and policy circles. This perspective serves a major purpose: dehumanizing a people in a region that an imperial power seeks to dominate, which allows the hegemon to manipulate the people and divide them against each other, while framing them as "backwards" and "barbaric," which in turn, justifies the Western imperial power exerting hegemony and control over the region; to "protect" the people from themselves.

Historically and presently, Western empires have divided people against each other, blamed the resulting conflict on the people themselves, and thus justified their control over both the people, and the region they occupy. This was the strategy employed in major recent geopolitical conflicts such as the breakup of Yugoslavia and the Rwandan genocide. In both cases, Western imperial ambitions were met through exacerbating ethnic rivalries, providing financial, technical, and military aid and training to various factions; thus, spreading violent conflict, war, and genocide. In both cases, Western, and primarily American strategic interests were met through an increased presence militarily, pushing out other major imperial and powerful rivals, as well as increasing Western access to key economics resources.

This is the lens through which we must view the unfolding situation in Pakistan. However, the situation in Pakistan presents a far greater potential for conflict and devastation than either Yugoslavia or Rwanda. In short, the potential strategy of "Balkanization" and destabilization of Pakistan could dwarf any major global conflict in the past few decades. It's sheer population of 187 million people, proximity to two major regional wars in Iraq and Afghanistan, its strategic location as neighbour to India, China, and Iran with access to the Indian Ocean, and its nuclear arsenal, combine to make Pakistan the potential trigger for a much wider regional and possibly global war. The destabilization of Pakistan has the potential to be the greatest geopolitical catastrophe since World War II. Thus, Selig Harrison's op-ed in the New York Times in which he describes the "likely" breakup of Pakistan along ethnic lines as a result of "ethnic differences" must be viewed in the wider context of geopolitical ambitions. His article lays the foundation both for the explanation of a potential breakup, and thus the "justification" for Western intervention in the conflict. His "predictive" capacities as a seasoned journalist can be alternatively viewed as pre-emptive imperial propaganda.

Fracturing Pakistan

The war in Afghanistan is inherently related to the situation in Pakistan. From the days of the Afghan-Soviet war in the 1980s, arms and money were flowing through Pakistan to the Mujahideen in Afghanistan. During the civil war that followed, Pakistan armed and financed the Taliban, which eventually took power. When the U.S. and NATO initially attacked Afghanistan on October 7, 2001, this was primarily achieved through cooperation with Pakistan. When the war theatre was re-named "AfPak," the role of Pakistan, however, was formally altered. While the previous few years had seen the implementation of a strategy of destabilizing Pakistan, once the "AfPak" war theatre was established, Pakistan ceased to be as much of a conduit or proxy state and became a target.

In September of 2008, the editor of Indian Defence Review wrote an article explaining that a stable Pakistan is not in India's interests: "With Pakistan on the brink of collapse due to massive internal as well as international contradictions, it is matter of time before it ceases to exist." He explained that Pakistan's collapse would bring "multiple benefits" to India, including preventing China from gaining a major port in the Indian Ocean, which is in the mutual interest of the United States. The author explained that this would be a "severe jolt" to China's expansionist aims, and further, "India's access to Central Asian energy routes will open up."

In August of 2009, Foreign Policy Journal published a report of an exclusive interview they held with former Pakistani ISI chief Lieutenant General Hamid Gul, who was Director General of the powerful intelligence services (ISI) between 1987 and 1989, at a time in which it was working closely with the CIA to fund and arm the Mujahideen. Once a close ally of the US, he is now considered extremely controversial and the US even recommended the UN to put him on the international terrorist list. Gul explained that he felt that the American people have not been told the truth about 9/11, and that the 9/11 Commission was a "cover up," pointing out that, "They [the American government] haven't even proved the case that 9/11 was done by Osama bin Laden and al Qaeda." He said that the real reasons for the war on Afghanistan were that:

the U.S. wanted to "reach out to the Central Asian oilfields" and "open the door there", which "was a requirement of corporate America, because the Taliban had not complied with their desire to allow an oil and gas pipeline to pass through Afghanistan. UNOCAL is a case in point. They wanted to keep the Chinese out. They wanted to give a wider security shield to the state of Israel, and they wanted to include this region into that shield. And that's why they were talking at that time very hotly about 'greater Middle East'. They were redrawing the map."

He also stated that part of the reason for going into Afghanistan was "to go for Pakistan's nuclear capability," as the U.S. "signed this strategic deal with India, and this was brokered by Israel. So there is a nexus now between Washington, Tel Aviv, and New Delhi." When he was asked about the Pakistani Taliban, which the Pakistani government was being pressured to fight, and where the financing for that group came from; Gul stated:

Yeah, of course they are getting it from across the Durand line, from Afghanistan. And the Mossad is sitting there, RAW is sitting there — the Indian intelligence agency — they have the umbrella of the U.S. And now they have created another organization which is called RAMA. It may be news to you that very soon this intelligence agency — of course, they have decided to keep it covert — but it is Research and Analysis Milli Afghanistan. That's the name. The Indians have helped create this organization, and its job is mainly to destabilize Pakistan.

He explained that the Chief of Staff of the Afghan Army had told him that he had gone to India to offer the Indians five bases in Afghanistan, three of which are along the Pakistani border. Gul was asked a question as to why, if the West was supporting the TTP (Pakistani Taliban), would a CIA drone have killed the leader of the TTP. Gul explained that while Pakistan was fighting directly against the TTP leader, Baitullah Mehsud, the Pakistani government would provide the Americans where Mehsud was, "three times the Pakistan intelligence tipped off America, but they did not attack him." So why all of a sudden did they attack?

Because there were some secret talks going on between Baitullah Mehsud and the Pakistani military establishment. They wanted to reach a peace agreement, and if you recall there is a long history of our tribal areas, whenever a tribal militant has reached a peace agreement with the government of Pakistan, Americans have without any hesitation struck that target. ... there was some kind of a deal which was about to be arrived at — they may have already cut a deal. I don't know. I don't have enough information on that. But this is my hunch, that Baitullah was killed because now he was trying to reach an agreement with the Pakistan army. And that's why there were no suicide attacks inside Pakistan for the past six or seven months.

An article in one of Canada's national magazines, Macleans, reported on an interview with a Pakistani ISI spy, who claimed that India's intelligence services, Research and Analysis Wing (RAW), have "tens of thousands of RAW agents in Pakistan." Many officials inside Pakistan were convinced that, "India's endgame is nothing less than the breakup of Pakistan. And the RAW is no novice in that area. In the 1960s, it was actively involved in supporting separatists in Bangladesh, at the time East Pakistan. The eventual victory of Bangladeshi nationalism in 1971 was in large part credited to the support the RAW gave the secessionists."

Further, there were Indian consulates set up in Kandahar, the area of Afghanistan where Canadian troops are located, and which is strategically located next to the Pakistani province of Baluchistan, which is home to a virulent separatist movement, of which Pakistan claims is being supported by India. Macleans reported on the conclusions by Michel Chossudovsky, economics professor at University of Ottawa, that, "the region's massive gas and oil reserves are of strategic interest to the U.S. and India. A gas pipeline slated to be built from Iran to India, two countries that already enjoy close ties, would run through Baluchistan. The Baluch separatist movement, which is also active in Iran, offers an ideal proxy for both the U.S. and India to ensure their interests are met."

Even an Afghan government adviser told the media that India was using Afghan territory to destabilize Pakistan. In September of 2009, the Pakistan Daily reported that captured members and leaders of the Pakistani Taliban have admitted to being trained and armed by India through RAW or RAMA in Afghanistan in order to fight the Pakistani Army.

Foreign Policy magazine in February of 2009 quoted a former intelligence official as saying, "The Indians are up to their necks in supporting the Taliban against the Pakistani government in Afghanistan and Pakistan," and that, "the same anti-Pakistani forces in Afghanistan also shooting at American soldiers are getting support from India. India should close its diplomatic establishments in Afghanistan and get the Christ out of there."

The Council on Foreign Relations published a backgrounder report on RAW, India's intelligence agency, founded in 1968 "primarily to counter China's influence, [however] over time it has shifted its focus to India's other traditional rival, Pakistan." For over three decades both Indian and Pakistani intelligence agencies have been involved in covert operations against one another. One of RAW's main successes was its covert operations in East Pakistan, now known as Bangladesh, which "aimed at fomenting independence sentiment" and ultimately led to the separation of Bangladesh by directly funding, arming and training the Pakistani separatists. Further, as the Council on Foreign Relations noted, "From the early days, RAW had a secret liaison relationship with the Mossad, Israel's external intelligence agency."

Since RAW was founded in 1968, it had developed close ties with the Afghan intelligence agency, KHAD, primarily to do with intelligence sharing on Pakistan. In the 1980s, while Pakistan was funding, arming and training the Afghan Mujahideen with the support of Saudi Arabia and the CIA, India was funding two covert groups which orchestrated terrorist attacks inside Pakistan, which included a "low-grade but steady campaign of bombings in major Pakistani cities, notably Karachi and Lahore." RAW has also had a close relationship with the CIA, as even six years before RAW was created, in 1962, the CIA created a covert organization made up of Tibetan refugees, which aimed to "execute deep-penetration terror operations in China." The CIA subsequently played a part in the creation of RAW. In the 1980s, while the CIA was working closely with the ISI in Pakistan, RAW, while wary of their relationship, continued to get counterterrorism training from the CIA.

In October of 2009, the New York Times reported that the US strategy "to vastly expand its aid to Pakistan, as well as the footprint of its embassy and private security contractors here, are aggravating an already volatile anti-American mood as Washington pushes for greater action by the government against the Taliban." The U.S. gave Pakistan an aid deal of $1.5 billion per year for the next five years, under the stipulation of "Pakistan to cease supporting terrorist groups on its soil and to ensure that the military does not interfere with civilian politics." President Zaradari accepted the proposal, making him even more unpopular in Pakistan, and further angering Pakistan's powerful military, which sees the deal as interfering in the internal affairs of the country.

America is thus expanding its embassy and security presence within the country, as the Embassy "has publicized plans for a vast new building in Islamabad for about 1,000 people, with security for some diplomats provided through a Washington-based private contracting company, DynCorp." The NYT article referred to how relations were becoming increasingly strained between Pakistan and the US, and tensions were growing within the country exponentially, as "the American presence was fueling a sense of occupation among Pakistani politicians and security officials," and several Pakistani officials stated that, "the United States was now seen as behaving in Pakistan much as it did in Iraq and Afghanistan." Futher:

In particular, the Pakistani military and the intelligence agencies are concerned that DynCorp is being used by Washington to develop a parallel network of security and intelligence personnel within Pakistan, officials and politicians close to the army said.

The concerns are serious enough that last month a local company hired by DynCorp to provide Pakistani men to be trained as security guards for American diplomats was raided by the Islamabad police. The owner of the company, the Inter-Risk Security Company, Capt. Syed Ali Ja Zaidi, was later arrested.

The action against Inter-Risk, apparently intended to cripple the DynCorp program, was taken on orders from the senior levels of the Pakistani government, said an official familiar with the raid, who was not authorized to speak on the record.

The entire workings of DynCorp within Pakistan are now under review by the Pakistani government.

As revealed in the Wikileaks diplomatic cables, U.S. Ambassador to Pakistan Anne Patterson wrote in September of 2009 that the U.S. strategy of unilateral strikes inside Pakistan "risk destabilizing the Pakistani state, alienating both the civilian government and military leadership, and provoking a broader governance crisis in Pakistan without finally achieving the goal."

In an interview with Press TV, Hamid Gul, former Inter-Services Intelligence chief revealed more of what he sees as the US strategy in Pakistan. He explained that with the massive expansion of the U.S. Embassy in Pakistan, and alongside that, the increased security staff, the Chinese are becoming increasingly concerned with the sovereignty and security of Pakistan. He claimed that the money that the US government offered (with heavy conditions) to Pakistan, $1.5 billion every year for five years, will be spent under the direction of the Americans, and that "they are going to set up a large intelligence network inside Pakistan," and ultimately "they really want to go for Pakistan's nuclear assets." He further claimed that the Indians are trying to destabilize Pakistan; however, he explained, this does not necessarily mean disintegrate, but rather:

> they are trying to destabilize Pakistan at the moment so that it feels weak and economically has to go begging on its knees to Americans and ask for succor and help. And in that process they will want to expect certain concessions with regards to nuclear power and also with regards to setting up their facilities here in Pakistan.

When he was asked what America's long-term goal was in regards to Pakistan, Gul responded that the goal:

> for America is that they want to keep Pakistan destabilized; perhaps create a way for Baluchistan as a separate state and then create problems for Iran so that this new state will talk about greater Baluchistan... So it appears that the long-term objectives are really to fragment all these countries to an extent that they can establish a strip that would be pro-America, pro-India, pro-Israel. So this seems to be their long-term objective apart from denuclearizing Pakistan and blocking Iran's progress in the nuclear field.

In Part 2 of 'Pakistan in Pieces', I will examine the specific ways in which the American strategy of destabilization is being undertaken in Pakistan, including the waging of a secret war and the expansion of the Afghan war into Pakistani territory. In short, the military and intelligence projections for Pakistan over the next several years (discussed in the beginning of Part 1 above) are a self-fulfilling prophecy, as those very same military and intelligence agencies that predict a destabilized Pakistan and potential collapse are now undertaking strategies aimed at achieving those outcomes.

7

R&AW in the Freedom Struggle of Bangladesh

The treaty had two main points. India will have its control over foreign and defence matters and Bangladesh would open its market for Indian products. Even after this, Indian newspapers continued to lobby for the merger of Bangladesh into India.

If European countries can become a united Europe, why can't India go to status-quo-ante, or the situation prior to 1947? Such were the views expressed in those newspapers.

RAW IN THE FREEDOM STRUGGLE OF BANGLADESH

Bangladesh which has an area of 55,598 sq. mile had a population of 118 million in 1990. A decade later the figure reached 126 million. Per capita income of Bangladesh is US $ 380 and its economic growth rate is 3.9 percent. Average life span there is 62 years, literacy rate is 39 percent and poverty is 35.6 percent. Though the land in Bangladeshi is very fertile, it, being located in extremely lowland on the bank of Brahmaputra and Ganga, frequently suffers from the floods.

These water problems also contribute to poverty. Though the people are highly industrious, poverty has stood in their way of building a prosperous society. Because of this, Bangladesh has been turned into one of the most poorest countries in South Asia. In case the earth's environment becomes unbalanced, snow in the northern part gets melted and sea level rises, nearly half of the country will be submerged. In the country with 98 percent of the people speaking Bengali as their mother tongue, 88 percent are Muslims, 10 percent are Hindus and 1.1 percent are Buddhists and Christians. Till the 12th century, the South and Southeast Asian region was at its peak of Aryan civilization and was known as Bangladesh.

The Muslims from the Middle-East made attacks at the end of the century and converted the Hindus into Christians forcibly. The Muslims of Bangladesh and the Hindus who continued to remain in Bangladesh and others who fled the country to the mountainous region were of the same country or clan. Had the attackers not changed their names and castes at the time of conversion, it would have been easier to trace down the lineage even after seven or eight hundred years. The Bengali language, the descendant of Sanskrit, however, continues to be spoken as a common language.

This is a matter of sorrow that some extremist elements who do not try to understand religion in its right sense have used religion as a tool for playing one against the other. Everyone wants to see that many Taslimas would be born, all would understand the essence of religion and all would treat each other with a sense of love and brotherhood. Just because of the religion, East Bengal in 1947 became a part of Pakistan. India and Pakistan got into war on Dec 3, 1971 and on Dec 15, Bangladesh emerged as an independent nation. A total of about one million people were reportedly killed during the civil war and ten times the number had to leave the country for India as refugees. Survived under the patronage of the erstwhile Soviet Union and India, Bangladesh has already had a lot of differences with them. Border disputes and differences over water resources are the areas where India and Bangladesh have locked their horns.

The Bangladesh episode corroborates the view that the imported politics will not work. The politics crafted by the people vis-à-vis the country's soil and geography is, in fact, democratic. Bangladesh, which is almost on all sides surrounded by India, has 21 districts. It spends nearly two percent of its national income in defence.

Sixty-seven percent of the total land is arable and paddy, jute and tea are the staple crops which absorb about 75% of the workforce. Oil and natural gas near the ocean top the list of minerals, while major industries include fishery, cement, jute, textile and chemical fertilizers. Industry absorbs 11% of the workforce, while the service sector absorbs 15%. In 1999, the average life span of man was 54 and that of women was 53. The population growth rate is 2.8%.

Following the independence of Bangladesh, it signed a seven-point secret treaty with India. According to the treaty, all types of employees including civil employees appointed during the Bangladesh civil war should be granted permanent status, other employees also could be appointed only by the Indian administrative service, a certain number of Indian soldiers will continue to remain in Bangladesh despite independence, Bangladesh will not have its own army, for its internal security, it will have only militias from among the freedom fighters who will work under the Indian military command, the trade between the two countries will be kept open and free, and matters pertaining to foreign affairs will be dealt only after close consultation with the Indian foreign ministry.

The treaty had two main points. India will have its control over foreign and defence matters and Bangladesh would open its market for Indian products. Even after this, Indian newspapers continued to lobby for the merger of Bangladesh into India. If European countries can become a united Europe, why can't India go to status-quo-ante, or the situation prior to 1947? Such were the views expressed in those newspapers.

The kind of treatment or relations India would like to have with Nepal is just the same. After the monarchy refused to succumb to the pressures of India for the sake of independence and sovereignty, India has gone at this institution ever since 1963 (2019 BS) and following the emergence of RAW, the attack has further intensified. India has a honey tongue but a heart of gall towards this institution ever since.

As per the grand design of SD Muni, the Maoists and the Nepali Congress have served up the illogic that there should be an option left for the people to choose between the monarchy and republic. 5.3 RAW's Efforts to Create Bangladesh Time is very powerful. Sometimes it so happens that an event taking place in one country may serve a threat to the politics and defence of another country. The political collapse of Russia created ripples in West Europe and in Nepal that brought about a change. The political disorder arising out of such ripples can be addressed only through political talks. Such works can be carried out with the help of spies in different countries.

India had already fought a "thine-mine" war with Pakistan. India was full of revenge against Pakistan. It wanted to weaken this country. East Pakistan was the main source of income for Pakistan. India had taken a calculated move to dismember it and weaken it. RAW entered East Pakistan and began inciting it against Pakistan. As a result of this, anti-Pakistani sentiments flared up here. The people, muktibahi (freedom fighters) and Pakistan itself were not aware of this for many years to come. One year before embarking on the operation in Bangladesh, a strategy was already framed to work in favor of Mujib. Shankar Nayer disguised as Colonel Menon had worked as a bridge between Mujib and RAW.

At the beginning, the conspiracy could not achieve success. India declared to take action against 28 persons involved in the conspiracy on charge of coup d'etat. The names of RAW's Colonel Menon and Major Tripathy were also published. After the first phase of the conspiracy came unstuck, joint-director PN Benarjee himself girded up his loins and spread a network of 100 spies in Bangladesh. He created cells along the borders and Menon continuously remained in his contact.

Kedar Siddiqui of East Pakistan was re-christened as Tiger Siddiqui and was brought into contact with RAW on behalf of the muktibahinis. After this, RAW provided trainings to hundreds of these freedom fighters in secret places. Weapons were also provided. Till they were strong enough to fight with the Pakistani army, this was not disclosed to anyone except Tiger Siddiqui. So may be the case with Nepal. Except one in the Maoist movement, nobody may be aware of such conspiracy because if the secret comes out of the closet, people will throw their guns. Everybody loves his or her country. I think Maoists also love. When the people of Bangal came to know of this after independence, they started to hate India. Thereafter, the relations between the two countries soured and got muddied like the flooded waters of the Ganges. Of course India brought Pakistan to its size, but in the long run, it proved a boomerang for it. One million people turned enemies. The Kashmir problem appeared stronger. Those who think ill of others will never find themselves better-off. This is the truth.

India should understand that centrifugal force also has same value as in the centripetel force. It may split over three dozen pieces if India fails maintaining balance with the neibours. 5.4 President Ayub Khan out of frustration delegated many of his powers to Yaya Khan and made an announcement to hold the elections on October 5, 1970. Immediately after this, RAW took stock of the special operation carried out in Bangladesh. It was only one day before the independence of Bangladesh that a Pakistani officer had known of the conspiracy.

After knowing that Pakistan was irate and got very provoked by the incident that it would teach Bangladesh a lesson that would never be blown over, RAW offered a suggestion to its chief and prime minister Mrs Indira Gandhi, as per which she had traveled around the world trying to gain support of the global community. She had appealed to the world to support her intervention in Bangladesh as her country was unable to cope with the pressure of a million plus refugees and it was urgently necessary to calm down the situation. On the other hand, Mujib, as per the Agartala conspiracy case of 1966, had put forth six-point demand with Pakistan.

The demands were as follows: 1. Pakistan would make its constitution federal and guarantee full autonomy to East Pakistan. 2.The federal government would take care of only defence and foreign matters, and in everything else, full autonomy will be granted. 3. Either to establish two central banks if the case is made one, or to maintain separate cases. 4. The right to collect taxes and revenue will be granted to the states and the center will be entitled to a small portion of it. 5. Economic, fiscal and legal improvement will be made. 6. East Pakistan will be entitled to keep para-military forces. Pakistan could not get even a wind of the tricks and shenanigans of India and had to suffer. If Pakistan had accepted the above six demands timely, there would have been its grips over East Pakistan. Similarly, the "Mutual Cooperation Agreement Between the Governments of Nepal and India" was presented to Nepal on April 1, 1990. But at that time, Nepal showed the sagacity and refused the proposal. But, as regards the domestic matters, it was a blunder to not allow to contest elections with the same symbol. Had the case been otherwise, the nation would not have to face the kind of crisis it is facing now.

RAW continued to receive information about hundreds of incidents after the Agartala conspiracy of 1968. Later the election in Pakistan was held on the same date as designated by RAW and the majority of the seats in parliament were captured by the East Pakistani candidates in favor of RAW.

In such situation anything RAW wanted to get done could be easily done. Now in Nepal, the same purpose lies behind the passage of the citizenship bill and delimitation of electoral constituencies not on the basis of political division but on the basis of population. Article 105 of the Constitution has been inserted with the same motive. 5.5 Though the Awami League unfurled the flag of victory after the elections of 1970, it had already got a hint that the majority attained through the crutches of foreigners would not count for much.

RAW had already got a tip-off that a military team led by Lt. General Tika Khan was heading for Chittagong well before the departure had taken place. Immediately after this information was received, an urgent notice was sent out. There was written ....Advise Menon......to bring in............our friend.........Muzib and .... Tazuddin .... Immediately, Mujib and Tazuddin and other leaders entered India and formed a government there. After this, a message that "the bird was caged" was forwarded. On the other hand, when Pakistan knew of the military action, RAW decided to make surgical intervention and accordingly a contingent of plainclothes soldiers was also dispatched. The contingent included the Nepalese soldiers from the Gorkha regiment.

The Mukti Bahini was only in name. In fact it was full of the Indian army. It had caused a significant damage to the Pakistani army. Some 25 thousand soldiers, 21 submarines and 600 bridges were lost in the war. It is because the Bahini had imported soldiers numbering 100,000.

In the second phase, yet another military action was taken. RAW had formed a central level coordination committee in order to make it more effective. The committee consisted of the foreign secretary, IB military deputy chief and those from the South Block and Air Force to coordinate the action. Yet another coordination committee was also formed with secretaries of the ministries of defence, home, finance and foreign affairs whose member secretary was RAW director Kao. Both these committees were under the close scrutiny of the prime minister.

All the people, regardless of their caste, class, section, profession or party, become united in India when it comes to safeguarding national interests. And it is not bad either. But, on the contrary, RAW does not allow its neighbors to become organized or united. Those who kick their national interests for petty interests and get caught in a bait offered by others are themselves anti-national.

Those who kill hens that lay gold eggs every day with the hope of getting all eggs at one go are simply fools. At present Nepal abounds in such fools. Even the bigger political parties have a majority of such fools. For instance, the Labor Act, which failed to get through and the Citizenship Act, which could not be amended, can be taken as a case in point. We can't say for sure that there were no such persons even among the constitution framers.

The subsequent outcome of this coordination committee was that the administrative decisions were freed of red-tapism which characterizes the Indian bureaucracy. On the other hand, Pakistan removed Tika Khan and appointed Mallick as the governor as a result of which RAW got an opportunity to consolidate itself. Analysts are of the opinion that the change of the governor basically lay at the dismemberment of East Pakistan. This may serve as an important example for administrators. The high-ranking officials or administrators of Nepal can learn significant and serious lessons from such events.

Stung by losing East Pakistan, Pakistan declared a war against India. The president, the prime minister, defence minister and finance minister of India at this time were out of the country. RAW without loss of any time gathered all these dignitaries. The army received an order of "Advance" and for 12 days at a stretch they fought on the western border of Punch and Chaso. The prime minister Gandhi declared that the war in Bangladesh has become a war on India.

RAW would provide trainings to 2,000 guerrillas in Bangladesh every six weeks. That the Maoists have also received such trainings has already been confirmed. Though the country's patriots are not fully assured that this has come to the notice of our feeble intelligence.

A plane of the Eastern Command which was instructed to bombard the quarters of the governor returned for not being able to identify the house. It succeeded only after RAW made available the detailed information including a map and other things about the quarters. 5.10 Even after the independence of Bangladesh, RAW did not leave the country. The disturbances and unrest there began to take a nasty turn. Consequently a one-party government was formed on Feb 04, 1974. Then the RAW got a wind that there was a possibility of a coup and therefore informed Mujib of it.

But he remained assured that such a coup would not take place since the persons including Zia-ur-Rahman were his disciples. However, a great massacre took place that lasted just three minutes. This was followed by yet another massacre. As a result, Bangladesh was pushed back, and continued to remain poor and deprived. The same thing repeated in Nepal also with the resulting backwardness, poverty and widespread deprivation. A revolution can be sustainable and the country can pick up momentum only if it is carried out by its own people.

All revolutions launched with the help of crutches of other countries are self-destructive and are bound to have the same fate of Bangladesh. Nepal should understand this well. All revolutions, rebellions, people's war or whatever have taken place during the six-decade long political history of Nepal, there is a hand of foreign conspiracy. They are far from rewarding or gratifying for the country.

The present state of governmentlessness can be logically construed as a result of such situation. 5.11 This applies everywhere that long, continuous efforts will pay off. Though this sentence sounds pleasing, the same sounds harsh in the case of RAW since its objectives are always driven with the objective of causing harm to or destroying others. As far as allowed by its powers, it wants Bangladesh, Sri Lanka, the Maldives and Nepal to suffer the fate of Sikkim, and if this is not possible, to make them Bhutan.

If this could not be done and if these countries continued to become sovereign, independent and prosperous, the dreams of becoming the great Chakravarti Bharatbarsha will be shattered. That is why, in order to fulfill its vested interests, RAW is indulged in many activities such as Chakma (Shanti Bahini), LTTE (Sri Lanka), Jammu-Kashmir and the Maoists (Nepal). All these outfits have been operating from the Indian soil. They have enjoyed not only food, shelter and clothing, they have also received trainings, guns and ammunition.

The Shanti Bahini guerrillas to be used against Bangladesh alone have received trainings from 25 different camps in Tripura of India. Yet another camp is in Dehradun and two are in Uttar Pradesh. It is estimated that the number of those fighting against Nepal is much greater. Furthermore, a place has also been prepared for the Chakma refugees.

In case the concerned country embarks on suppressing the guerrilla warfare created by itself, it (India) also appeals to the world community to discontinue foreign assistance, grants and loans to such country on charge of human rights violation. It had recommended discontinuation of foreign assistance by making a film about Chakma warfare.

After failing to make a dent into sovereignty of Bangladesh, the Chakmas have been incited to have a separate nation and capture the Chittagong port so that it could be used for north-east states of India.

RAW is always on the lookout for shortcomings or weaknesses, excuses and slogans. It has also incited the Nikhil Banga Civil Organization, Bangal Liberation Tiger, etc to carve "Bangabhoomi" out of Bangladesh as a separate state with one third of the total land.

As Bangladesh was surrounded by India on three sides and by water on one side, India, after the independence of Bangladesh, had taken a stand that there was no need for it to have a separate army. It had also served up a logic that India, being a friendly country, could pose no threat to Bangladesh. But clever Mujiber Rahman did not budge from his stance of building an army and also succeeded in it.

And this became the cause of his murder. For 18 times, he escaped the attempts on his life but he could not save himself from the 19th attempt. In fact, in this age of ours, army has become an indispensability to safeguard the state's independence, sovereignty and national integrity. Had Sikkim had a strong army, it would not have been so easy for India to annex it. Just because Sri Lanka had a powerful army, it was able to stand up to the Indian pressures.

But, to the contrary, even for quelling a petty rebellion, the Maldives, for not having an army, had to invite the Indian army overnight. Had Bangladesh agreed to not have an army, it would have been gradually reduced to the state of Bhutan and Sikkim. If that were the case, Nepal and Sri Lanka would be the only countries to bear the brunt of India. That's why, India, despite being the one of the poorest country if looked at from people's level, continues to make whopping investments on defence.

After RAW failed in its bid to merge Bangladesh into West Bengal, it has been trying to fish in troubled waters by raising the issues of Hindu, Muslim and Bengali language and culture, and that of nationality. By inciting the Chakma indigenes, it has created a domestic conflict. This has intensified to the extent of demanding a separate homeland as has bee done by the Tamils in Sri Lanka.

So RAW hopes that in case this issue picks up momentum as planned, Bengal may become one unified state. But RAW should also understand that if it gets into such a risky game, there may also emerge yet another independent, wholesome Bangladesh consisting of East and West Bengals. This analysis cannot be given a short shrift. Problem with Bangladesh Bangladesh also suffers from the problems of border encroachment.

Bangladesh, surrounded on three sides by India like Nepal, has many border problems with India. Under the pretext that many Bangladeshis have entered India rather than taking up the issue of smuggling, the border has been fenced with huge barbed wires.

Farrakka dam and disputes over downstream benefits, issue of Chakma rebellion, Bangabhoomi activities, the problem of Indian immigrants, smuggling, border clashes which often take place, abduction of Bangladeshi citizens and intervention in its sea are the major problems of Bangladesh.

Like in Nepal, educational materials in Bangladesh also are likely to encourage Indian dominance. Sub-standard Indian publications enter the country without any checks. So-called intellectuals and businessmen having a lust for money are importers of such items.

The provisions for tax-free customs and for making available books on credit for 6-8 months to the businessmen has crippled the ability of these countries to compete. For indigenous publications they are provided with 3-25% in commission, whereas the Indian publications provide them 40-80%.

This is why the businessmen naturally tend to give more priority to the books of Indian publications. Educational institutions in Nepal are rife with RAW agents. Since the governments of these countries impose tax on newsprint nine times more than on the books, indigenous publications automatically become more expensive and it is all because of the RAW. In fact, the reverse should be the case. Behind the fleeing of Bangladeshis who had shed their blood and tears for the independence of their country lies the plundering and loots by the Indian army who had entered Bangladesh with a view to 'liberating' it. Whatever they could lay their hands on were looted. Everything from the ceiling fan to spouts of taps were not left.

Hundreds of public trucks and the vehicles from businesses and industrial estates were loaded with the plunder. The scholars there argue that there cannot be such a large scale plundering without the support of upper echelons of India. India treated Bangladesh as a colony.

If India had given a fair deal to Bangladesh, nobody would have said anything against her. But India, through her notoriety has proved time and again that she is not our friend but an rubbish foe. 5.17.1.Bangladesh (Water Politics)Besides the Ganges and Brahmaputra, 11 other rivers also flow down Bangladesh whose total capacity is 82,000 cusec. Bangladesh has used these rivers.

But as they continued to be exploited by the people of India in the north of Bangladesh, it had a serious impact on all aspects including agriculture, industry and energy sectors of Bangladesh. The dam over the Muhara river can be taken as an example. Some 1,100 acres of land of Bangladesh required for the dam has been under the control of India, just as it did in the case of Tanakpur in Nepal. Similarly, India has also forcibly seized the 12 sq. mile of Silhat, Bangladesh for the dam constructed over the Kusihara river. 5.17.2. Farrakka Dam India is creating scenes by raking up the issue of the upper riparian country rights from the Farrakka dam, which is 17 kms from Bangladesh.

In fact that water flows down from Nepal. Just the opposite, with regard to Nepal, India is frantically crying for its lower riparian country rights and has even gone to the extent of inciting donors to prevent them from providing loans to projects for generating hydropower and for irrigation from the rivers with their source in Nepal itself. India's such attitude has caused Bangladesh an annual loss of some Rs 8 billion.

Similarly, Nepal also has got to cope with an annual loss of some Rs 30 billion through India's forcible intervention and dishonesty in such rivers as Rapti (Sikta), Karnali, Seti, Kankai, Arun, Mahakali, Koshi and Gandaki. 5.17.3. India has sought to construct a canal linking the Ganges and Brahmaputra from Jogipopa of Assam to Subarna Sinri of West Bengal. The link canal will be 324 km long, one km wide and 30 feet deep.

The proposed canal will be 30 km north of the Farrakka barrage. While constructing this canal, a 60-feet high dam should be built on the Bangladesh side. This will absorb all the waters of all the 11 rivers and of the Ganges and Brahmaputra. From this India will generate hundreds of thousands of megawatt electricity, use the water for irrigation and even the army will take advantage of it. On the other hand, 161,280 acres land of Bangladesh will be submerged and 700,000 people will be turned homeless. The entire country will be divided into two blocks. Unless Bangladesh agrees to abide by these conditions, it will continue to be as in the case of Farrakka.

RAW USES FORD FOUNDATION IN ANTI-BANGLADESH CAMPAIGN

Jaideep Saikia, an outward analyst, but virtually an Indian intelligence operative, hailing from Assam, abruptly tunes to India's anti-Bangladesh campaign that the demography of Assam is being rapidly changed due to the alleged infiltration of the Bangladeshi Muslims into Northeast India, particularly in Assam in his recent book, "Terror sans frontiers: Islamist militancy in Northeast India".

Educated, better to say trained, in school at the Rashtriya Indian Military College in Dehra Dun, Saikia recently researched on so-called Islamic Militancy in North East India under the aegis of a Ford Foundation fellowship, which was awarded for the year 2003. The research was conducted at the Program in 'Arms Control, Disarmament, and International Security'(ACDIS) at the University of Illinois at Urbana-Champaign. It is an astonishing and utter folly how 'For Foundation' could sponsor and allow Saikia to use his fellowship on such an issue, which is not only controversial, but also baseless and false and a part of India's anti-Bangladesh media campaign.

Saikia's effort cannot be termed as research work, as this type of stories is written almost daily in India. India's electronic and print media, including websites, are poured with such fabricated anti-Bangladesh items. It is assumed that Indian intelligence outfit RAW(Research & Analysis Wing) managed and possibly financed 'Ford Foundation' to award fellowship to Saikia, which he used not only to defame Bangladesh, but also to prepare a ground for India to invade Bangladesh.

Without deep and careful study it can easily be questioned, how Saikia, being a researcher could write, like his all other fellow-Indians, an essay having minimal statistics and historical facts, which he on the other hand, distorted in every possible ways. He tuning to his mentors in New Delhi chorused that Bangladeshis deliberately infiltrate into Assam to change the demography of the state either to form a new Muslim state out of Assam or merge the Muslim majority areas of the state with Bangladesh. To justify his claim, Saikia says, "The Muslims now constitute more than 70 per cent of the population of Dhubri district of Assam. But Saikia did not mention from which source he collected this religion-based demographic information, as the Indian census of 2001, did not enumerate its citizens on the basis of religion.

Secondly, he should know that at least five districts of Assam adjoining Sylhet had Muslim majority in 1947, when the subcontinent was partitioned. These districts were Goalpara, Hilakandi, Cacher, Dhubri and Karimganj subdivision of Sylhet. For this reason, the Muslims constitute about 30 per cent of the population of Assam. So whatever might be the percentage of the Muslims in any district of Assam it cannot be termed as a threat to Assam or India.

Thirdly, Assam or any other state is not richer than Bangladesh, rather many states of India, not to speak of Assam lag far behind Bangladesh to a great extent. So why should the Bangladeshis leave for a poorer region to lead a poorest life.It is to be mentioned that Assam Gano Parishad, (AGP) is the prophet of anti-immigration crusade in Assam. But during its 2-term rules, AGP government under Prafulla Kumar Mahanto could identify few Muslims as illegal infiltrators in Assam. Even the current Congress Chief Minister Tarun Gagoi and Former Chief Minister late Hiteshar Saikia officially acknowledged that there is no illegal infiltration of the Muslims in Assam.

Meanwhile, the Ahoms, including the mainstream secessionist outfit ULFA (United Liberation Front of Assam), comprehended the design of RAW to divide the people of Assam into several antagonistic groups and crush them using one against the other mainly to frustrate the freedom struggle of Assam.

Realising the duplicity of Indian government, ULFA in July 1992 publicly declared the Bengali speaking migrants, which also include the Muslims, as friends. In a publication addressed to the 'East Bengal migrants' ULFA stated: "East Bengal migrants are considered Assamese. Without these exploited lot, ULFA cannot be successful. These are people who are educationally, economically backward. They cannot be our enemies.

These hardworking people are ULFA's protection shield. Their contribution to the national income is immense. They can produce essential things from a small piece of land, sell without any profit, work hard for the betterment of Assam, sacrificing them for the future of the state. They are our real well wishers, our friends, better than the Indians. ('The Revolution Comes Full Circle: Bibhu Prasad Routray.) In the same publication, ULFA went on to define the term 'Bidekhi'(foreigner). "Those who do not regard this state as their own, accept it as their motherland, are not ready to sacrifice their lives for the sake of this country, are aliens, 'Bidekhis for us." Saikia should have read this statement of ULFA. He should also know that the Bengali Muslims accepted Assamese as their mother tongue and identify them as Ahoms not as Bengalis. The new generations of the Muslim Ahoms even do not know Bengali. They are not antagonistic to the interest of Assam. All these factors prompted ULFA not to brand the Muslims as foreigners.

Being failed to brand the Muslims as infiltrators or outsiders, very recently India floated another allegations that Bangladesh designs to secede the Muslim majority districts of Assam either to merge with her territory or create an independent Muslim state in Assam. Virtually, the campaign is made to create anti-Muslim sentiment among the Ahoms so that the unity among communities becomes far a cry.

Saikia and other Indians not only floated the allegation of infiltration of the Bangladeshi Muslims to Assam, but also allege that Bangladesh in one of the mentors of the decades old secessionist militancy in Northeast. According to the allegation, which Saikia also did not forget to forefront in his book, Bangladesh provides shelter, training and even arms to different militant groups of the region, particularly ULFA, ATTF (All Tripura Tiger Forces), etc.

But being an Ahom and above all a researcher, Saikia should know that secessionist insurgency in Northeast when India got its independence from Britain in 1947, well before the birth of Bangladesh. People of this region do not feel them as Indians. They are fighting to end what they call, "Indian occupation." Previously India blamed China, Burma (Now Myanmar), Pakistan and even America. But they shortened their list over the years and ascribe the allegation on Bangladesh and Pakistan. Some of the Indians now consider Bangladesh more dangerous for northeast than Pakistan. This allegation against Bangladesh was brought to the forefront, because it will be easier to squeeze weaker Bangladesh than any other country that India blames

But India could never prove any of her allegations against Bangladesh. India officially challenged that there are 195 camps or training centres of the Northeast insurgents in Bangladesh and supplied a list mentioning their whereabouts. According to the list, training centres and camps are situated in hospitals, police stations, residential colonies, government offices, playgrounds, etc. Bangladesh repeatedly requested India to come and show on-spot the existence of these camps and centres. But India never accepted the offer, as Indian policymakers know that there is not even single such centre or camp of the northeast militants, not to speak of 195.

Still the propagandists in New Delhi deliberately continue their fabricated allegations against Bangladesh, whose brief ulterior reasons I have mentioned earlier. I really feel pity for Saikia as well as Ford Foundation for being used as the tools of RAW. How Ford Foundation could accept such a baseless research work which goes against a country, which is a main target of Indian expansionist design. I would request Ford Foundation to send a 'fact finding mission' to Assam and Bangladesh as well to inspect the ground realities. Such mission will surely find that all the allegations that Saikia mentioned against Bangladesh in his so-called research work are the products of exaggeration and misinformation. Ford Foundation, to uphold its neutrality and worldwide reputation and acceptability, should consider my suggestion and act accordingly.

August 17 Blasts: Is there external linkage?

The controversy over Tarique Zia's seemingly misquoted comment in the BBC interview that al-Qaeda 'may' have been involved in the August 17 serial blasts notwithstanding, despondency is bound to set in as the investigators have not yet unearthed any significant leads to the attacks' masterminds (and their political goals) despite over 300 arrestees' testimony having been recorded and a slew of clues found. Such uncertainty does give rise to an obvious concern: Is there an external link to the blasts and, if so, who could have pulled the strings from behind the nation's borders, and why?

A study of the post-blast behaviour of the Indian media and the intelligence apparatuses can go a long way toward understanding why terrorist incidents in Bangladesh seem to matter so much to our neighbour. Since the attacks, the Indian media has launched a virtual crusade against Bangladesh, spearheaded by the Telegraph that wrote, 'Delhi should urge major donors to impose economic sanctions on Bangladesh.' The paper also reported that Indian security agencies had advised the central government to 'force Khaleda Zia to clamp down on Islamic fundamentalist outfits'. The government of Bangladesh did respond earnestly to such pressures and diatribes and conducted a virtual witch-hunt in the preceding weeks against Islamists of suspicious hues, although the end result of the ongoing manhunt seems destined to be as much a failure as the previous ones.

Meanwhile, a just concluded study of Bangladesh's post-blast security situation by major Indian intelligence outfits pointed the finger of suspicion for the August 17 blasts at familiar groups like the Jagrata Muslim Janata and the Jamaatul Mujahideen, which are, says the study, 'banned, and are known to have fanned anti-Indian sentiments'. Coincidentally, the police in Dhaka say the same thing but cannot trace the attacks' elusive masterminds.

The masterminds of a series of such attacks over the years not having been traced, one cannot resist the temptation of being suspicious about the latest attacks' genesis and the ultimate motivation of the masterminds.

The Indian intelligence bodies' study, however, has made some interesting observations. 'There were 370 explosions in 63 of Bangladesh's 64 districts. The kind of explosives used and the impact of each blast were similar to that on August 13 at a Muslim shrine in Akhaura in which one person was killed and 30 others were injured…There are insinuations that an earlier blast in August 2004 was suspected to have been inspired by India's Research and Analysis Wing (RAW). It is possible that efforts will be on to malign India again by pointing fingers at Delhi,' the study opined.

In conclusion, the study noted that 'the outfits were emboldened because of the lack of tangible action by the Khaleda government… The blasts are intended to be a message to Dhaka and to discourage the government from succumbing to international pressure to clamp down on the outfits.'

Reportedly a separate detailed study, circulated among the top echelons of the Indian security establishment, says, 'Delhi should actively consider economic measures against Bangladesh.'

The tirades of the Indian media and comments of the intelligence agencies aside, everyone knows that the Jamaatul Mujahideen had left leaflets on the sites of bombing and many of the arrestees have reportedly confessed to having carried out the attacks at its behest. Yet BNP Deputy Minister Ruhul Quddus Talukder (also an MP) had a different view of the events. He had said earlier, 'I don't think they (the JM) have such a strong network. Awami League must have done this, using fake leaflets, to blacken Bangladesh's image internationally.' Does the Minister know something that others don't?

A somewhat similar claim came from Mufti Fazlul Haq Amini, chairman of the Amini faction of the Islami Oikya Jote and a constituent member of the ruling four-party alliance. He said on August 19, 'Swearing upon Allah, I say the 14-party alliance of Awami League and left parties launched the bomb attacks in a planned way to uproot the Islamic forces, but Islamic forces can never be eliminated.'

To confound confusion further, both India and Israel were whisked into the scene by the Jamaat-e-Islami's Amir and Industries Minister Matiur Rahman Nizami. He blamed India's external intelligence agency, Research and Analysis Wing (RAW), and Israel's Mossad for 'playing an important role' in the August 17 attacks. He added, 'They are the patrons of the serial blasts as they don't want good relations between Bangladesh and China. That's why the incident occurred when Prime Minister Khaleda Zia was on a visit to Beijing.'

Juxtapose the above with the embedded Indian concerns over Bangladesh's political developments over the years. The copy of a 2004 RAW report obtained by this author reads, 'Pakistani intelligence officers in Dhaka are becoming increasingly active in espionage against India. In 2002, three modules (sic) being run by them from Dhaka, and using some Bangladeshi operatives, were busted. A large number of secret documents and photographs of sensitive defence locations were recovered from one Ziauddin Ahmed Biswas (resident of Murshidabad in West Bengal), arrested on November 17, 2002. Later, the arrest (December 2002 in Lucknow, UP) of Bangladeshi national, Mohammad Mamunur Rasheed, led to the recovery of fake travel documents and also incriminating documents indicating a plan to recruit Indian Muslim youths for training in Bangladesh and Pakistan for subversive activities within India.'

Another RAW report of 2004 implicates the Dhaka regime more directly. It says, 'It is hardly any secret that the Inter-Services Intelligence (ISI) of Pakistan has close links with Bangladesh's Directorate-General of Forces Intelligence (DGFI) and operates openly and freely in that country. It (ISI) not only helps coordinate the activities of al-Qaeda and fundamentalist Islamic militant groups through the DGFI, but backs a Bangladeshi Taliban group named HUJI that runs six training camps for ULFA terrorists in the Chittagong Hill Tracts.' A West Bengal intelligence outfit goes a step further: 'While ULFA training camps have been organised by the sector headquarters of the Bangladesh Rifles (BDR), training camps of the CNLF have been organised partly by 103 and 105 infantry brigades of the Bangladesh Army at Khagrachhari and

Rangamati,' the report claims. From hindsight, the pattern of such accusations seems a corollary to many such reports circulated in the past. For instance, prominent security experts of India have been crying wolf since the late 1990s (long before the incidents of 9/11 that acted as a harbinger to the global hunts for Islamist terrorists) that activities in Bangladesh posed a serious danger to India's security and national interests.

Particularly, Assam Governor Lt Gen (retd) SK Sinha wrote in his report to the central government in March 1998, 'The long cherished design of Greater Bangladesh, making inroads into the strategic land link of Assam with the rest of India, can lead to severing the entire land mass of the North East from the rest of the country.' In another report submitted to the President of India in November 1998, Sinha wrote, 'Continued silent demographic invasion of the North East poses a great threat both to the identity of the Assamese people and to our national security.' Influenced by such reports, India decided to fence the entire Indo-Bangladesh border at a cost of over $500 million and nearly 70% of border fencing was completed by mid-2005. The Indian Border Security Force also killed more than 500 innocent Bangladeshis over the years since General Sinha filed his first report.

India now claims that since 1990, Assam has seen the birth of 9 Muslim militant outfits owing allegiance to Harkat ul Mujahideen and Lashkar-e-Toiba, the groups that run ferocious operations against Indian forces in Indian-occupied Kashmir. Indian intelligence outfits believe the groups have their rear bases inside Bangladesh. Is India looking for a pretext to launch pre-emptive military assaults on Bangladesh at some point in the future, based on such reports? Policy-makers in Dhaka must mull over this prospect seriously.

Coming to the August 17 blasts in particular, one wonders why the Islamists, whose 'profound' aim is to create a 'Greater Bangladesh' by creating demographic imbalance in the neighbouring Indian states of Assam and Tripura in particular (according to Indian reports), should resort to blasting of 'innocuous' bombs inside Bangladesh and leave behind signatures for identification? How is the mission of creating a greater

Bangladesh served by such blasts? Isn't it more plausible that, in the absence of any verifiable and authentic conclusion, the blasts have occurred to prove to the world that Bangladesh is infested with Islamist Jihadis determined to take on India by using Bangladesh as a launching pad? At the least, such a hypothesis does mesh well with the embedded Indian perceptions of Bangladesh, as has been learnt from the intelligence reports quoted above.

It is under such contexts that one must compare the Indian mindset with the comments made by some Bangladeshi politicians after the August 17 blasts (quoted above), and try to guess the 'untold' reasons behind the authorities' inability to reach any conclusion with respect to the attacks' masterminds.

THE FALL OF DHAKA: LESSONS FOR PAKISTAN

"We formed a Sangram Parishad led by Bangabandhu to free East Pakistan through armed protest," said Shawkat Ali, the Speaker of Bangladesh parliament in a court hearing.

Shawkat Ali is one of the accused that was implicated in Agartala Conspiracy Case, a sedition case brought forward by the Government of Pakistan in early 1968 against Sheikh Mujibur Rahman, the leader of the Awami League and 34 other persons.

As a reporter of the events that happened, I believe in the proclamation of truth. In 2011, I had a chance encounter with a renowned former student leader of Dhakka University and it bloomed into a friendship based on mutual respect. Naive to the socio-political realities of what purported to the great tragedy of 1971, I learnt alot from that person. I can still remember his words, "If Mujib would have wanted, Pakistan would never have been broken." Since the past 40 years, Pakistan has been solely held responsible for the secession of East Pakistan. Notwithstanding that to some extent certain political bigwigs of Pakistan succumbed to dispel doubts inculcated in Bengalis minds, the focus of this essay would revolve around India's illegitimate role in the creation of Bangladesh in 1971.

Experts suggest that the first instances of State Sponsored terrorism reported in Asia, to destabilize other nations harmony originated from India. The intimate involvement of RAW (Research and Analysis Wing) in dirty deeds includes drugs trafficking, human trafficking, arms trafficking, coup d'état in foreign nations, subversive activities, assassinations, nuclear proliferation, and downright recruiting, FUNDINGand training of terrorists in different countries. The documented evidence of India's illegal measures were presented by Rabinder Nath, a double agent of CIA when he ultimately defected from RAW. This continued fetishism of India with terrorism, hidden beneath the banner of political talks has fostered dangerous notions in the terrorist elements of Asian region. Candid revelations of the intelligence community worldwide acknowledge that proxies like Baloch Liberation Army, Sindhu Desh Liberation Army, Tehreek e Taliban et cetera are funded and trained by Indian army. A killer Ajmal Pahari belonging to the terrorist wing of a political party MQM, caught by the police confessed about being trained by Delhi. Not only of her arch rival Pakistan, integrity of countries like Burma, Sri Lanka and Nepal have also been violated systematically by India to no avail.

But they got successful once.

The day when Bangladesh came into existence.

How Bangladesh came about?

The answer to this lies in the adoption of Chanakya Doctrine by India. Considered as a Hindu Machiavelli, Kautilya alias Chanakya, a Chandragupta's minister who developed a strategy of destabilizing and weakening neighbouring states around 320 B.C. The continued successes of Chandragupta and Asoka, is considered as a result of this doctrine. After the humiliating Indian defeat in 1965 Pakistan-India war, this theory was put to test by Indian forces and the factories to create traitors were set in Bangladesh.

India has a long history of activities in Bangladesh since 1960s, and it reached its zenith at the time of Bangladesh creation. It most significant development was the creation of Mukti Bahini, a secessionist force made up of nationalists to counter the writ of Pakistan through armed struggle. Intelligence documents revealed that India had engaged these people from as back as 1967. The Six Points of Mujib that demanded certain autonomy for Eastern

Pakistan came afterwards. Pragmatism demands us to raise our eyebrows on thoughts like "Why was India involved in Bangladesh at the time when there was relative calm in the society?" "Were they planning to aggravate the situation further?"

In the meanwhile, the Eastern Command of Inter Services Intelligence uncovered a plot. It was discovered that a navy steward Mujibur Rahman and the educationist Mohammad Ali Reza went to Agartala, a city in India to seek Indian support for an independent Bangladesh. On January 18, Sheikh Mujib was named as one of the accused. He and others were arrested on 9 May1968. The trial began on 19 June 1968 in Dhaka Cantonment under a special tribunal. The charge sheets of 100 paragraphs were presented before the tribunal, with 227 witnesses and 7 approvers. The accused maintained the stance of false implication. Being labelled as a traitor and separatist by Pakistan, Mujib's followers instigated the masses and a massive upsurge of people thronged the streets. They organized mass movement and demanded immediate withdrawal of the case and release of all prisoners. The final date for the case decision was 6 February 1969, but it was deferred and Mujib ur Rehman was eventually released; to be commemorated by the Bengalis as hero.

The ranks of Mukti Bahini in the meanwhile multiplied. The already disenchanted leftists wary of Islamic Republic of Palistan, were made to join on the promises of a separate ethno centric land based on secular values. The creation and training of this proxy force was code-named Operation Jackpot. Training was provided to them in the Jungle Warfare and Counter Insurgency school at Vairengte, India. Later Field Marshal Sam Manekshaw revealed in his book "Soldiering with Dignity" that 80000 Hindus were also inducted in the ranks of Mukti Bahini.

This war was brought upon the Bengalis by India. Creation of Mukti Bahini and Agartala Conspiracy are a stark reminder of how Indian militiary and civilian leadership functions.

On 26 March 1971, the State of Pakistan launched Operation Searchlight in Eastern Pakistan against Mukti Bahini. This is widely considered that Bengalis were murdered by Pakistani forces, irrespective of the fact that the Bengalis killed were miscreants of

Mukti Bahini. When the miscreants of Mukti Bahini were pillaging the houses, raping the women and killing men of Behari nationality; nothing more could have been expected from the army that is taught to value civilian lives. Later on to cover the rapes committed by Mukti Bahini, the government of Bangladesh accused Pakistan army. Later it was proved wrong when Sarmila Bose, a senior researcher in her book "Dead Reckoning" stated,

"During my field research on several incidents in East Pakistan during 1971, Bangladeshi participants and eyewitnesses described battles, raids, massacres and executions, but told me that women were not harmed by the army in these events except by chance such as in crossfire. The pattern that emerged from these incidents was that the Pakistan army targeted adult males while sparing women and children." As finally signs of progress started emerging and the chances of Mukti Bahini defeat got brighter, India violated the sovereign integrity of Eastern Pakistan by declaring support for the miscreants, and engaged in direct warfare with Pakistan army from both the East-West front. The proposal of ceasefire was also forwarded in the United Nations by Pakistan to which India didn't respond. Clearly this operation was purely designed to disintegrate Pakistan, as India's no response, as well as USSR veto tells a different story.

RAW IS TURNING BANGLADESH INTO A BATTLE FIELD FOR INDIAN INTEREST

Bangladesh is thrown under a massive battle; internal and externally where as it needs internal unity, peace and strength for survival and advancement for its citizens. Let us summarize the political situation of Bangladesh.

1) Some weak and known political figures are facing with embarrassing situation and always fighting with each other. But the main shows are being controlled by a most corrupt, greedy, liar, cruel syndicate of Political-Administrative-Business-Army- Currency launderers-Smugglers-Police-Educationists-Youths-Intelligence and Judicial groups.
2) They are assigned to turn Bangladesh vulnerable as soon as possible, before the war appears in borders between

India vs. China-Pakistan for a muscle show before it can be counted as a regional super power. American and European war industries need to egg these powers to war in order to keep Asia weak in economy.

3) Bangladesh Armed forces, Intelligence directorates, police and RAB will be re-set up gradually and bringing under Indian command and control.
4) The ownerships of the export oriented Industries are gradually being transferred to Indians and the continued strikes and the setting of fires in the rest of the industries are acts of sabotage by RAW operatives.
5) All exports channels are to be jammed (the recent problems at Chittagong port is an example).
6) The Hospitals and Universities are being set up to bring poisonous drug addiction in a commando form of distribution network.
7) Avoiding democratic norms and practice and terrorizing the non pro-Indian society, the administration and law and order officials.
8) Leaders of BNP and Jamaat parties are being pushed to numbness.
9) The general public are becoming frustrated by Indian dominance and are already venting reactions.

Let us touch some points of the regional muscle power competitions, such as;

1) Indian Military Chief General V K Singh on 15th October, 2010 declaring the possibility of a conventional war against China and Pakistan and also the possibility of using Nuclear weapons.
2) Indian Ambassador in Washington DC, Meera Shankar expressed concerns about the Chinese heavy military enforcement in Indian Eastern and Western borders and the building of powerful Rail stations and Rail communications closest to India-Pak and India-China borders.
3) Pakistan has exposed their strong alignment with China in all respects; Military, financial, communication and gas

pipe line. The newly built Pakistani Gwadar sea port is being transferred to the Chinese authorities which makes easier for its naval moves in the Indian Ocean and the multi-diversified routes to central Asia also.

4) CNN circulated news of Bin Laden's stay in Pakistan. Ex-President of Afghanistan Borhanuddin Rabbani becomes the President of the Afghan Peace Council for a Taleban-Afghan government formal negotiations in order to quiet down the war and establish peace in Afghanistan.
5) Pakistan stands with major roles and Iran also supports the NATO in peace making.
6) Defense Secretary Robert Gates has announced his support to the peace process in Afghanistan from the NATO Headquarters in Brussels (Alzazeera, Reuters).
7) India has been demolishing the natural design of power routes of Bangladesh (Muslim majority country and enemy) for turning it permanently disabled.

Afghanistan is located in a strategically connecting route to Central and South Asia and close to Russia and Iran. Bangladesh is the strategically connecting route to South and East Asia and close to China and India. RAW is frustrated in Afghanistan and is now stationing in Bangladesh as a regional center.

"India-Pakistan recent debate on war issue: China irritating and worrisome to India" was the news headline of Tibetan Review.net on October 17th, 2010. The Indian Army Chief, General V K Singh, on October 15th, called the terror infrastructure across his country's western border and China's rising military prowess as irritating and worrisome, reported the Times of India online on October 15.

Addressing a seminar on "Indian Army: Emerging Roles and Tasks in New Delhi", Singh has said, regarding China, we have a rising China, both economically and militarily. Although we have CBMs in place, although we have a very stable border, yet we have border disputes. He has said, a conventional war with China or Pakistan was highly uncertain but explained that skirmishes can occur. "Pak, China irritants for India: Army Chief

" was another headline of the Deccan Chronicle. The entire news is detailed for the viewers.

New Delhi, Oct. 15: In a candid declaration on Friday, the Army chief, Gen. V.K. Singh, described Pakistan and China as two irritants for Indian national security.

On China, the Army chief cautioned that India has a border disputes with a rising China and said Chinese intentions need to be examined.

On Pakistan, he said there was certain amount of support for terror groups in that country and that India had something to worry about as long as the time terror camps in that country were intact.

The Army chief also said that while conventional war was not certain, skirmishes were possible and that India should have substantial conventional war-fighting capabilities along with the ability to fight in a nuclear scenario. He said, We have a rising China with economic and military capabilities. Although we have Confidence Building Measures (CBMs) in place and a stable border, we have a border dispute (with China). The intentions (of China) need to be looked at.

The Indian Army already has a doctrine in place to fight a two-fronts war in case of the eventuality of any joint aggression by India's neighbors. But interestingly, the IAF chief, Air Chief Marshal P.V. Naik, warned later in the day that a country (adversary)-specific policy could lead India into an arms race and that therefore, the armed forces need to have a capability-specific policy rather than country-specific policy ".

The two statements are being interpreted in some quarters as a possible difference in perception on the issue by the two service chiefs. Pakistanis reaction was published in the Indian Express on October 16th, 2010. Pakistan on Saturday reacted angrily to the Indian Army chief's remarks describing the country as a major irritant for India's security and about the possibility of a war in a nuclear scenario, saying they were 'jingoistic' and 'unwise'.

Rejecting the allegations made by Indian Army chief Gen V K Singh, Foreign Office spokesman Abdul Basit said in a statement:

"The government of Pakistan takes a serious exception to the reported statement of the Indian Army chief about his threat perception from Pakistan, war under a nuclear scenario and uncalled for and gratuitous comments on the internal affairs of Pakistan."

The repetitive mentions by Indian Army's high command "about war under the nuclear scenario is not only irresponsible but also jingoistic and unwise," Basit said. "Such statements and grandstanding by India are evidently unhelpful to the cause of promoting peace, security and stability in South Asia," he added.

The statement and counter statement gradually fueling the angers of two enemy countries -India and Pakistan and the Bangladeshis have been witnessing the symbol of such preparation from couple of years since the affairs of Indian Horses and a full General in Bangladesh which appeared more clearly with the Pheelkhana attack in Dhaka in February 25-26, 2010 under the democratic champion regime of Sheikh Hasina.

In which direction Bangladesh Government moves? Hasina Government and India have been exercising all efforts in executing the points of treaty with Indo-BD Govt. in 1971 in different style. Though that Colonial Roadmap was not followed during the regimes of Sheikh Mujibur Rahman and Ziaur Rahman when they were leading Bangladesh. However, both were assassinated under covert sabotage of the foreign powers.

As Hasina and Khaleda are Indian loyalist politicians and the former one is a 100% useful when the latter is found to be worthless, India has chosen the right ally for them in the right time and extends 12 hands to create vulnerabilities in Bangladesh categorically as per their routine. RAW has already set up their operatives in all spheres of the society and the state administration.

Bangladesh is the icon to the bordering neighbours On the other hands, It is widely known to the leaders of the world that Bangladesh has become the icon to the people of her neighbouring Indian provinces who have been living in the poorest region and vulnerable states of India and Nepal, Bhutan and Arakan state of Burma. The Private sectors are booming fastest and the neighbours are rushing in to get jobs and higher social lives in Bangladesh.

Indian policy makers have been witnessing the rapid growing economy in Bangladesh with anger as their people of the Northern states are gradually depending on Bangladesh. All most 50% of the Indian region is influenced by the socialists and communists. This vast area been discriminated by the Indian mainstream politics since the National Congress government took over the governance of India in 1947.

That area holds common historical and cultural commonness with present day Bangladesh and there are differences with the Delhi line of administration. In due course this vast region, which has been heading up and engaged in guerrilla warfare for Independence, is becoming the important consumers of most Bangladeshi products where as the Indian government has been trying to keep Bangladesh as a hub of internal smuggling zone and a buffer state.

War-torn Bangladesh is the demand of the RAW. RAW represents the military, political and economic interests of the Indian Aryan capitalists. So, they are now engaged in a radical operation to distabilise Bangladesh through 'friend and enemy' Channakyo tactics.

It is not fighting terrorism but rather engaging Bangladesh in war:

Mr. R K Meghan alias Sanayima, the Chairman of United National Liberation Front (UNLF) Meitei rebel group was been arrested from Lalmatia in Mohammadpur, Dhaka city on September 29th, 2010. He was taken in a swoop by a joint operation of the Bangladesh and Indian Intelligences. The news was published in Indian Express.com website.

This UNLF was established in November 24th,1964 and has been fighting for liberating Manipur and building a socialist society. It is the oldest Meitei group and might have the link with National Socialist Council of Nagaland (NSCN), KUKI Nnational Army, United Liberation Front of Assam (ULFA) and other guerrilla groups.

Raj Kumar Meghen is the current Chairman of the UNLF. Bangladesh Government has never dealth in any business with them but this rebel leader might have taken shelter with a disguised name in Bangladesh as thousands of Indians enter and stay here without valid passport for the safeyt and sound life of their families. But there are lot of doubts to use Meghen to propagate against Bangladesh which RAW used to do for targeting the country in keeping pressure. Though it will be useless effort.

My views: My personal opinion is that a guerrilla leader who cannot support himself from saving from enemies, he is not capable to support his poor and backward nation for their liberation. He should accept the death in smile. I am guerrilla fighter and we liberated Bangladesh. RAW supported us as it was in Indian interests to break and cut off Pakistan, a Muslim enemy country.

Now, Mr. K Meghan is dishonoured and might be killed because the Indian government never honours the humanity and spirit of liberation.

On what legal basis are these joint operations being carried out in Bangladesh?

There must be some legal agreement allowing RAW to operate in tandem with the DGFI or NSI on Bangladesh soil.

When was this agreement signed and by whom?

More importantly is there a reciprocal agreement allowing DGFI and NSI to operate alongside RAW in India? If not then why have we allowed this liberty to Indian foreign intelligence for them to operate in Bangladesh?

MBI MUNSHI a young Barrister and a researcher from Dhaka wanted to know the answers of these questions and invited some one to share their thoughts on it.

I feel honoured in sharing with my friend. Once I was a special guest in the National Press Club, Dhaka during my visit to Bangladesh. Possibly from the present Government side everybody will keep shut their mouths as this is the culture of the slaves vis a vis their lords, and on the other hands the cabinet has no liberty to comment on this issue. The top gambling issues are limited to the top circle affairs. So blaming of the DGFI and NSI for such covert action is not acceptable in any way as they are carrying out the orders of the supreme authorities.

Remember Please, untold small and important clue for the Analysts of the Indo-BD relations. General Ataul Gani Osmani, the Chief of Mukti Bahini and the Chief of Bangladesh Armed forces was allowed to enter in Dhaka but not to enter Dhaka Cantonment until and unless the Indian Army vacated Bangladesh. The Chief of Army Staff had to open up the Army Headquarter in a small room in an old building on Minto Road, Dhaka. The original handwritten lists of the Indian trained Mukti Bahini was taken away forcefully from that office by Sheikh Kamal and were burnt as RAW decided of creating the situation to let Bangladeshis know it was the Indian war against Pakistan and India won the battle. All the office staffs witnessed the anarchic demonstration and the matter was reported to Sheikh Mujibur Rahman.

Major Mohammed Abdul Jalil, the brave sector commander of the 9th Sector during the liberation war of Bangladesh, was arrested by Indian Army with the consent of BD Government when Major Jalil opposed them in passing our million dollars valued weapons and ammunitions to India from Bangladesh. The Indian Army carried everything even the window cover, pillow cover, bad sheet, chair, table, electric wire, light bulbs, kitchen staffs, bathroom fittings etc, what ever they found nearby and did not allow any Bangladeshi Army officer to enter in the cantonment zone.

Bangladesh Government did keep silent and did not stand with Major Jalil in saving the national properties. Every one of the top layer of the politics was engaged in saving their own skin as if their only job was to prove their utmost loyalty to the Indian Army.

These all are the consequences of a covert treaty between India and Bangladesh government signed by Indian and the Bangladesh government in exile in October 1971. This treaty was initiated by Indian foreign Intelligence- RAW. Honourable Premier Tajuddin Ahmed was active to collect the signatures from all the ministers of the exile BD Government. The honourable acting President Syed Nazrul Islam became sick and nervous after going through the documents of the treaty which he signed earlier at the Prime Minister's request and without reading it. The fact was disclosed by the then Chief of Bangladesh Mission in Delhi Mr. Humayun Rashid Chaudhury (later Foreign Minister during General Ershad's rule) in his interview (Masudul Haq; RAW and CIA in the liberation war of Bangladesh).

We know it has happened because of the lack of statesmanship and the lack of military thinking at the level of the then politicians who had no experience even to run a provincial government of East Pakistan. Mr. Tajuddin Ahmed was a pro-socialist believer and Pro Indo-Soviet liner. He did not consult with the Mukti Bahini sector commanders.

USA Ambassador Boster saved Mujib and Bangladesh

It was fact that Sheikh Mujib managed Finance Minister Mr. Tajuddin to resign from the Government position in the same day, the document was taken to Prime Minister in his breakfast table by Khondkar Mostaque Ahmed.

The then HE American Ambassador Davis Eugene Boster in Dhaka promised and extended his full support in having the clear consent of the President of United States of America in saving the life of Prime Minister Sheikh Mujibur Rahman on that day when he was invited and requested for the American support in case of any Indian attack on him (Shekh Mujib) and Bangladesh.

White House did the accurate act when it was needed. (This fact was collected and reconfirmed by responsible Intelligence Sources).

The Indo-BD treaty was signed in October 1971 in Delhi. The main 7 points of the treaty are as follows;-

1) After the establishment of Bangladesh, the administrative officers who actively participated in the war of liberation would remain in their posts. The rest would be terminated and vacant posts would be filled up by the Indian administrative officers.
2) After the liberation of Bangladesh the required number of soldiers would remain in Bangladesh (No time limit was laid down).
3) Bangladesh would not form and maintain any formal regular Armed Forces.

4) To maintain internal security and law and order a militia would be formed comprising of the freedom fighters.
5) The Chief of Staff of the Indian Armed Forces would lead the probable war with Pakistan. The Mukti Bahini (Freedom Fighters) would work under the command of Indian Armed forces.
6) Trade Transactions between the two countries would be free and open. The volume of trade would be calculated once in a year and the price would be paid in pound sterlings.
7) The Foreign Ministry of Bangladesh would maintain a close liaison with the External Affairs Ministry of India and the latter would assist the former as per as possible.

This information of the treaty also was mentioned in the book of Dr. Kali Das Baddyo who was dedicated in keeping liaisons for Bangladesh liberation, having the trusted connections with Awami League leaders and RAW and became an Indian citizen after his assigned mission was successful. His next mission has the name of Bangobhumi: separating Hindu inhabited regions of Bangladesh.

The leaders are lying everyday and shamelessly appearing to the public with their terrorizing attitude against their competitors. These snake-charmers never care about those snakes that are already staying around and inside both the political power circles and waiting for the appropriate time to bite and kill.

Projects and failures:

a) Bangladesh is already isolated from the Muslim world, especially Saudi Arabia and Malaysia, with collapsing of remittances from these two major manpower markets. Money launderers are supported by the government. Crime world is awarded an upper hand. Smuggling routes are kept unguarded. Major Garment factories are being transferred to Indian owners. Manpower exporting channels are being mishandled. Indian Hindu and non-Muslims are found being exported to Muslim countries with fake Muslim names for sabotage against Bangladesh. Internally terrorizing the Muslim citizens and encouraging non-Muslims and Indians (with fake identity) in important

Govt. positions of the country and allowing Indian RAW operations in freehand across the country to take control.

b) The State Bank of India is going to replace Bangladesh Bank to collect the remittances from abroad following the case of Bhutan. The Bhutanese are collecting local currencies from local banks against those remittances. The Bhutanese have to remit in the State Bank of India. Finance Minister M A Muhit already exposed the Sonali Exchange abroad as a loosing concern in a reception meeting organized by Dhaka University Alumni Association, USA in Jackson Heights, and NewYork on October 11,2010 which is a motivated campaign on the basis of the govt. policy. Sonali Exchange might close if the RAW guidance functions accurately.

Conclusion

RAW is already stationed Dhaka. It must be closed soon. But that will need the changed situation which will be enough to compel them to return back. May be their insecurities or other alternative. CIA might play a negotiating role in it. The Intelligence agencies of Bangladesh should be utilized to collect the information to secure the country's interests; the industries, trades, educational systems, health and communications and sea lanes and to protect the country from smuggling of poisonous drugs, arms etc and saving from the regular attacks from the Indian and Myanmar sides in the border areas.

Intelligence agency is needed to save exports and manpower markets and to secure the routes of remittances and other interests in abroad. We do not permit anybody to rent our Intelligence directorates to India for their internal vulnerabilities. The patriot intellectuals, bureaucrats and diplomats are welcome to turn about and take lead to change the political decisions and bring back the steering of the country towards the safest journey.

8

R&AW in Balochistan

Balochistan Chief Minister Jam Mohammad Yusuf on Monday said that involvement of external elements, including the Indian intelligence agency Research and Analysis Wing (RAW), in the current acts of terrorism in Balochistan could not be ruled out.

Speaking at the Meet the Press programme of Karachi Press Club, he defended the construction of Gwadar port and military cantonments, and blamed 'anti-Pakistan forces' for fomenting trouble in the strategically located Balochistan.

"Though dialogue for normalization is continuing, as long as Kashmir is not settled they will continue to create difficulties for Pakistan," said Jam Yusuf in an apparent reference to the Indian RAW.

In support of his contention with regard to foreign involvement, Jam Yusuf referred to various training camps in which, according to him, terrorists were being harboured and paid huge sums to create trouble.

He said that none of the Baloch wadera had the capacity to finance such an operation. He said that some of those involved in terrorist activities had fled to the Gulf. "Conspiracies are hatched against Balochistan by anti-Pakistan forces who do not want Gwadar port to become economic hub in the region," he said.

The Balochistan chief minister said that RAW was running terrorist camps in Iran and Afghanistan. "It has now set up 30 to 40 such camps in Balochistan, each with training facility for 30 people who are paid Rs10,000 monthly.

"The monthly expenses of each such camp are over Rs0.4 million. The money is being supplied from abroad," he alleged. He promised that names of the held terrorists would be disclosed once the ongoing investigations concluded.

He told a questioner that "Al Qaeda is not involved in these activities." He also accused terrorists, trained in Punjab, of causing sectarian violence in his province. He denied that any operation had been launched by the army in Balochistan but conceded that an 'operation cleanup' had been launched by the local administration with the assistance of Frontier Constabulary, Levies and the Navy.

"Several terrorists have been arrested in this operation and arms, ammunition, satellite phones, wireless sets, maps and anti-Pakistan literature recovered from their camps. Some terrorists have also given up voluntarily," he said.

Jam Yousuf said that nobody should object to establishment of army cantonments in Balochistan. Wherever felt necessary, cantonments would be established in the province, he said.

He pointed out that cantonments had existed at many places in the province before but no hue and cry was made. Replying to a question, he said China was a time-tested friend of Pakistan and didn't raise any unnecessary hue and cry over the killing of its engineers working on the Gwadar port project in last May.

"If US engineers were killed in Gwadar, it would have declared Pakistan a terrorist country," he added. He said that Gwadar port would become the hub of economic activity in the future and help the province in increasing revenue. He hoped that it would one day demand share in the NFC on revenue generation basis, as was being done by Sindh.

He advised the opponents of the mega project to "swallow the bitter pill" because some sacrifice had to be made for future development. He stressed that nobody would deprive the Balochis of their land but at the same time pointed out that people themselves had sold their land to investors.

Replying to a question, Jam Mohammad Yusuf maintained that he considered all Baloch politicians, including Nawab Akbar

Khan Bugti as 'loyal Pakistanis' and urged them to play their role in the development of their province.

"Every Baloch is a nationalist and they love their land as much as any politician. Balochistan is not a personal property of anybody. The past governments did nothing for its development except making hollow promises.

He said that a dialogue with the opponents of mega projects had started with Baloch leaders and hoped that soon some positive outcome would emerge. "People of Balochistan want progress and development in their province but people from outside don't.

The president has given Rs5 billion for Gwadar Development Authority and assured that locals would be provided all possible opportunities. The Balochistan chief minister announced a donation of half a million rupees for the KPC.

COAS VOWS TO CRUSH INSURGENCY IN BALOCHISTAN

Army Chief Gen Raheel Sharif warned 'foreign governments and intelligence agencies' on Wednesday against their involvement in the insurgency in Balochistan and announced continuation of development projects in the province by military organisations despite insurgent attacks.

'The army chief warned foreign states, intelligence agencies against trying to destabilise Pakistan by supporting terrorists in Balochistan. We'll defeat them comprehensively, military spokesman Maj Gen Asim Bajwa quoted the army chief as saying.

Gen Sharif made these comments during a trip to Balochistan, where he visited Frontier Corps headquarters and met Balochistan Governor Mohammad Khan Achakzai, Chief Minister Abdul Malik Baloch and Commander Southern Command Lt Gen Mohammad Naseer Khan Janjua and discussed the security situation with them.

Progress in counterinsurgency operations wasalso reviewed.

Gen Sharif's trip to Balochistan came against the backdrop of insurgent attacks on a labour camp near Turbat in which 20 labourers were killed.

On his return from Quetta, the army chief met Prime Minister Nawaz Sharif and discussed with him the security situation in the province.

The government and lawenforcement agencies have time and again alleged involvement of a foreign hand in the Balochistan unrest, but have never shared proof to substantiate their claim. By alluding to external involvement in the unrest, the law-enforcement agencies (LEAs) generally mean to be referring to Indian intelligence agency RAW. Other intelligence agencies suspected of contributing to the Balochistan unrest are Afghanistan's NDS and those of certain countries in the Gulf and West.

After the labour camp carnage, Balochistan Home Minister Mir Sarfaraz Bugti had also alleged that Indian secret service Research and Analysis Wing (RAW) was FUNDING anti-state elements in the province.

Gen Sharif reiterated full support of the armed forces to the Balochistan government in tackling the problem.

The army chief 'commended' performance of ISLAMABAD: Army Chief Gen Raheel Sharif warned 'foreign governments and intelligence agencies' on Wednesday against their involvement in the insurgency in Balochistan and announced continuation of development projects in the province by military organisations despite insurgent attacks.

'The army chief warned foreign states, intelligence agencies against trying to destabilise Pakistan by supporting terrorists in Balochistan. We'll defeat them comprehensively, military spokesman Maj Gen Asim Bajwa quoted the army chief as saying.

Gen Sharif made these comments during a trip to Balochistan, where he visited Frontier Corps headquarters and met Balochistan Governor Mohammad Khan Achakzai, Chief Minister Abdul Malik Baloch and Commander Southern Command Lt Gen Mohammad Naseer Khan Janjua and discussed the security situation with them.

Progress in counterinsurgency operations wasalso reviewed.

Gen Sharif's trip to Balochistan came against the backdrop of insurgent attacks on a labour camp near Turbat in which 20 labourers were killed. On his return from Quetta, the army chief met Prime Minister Nawaz Sharif and discussed with him the security situation in the province.

The government and lawenforcement agencies have time and again alleged involvement of a foreign hand in the Balochistan unrest, but have never shared proof to substantiate their claim. By alluding to external involvement in the unrest, the law-enforcement agencies (LEAs) generally mean to be referring to Indian intelligence agency RAW. Other intelligence agencies suspected of contributing to the Balochistan unrest are Afghanistan's NDS and those of certain countries in the Gulf and West.

After the labour camp carnage, Balochistan Home Minister Mir Sarfaraz Bugti had also alleged that Indian secret service Research and Analysis Wing (RAW) was funding anti-state elements in the province.

Gen Sharif reiterated full support of the armed forces to the Balochistan government in tackling the problem.

The army chief 'commended' performance of LEAs in 'improving the law and order situation'.

Balochistan has consistently lagged behind in the implementation of the National Action Plan and has suffered more casualties this year than suffered jointly by the other three provinces in terrorismrelated incidents.

Gen Sharif attributed poor progress to 'security challenges of vastBalochistan' The army chief called for adopting an integrated approach by civil and military leadership and LE As for achieving peace in the province. Reiterating military's commitment to fighting terrorism and insurgency, he said: 'We will unearth terrorists, abettors, sympathisers and FINANCIERS. None will find place in the country to hide. We will go to any length to restore the writ of the state.

BATTLE IN INDIA OVER BALOCHISTAN

Hell has no fury like an offended far-right nationalist. And even a democracy can deny one the power to dissent when ltra-nationalists are out to exploit an issue involving a country's traditional "enemy." India provides a current illustration. For days now, the country's parliament has been rocked by a controversy over a joint statement of the prime ministers of India and Pakistan. As noted in these columns before (A Piece of Paper and South Asian Peace, July 20, 2009), the enemies of South Asian peace began by attacking the document for "delinking" the issue of terrorism from the India-Pakistan "composite dialogue" suspended since the Mumbai outrage of eight months ago.

The focus of the far-right fury has now shifted to the last lines of the statement lambasted as a "sell-out." The brief document is denounced as all the more of a "betrayal" for mentioning Pakistan's province of Balochistan, with a hint at India's alleged hand in the Baloch insurgency.

The statement, issued on July 16 after a meeting between Manmohan Singh and Yousaf Raza Gilani at the non-aligned summit in Sharm el-Sheikh (Egypt), ends with the words: "Prime Minister Gilani mentioned that Pakistan has some information on threats in Balochistan and other areas." Working itself up into a white heat of rage over this, the main opposition Bharatiya Janata Party (BJP) and its allies have staged a series of walkouts in the two houses of the parliament, with its media friends trying to whip up a furious campaign on the issue.

"This has never happened before" was their near-hysterical outcry. This is not the first time Pakistan has complained about India's involvement in its south-western province. From 2004, in fact, both local and national leaders, including former President Pervez Musharraf, have leveled the allegation in an increasingly strident manner. India has been charged not only with subversive operations from within Balochistan, but also with running camps for training Baloch insurgents in neighbouring Afghanistan.

It is true, however, that Balochistan has never figured in an India-Pakistan joint statement before, Nor indeed has Islamabad taken its complaint on this count to any international forum, including the United Nations. But Pakistan may not have gained from inclusion of the issue in the joint statement, as we shall see just in a while. Meanwhile, the BJP seemed to receive fresh ammunition from reports in the Pakistani media that Gilani confronted Singh with a dossier detailing India's covert subversion in the restive province. According to the reports, the dossier listed the safe houses being run by India's external intelligence agency, the Research and Analysis Wing (RAW) of its External Affairs Ministry, in Afghanistan for training Baloch militants for "missions in Pakistan."

According to one report, Pakistani Foreign Secretary Salman Bashir told Indians in Egypt that, if India did not agree to the "delinking," Pakistan would be forced to produce before the international media at least "three Indian Ajmal Kasabs" who were directly or indirectly part of the terrorist activities in Balochistan. This alluded to Ajmal Kasab, a Pakistani who is the only militant involved in Mumbai caught alive and is undergoing a trial now in India.

The alleged dossier has slowly disappeared from the debate. First, it was claimed that the dossier was only shown, and not given, to Singh. Now it has been denied by both sides. What happened in the meeting, then, to warrant those lines? Singh's explanation in the parliament on July 30 was: "When I spoke to Prime Minister Gilani about terrorism from Pakistan, he mentioned to me that many Pakistanis thought that India meddled in Balochistan. I told him that we have no interest in destabilizing Pakistan.... If Pakistan has any evidence,... we are willing to look at it because we have nothing to hide."

Gilani - whatever else might be his game - was not wrong about the perception on the issue in Pakistan. Indian peace activist and Magsaysay award-winner Sandeep Pandey, just back from a visit to Pakistan, says: "Manmohan Singh has merely acknowledged something which is common knowledge in Pakistan." It is not something unknown to concerned Indian agencies and quarters close to them, either.

It would be terribly unfair, of course, to tar all Balochs fighting for independence or autonomy as terrorists. Balochistan is the largest as well as the least-developed province of Pakistan. It is certainly not without reason that insurgency has continued here relentlessly since the late 1940's. All this, however, is no argument for rejecting evidence of at least India's past role in Balochistan, available from Indian sources of proximity to undeclared policies. A journalist known for closeness to security and intelligence agencies, Praveen Swami, wrote a year ago: "As the Nawab Akbar Khan Bugti-led Baloch insurgency against Pakistan escalated from 2004, Islamabad's allegations grew more strident. In August 2004, Balochistan Chief Minister Jam Mohammad Yusuf declared that India was running 40 terror camps targeting the province.... At the beginning of July 2006, Mushahid Husain, the chair of the Pakistan Senate Standing Committee on Foreign Affairs, asserted that RAW was 'training 600 Balochis' in Afghanistan."

Significantly, Swami adds: "Were these charges true? It is hard to say. Credible allegations exist that India offered low-grade funding for Baloch insurgents in the wake of the 1971 Bangladesh war of liberation - but then withdrew support to avoid destabilizing Prime Minister (Zulfikar Ali) Bhutto. It is probable, though not proved, that India also held out some financial support to Bugti and other Baloch nationalist leaders."

In February 2006, the well-informed Swami had something more shocking to say: "Musharraf has not made public the evidence he claims to possess on Indian involvement in Balochistan, and leaders of the insurgent groups there have been dismissive of his assertion.... Yet, it is also true that Indian frustration with Musharraf's refusal to deliver on his promises to end Islamist terrorism in Jammu and Kashmir has been growing. Many in India's intelligence establishment believe that the time has come to use what are called offensive covert means."

Explains Swami: "In the past, India has demonstrated the capability to do so, and with good effect: two Research and Analysis Wing (RAW) groups, CIT-'X' and CIT-'J', had, for example, carried out a series of bombings in Lahore and Karachi as retaliation for strikes by Pakistan-backed Khalistan terror groups. India's offensive covert operations were closed down early in the tenure of Prime Minister I. K. Gujral, but the weapon, as Musharraf well knows, could be unsheathed again." This could be done, he meant, in Balochistan.

Security analyst Ravi Visvesvarya Prasad voices a similar grievance about Gujral, vindicating critics of India's past activities in Balochistan. In a newspaper article of July 27, 2009, he writes: "... India's covert capabilities in Pakistan, painstakingly built up during the regimes of (former Prime Ministers) Indira Gandhi and P. V. Narasimha Rao, were unilaterally shut down by then-Prime Minister I. K. Gujral in 1997-98 as part of his peace initiative. As a result, India today has virtually no reliable and capable human intelligence assets within Pakistani territory."

A related point, with an added religious dimension, is made by former RAW operative and security expert B. Raman in a recent analysis. Says he: "The Hindu population of Balochistan has considerably come down in recent years due to their forcible ejection from there by the Army after it launched the project for the construction of the Gwadar port with Chinese assistance. The Inter-Services Intelligence looked upon them as potential Research and Analysis Wing agents and forced them to shift."

Raman adds: "But the Hindus who have managed to remain have continued to enjoy the protection of the Baloch leaders and people. When Nawab Akbar Khan Bugti was killed by the Pervez Musharraf government in a military operation in August 2006, among those who died with him were Baloch Hindus whom he had taken under his protection."

Raman outdoes the BJP in that he considers the joint statement a betrayal of Baloch "freedom fighters" as well, since it equates them with "terrorists" and thus serves the interests of Islamabad. But, as mentioned before, Balochs themselves do not seem to share his bitterness.

An organization of the indigenous Marri people of the province, Anjuman Ittehad Marri (AIM), says: "The mention of Baluchistan in the joint statement... has brought the goal of an independent Baluchistan even closer as it has helped internationalize the Baluch question..."

Hamid Mir of Pakistan's increasingly influential Geo TV agrees with the AIM assessment, while explaining why Pakistani rulers have been reluctant to expose India's role in Balochistan. Says he: "... Balochistan is not a serious dispute like Jammu and Kashmir; it is a problem of provincial rights. Instead of internationalizing the issue, therefore, Islamabad should address the problem realistically. It cannot get away by blaming India alone for the unrest in the province."

It would serve better the cause of both the countries - and South Asia - if they go for bilateral talks on both issues instead of internationalizing the disputes further. They cannot succeed, however, if they seek to do so behind the backs of the people of either Kashmir or Balochistan.

INDIAN RAW'S IN BALOCHISTAN

After the RAW got immense success in East Pakistan and due to the lack of abilities on part of Pakistani leadership to handle the crises in Eastern part of the country, a new country was created with name of Bangladesh in 1971, just within some 30 months of the inception of RAW, Rameshwar Nath Kao sought Prime Minister Indira Gandhi's permission to launch KBP-II for the separation of Balochistan from Pakistan.

The Daily Mail's investigations indicate that though Kao and the *'Kaoboys'* of RAW were feeling over excited with their success in breaking Pakistan into two and wanted an immediate go-ahead from the PMO for the implementation of the 2 nd phase of the Kao plan (KBP-II), the Indian Prime Minister was being extraordinary cautious in taking any further step in this direction as she got the information that the American CIA and the Chinese intelligence, both were monitoring the RAW moves very closely and both the Chinese and the US government had in a way conveyed to the government of India that any repeat of East Pakistan like mischief by India in West Pakistan would not be allowed and tolerated at all.

These finding further indicate that at that particular stage, Indian government was very eagerly looking forward to the Shah of Iran for 2 soft loans amounting to the tune of not less than $ 25 millions. Indira Gandhi also knew that any Indian move in Balochistan, at that particular stage, could have easily annoyed the Shah of Iran as he was a very close friend of Pakistan, resulting into the refusal of the 25 million dollars loan from Shah. India was already persuading the sister of Shah of Iran, Madame Ashraf Pehlawi for pursuing Shah to approve loan. According to the records, Shah's sister was given a kickback of $ 6 million for the sanctioning of the loan.

The Daily Mail's investigations indicate that keeping all these reservations, Indira Gandhi asked the RAW Chief Kao to hold his horses and shelve the Balochistan plan until the circumstances get changed and especially until the loan from Iran was transferred into Indian government's accounts. These findings further indicate that this reply from Prime Minister came as a great dejection for both Kao and his 'Boys' at the RAW headquarters, though Indira Gandhi allocated huge funds to RAW for its expansion worldwide after getting the Iranian loans, yet many officials of RAW still belief that it was just a bid to appease RAW after ordering it to keep the Balochistan operation on hold while the RAW officials were very much excited about launching it as soon as possible, without letting the Pakistani counterparts to get out of the shock of Kao's Bengla plan.

According to some senior International journalists as well as certain security experts and former intelligence official, the RAW and specially its Kaoboys were never actually waiting for a formal nod from PMO and they in fact had already starting working on Kao Balochistan Plan (KBP-II). RAW had already started contacting Baloch leaders through social activities in foreign countries and a PSYWAR was launched amongst the Baluchistani people with a crystal clear reference to what happened in East Pakistan and how India helped East Pakistanis to have a spate, independent country. In the meantime RAW also sought agency-to-agency help from its counterpart in former Soviet Union and KGB replied in a positive manner to help RAW implcment its Kao plan for Balochistan.

Soon after entering into the Balochistan game, Kao and his team realized that the things in Balochistan were never as easy as those were in East Pakistan. They discovered that they had no advantage of having a road link in Balochistan that they had in East Pakistan and secondly the disadvantage was that Pakistani army had total control and very strong road link to any part of Balochistan, something that it lacked in case of East Pakistan. The only encouraging point for RAW while starting the Balochistan game was that here they did not had to launch and fund the movement at the grassroots level like in case of the East Pakistan but in fact in Balochistan, they just needed to lure a handful of Baloch tribal leaders, specially young ones who were very much attracted towards fun life of West, and rest was to be done by these tribal leaders. After making this assessment, RAW decided to go-ahead with the KPB-II.

However it got a shocker from KGB when KGB expressed its inability to provide any strategic or tactical help for Balochistan plan due to KGB's lack of resources to carry out any deep sea covert operation in the hot waters of Indian Ocean and the Arabian sea however it promised every help and support for the cause in any other shape, at a later stage. Some experts say that KGB's abrupt nod for joining RAW in Balochistan game could also be seen in the backdrop of cold war era rivalry between CIA and KGB as KGB was constantly looking to hit CIA hard anywhere in the world at first available opportunity during that era and since KGB knew that CIA would feel deeply hurt by its any joint operation with RAW in Balochistan and thus it straight away offered all its help and support, even without approval from the highest level of the Soviet government. It remains another fact that over the years, things got drastically changed and today CIA itself is fully embedded with RAW in the Balochistan game.

The Daily Mail's findings indicate that the top boy amongst Kao's *'like-minded'* Kaoboys was an IPS officer B. Raman and was known as *'Kao's Special Boy.'*

Raman served in RAW and earlier in the IB for about 27 years and got retired from RAW in August 1994. When RAW was making an assessment to enter into Balochistan game, the agency's head Rameshwar Nath Kao decided to explore a new avenue to begin the game, without waiting for PMO's word in this direction. After the careful assessment of all the options, Kao decided approach the French Intelligence. The French external Intelligence, then known as SDECE and is these days know as DGSE. In French language SDECE means Service for External Documentation and Counter-Espionage while DGSE stands for Directorate general of External Security.

Research indicates that the then SDECE was headed by Le Comte Alexandre de Marenches, an ex army officer of France. As mentioned above as how RAW manipulates Indian diplomats across the world, RAW opted in this case to use the services of the then Ambassador of India to France who himself was an ex-army officer of India and was married to a French speaking lady from Luxemburg that had enabled him to become a close friend of the then French Interior Minister Michel Poniatowski. Kao used the Indian ambassador to have a meeting of top RAW officials with their French counterparts through Michel.

The ambassador 'obliged' the RAW chief and a meeting was fixed between French and Indian spy masters at Paris. During the meeting, the RAW side, headed by Kao, proposed for a liaison between French and Indian intelligence agencies for the collection and sharing of intelligence with regards to the movement of US and Soviet as well as the Chinese Navies in the water regions of Indian Ocean and Arabian Sea. An agreement in this regard was finalized straight away and France agreed to establish a liaison office at Paris in this regard and showed its complete willingness to the project, without knowing that RAW had some Balochistan related motives behind this move as it no interest at all in the movement of the Naval fleets of soviets or Americans or even the Chinese. The research indicates that RAW wanted to use the project for transporting arms and heavy weapons to Balochistan through this project as it had already been able to lure certain Baloch leaders to launch an insurgency movement. The French and Indian intelligence agencies agreed to establish at least four Technical Intelligence (TECHINT) stations in India's spotted water regions in Indian Ocean and Arabian Sea. Though the Indians claim that the project was soon abandoned, yet it remains a fact that these stations still exist and are operational under Indian control. However France pulled out of the project after quite some time. Some intelligence experts believe that France developed some serious doubts about RAW's movement under the garb of the said Technical Intelligence Stations after the French intelligence managed to retrieve volumes and volumes of highly classified documents relating to the covert operations of RAW from the Indian Prime Minister's Office. There are some stories in this direction out which one says that it was the job of some French under cover secret agents who developed some special relations under the disguise of gays with RAW's liaison officer in France for the said project B. Raman and they managed to get some way to access to the classified document in Indira Gandhi's office.

Research indicates that after French and Indian intelligence agencies agreed upon establishing a liaison office at Paris, B Raman maneuvered a lot to motivate the RAW Chief Kao to post him to Paris as the liaison officer as at that time, France was known as the Paradise of the gays. Kao who did not want to send Raman out of sight for a longer period due to his *'special feelings'* for Raman, finally agreed upon sending Raman to France on deputation. In this direction first RAW tried to send him Raman to France in the disguise of media representative from India, a practice that RAW is still exercising across the world with a great success, and all arrangements were made with the collaboration of an Indian newspaper The Hindu, yet at the eleventh hour the plan was changed and Raman was sent to Paris under the diplomatic cover, the other major practice of RAW that is still very much in fashion.

At Paris, Raman's duties to the knowledge of the French intelligence were to perform liaison officer for the TECHINT project while the host government knew him as diplomat t he Indian embassy. However, RAW had assigned him some other responsibilities. He was sent to Paris to communicate with Baloch tribal youngsters living and studying in England and France and to lure them to join the Kao plan for Balochistan. In the process, Raman met with a young Iranian gay at Paris. In one of his latest books, Raman admits that he met the Iranian boy in Paris and he lured him and developed special relations with him. Raman writes, one night his Iranian friend, suddenly developed some serious medical problems and he, despite being an Indian diplomat, rushed the Iranian boy to the hospital in the emergency and got him treated there and also paid all the bills at the Paris hospital. Though Raman refrains from explaining his relations with the Iranian gay guy in details, he however writes that the same Iranian guy, proved very helpful to him for his covert operations during his stay in Paris. According to certain media and intelligence reports, during his stay in Paris, Raman used the Iranian boy to the maximum to establish special ties with certain Balochistani youngsters, mostly the sons of Baloch tribal leaders and he remained successful in luring them to get embedded with RAW for the successful implementation of the Kao Plan for Balochistan.

Back home at New Delhi, when RAW had finalized the aggressive implementation of the Kao plan in Baluchistan, Prime Minister Indira Gnadhi got into some internal political turmoil and she finally declared the state of emergency in the country, a move that prevented RAW from pursuing the Kao plan at that very moment.

Research indicates that during the state of emergency, Indira Gandhi misused RAW to the maximum to fix her political opponents. However, she finally went to the polls and met with the defeat in the General Elections. This resulted into the bringing of Moraji Desai as the new Prime minister of India. Desai did not have any respect for RAW has he knew that Indira Gandhi had used RAW against him as well. However he did not touch the affairs of RAW much. In the meantime, when RAW moved the file of Kao Plan for Balochistan, he got furious and asked RAW to focus on country's security instead of remaining busy in hatching conspiracies against other countries. He however kept the Kao plan file in his office. Some close associates of Desai attribute this development to Desai's hateful feelings towards RAW and he thought that Kao plan was a baby of his first degree opponent and thus he should stay away from it. Some others think that Desai snubbed RAW over the Kao plan owing to his peace initiatives with Pakistan and because of his very cordial relations with then military ruler of Pakistan, late General Zia-Ul-Haque. It is said that during his visits to England and France, Desai asked the RAW officers posted those countries to give him details of their responsibilities in those countries in writing. Both the officers refused to give any explanation to Desai in back and white.

RAW did not succeed in getting a formal green light for the Kao plan for Balochistan during Desai's era and the agency decided to suffice on wait and see policy. In the process, new elections were held in India and as result of these polls; Indira Gandhi again came into power as the Prime Minister of India. Once again, at a suitable stage, RAW moved the Kao plan file to the PMO. People associated to the Indian Prime Minister's office say that upon receiving the file, Mrs. Gandhi summoned the RAW Chief and directed him that the agency should first address the new menace that had hit the country. This was the growing Sikh separatist movement in Indian Punjab. Indira asked to deal with the issue as top priority of the agency and to use all resources for the purpose. RAW got engaged in the new top priority assignment and the Kao operation was again put on the back burner. However, reports suggest that RAW, on the parallel, continued its unauthorized interference in Balochistan and kept the Kao plan alive and in the meantime, it managed to shift maximum weaponry into Balochistan through the France-blessed TECHINT sea stations. It also got the immense support from KGB and its extension in Afghanistan after the former USSR invaded Afghans. The reports suggest that KGB played the major role in training the Baloch militants, given to RAW by certain Baloch tribal leaders, to use the arms and weapons shipped by RAW through sea routes to Balochistan over the years.

The reports also indicate that it was not possible for RAW to successfully form the militant outfits in Balochistan without the strong help and assistance of KGB as both RAW and KGB managed to install militant forces like the Balochistan Liberation Army (BLA) and Balochistan Liberation Front (BLF) etc. there were comprehensive training facilities for these militants by KGB in adjoining Afghanistan and loads of money for their mentors by RAW.

Back in India, RAW remained busy in tackling the Sikh movement. The details of the Sikhs' movement in India would be discussed at a later stage but it is to be worth mentioning that RAW's inability to handle the genuine movements like the Khalistan movement by Indian Sikhs was exposed to everyone across the world and particularly amongst the global clandestine community. RAW made many goof-ups in implicating Pakistan and its top security agency, Inter Services Intelligence (ISI) into the Khalistan movement. It remains a fact that the ISI did get some security benefits out of the Khalistan movement but the volume of the ISI role in the movement, portrayed by RAW was no where near the ground realities.

Just one incident out of dozens, is enough to prove that how panicked and furious the RAW got to implicate ISI and Pakistan into the Khalistan freedom movement and that how unable the RAW was to create even fake cases against ISI to convince the global community. In one incident, some alleged members of the Sikh freedom movement, hijacked an Indian passenger aircraft and took to Lahore. Pakistan refused to hold talks with the hijackers and the plane was then taken to the UAE. From UAE, somehow RAW managed to take the custody of the hijackers and took them to India.

After a few days, Indian government came out with the claims that hijackers had confessed that they hijacked the said aircraft from India with a toy pistol but later, during their brief stay at Lahore airport, some ISI officers gave them the real pistol which was retrieved from the UAE authorities later and after contacting a French arms company in the backdrop of the make and serial number of the said pistol, it was revealed that the said pistol was officially imported by Pakistan army and the episode proves that ISI was behind the hijacking and the entire movement of Khalistan. This outrageous episode earned India merely a big, loud laughter across the world and very badly damaged the credibility of RAW and Indian government's allegations against Pakistan which is still haunting New Delhi as well as RAW.

The research reveals that as RAW completely failed in countering the Khalistan movement, it finally advised Prime Minister Indira Gandhi to go all out for a comprehensive military operations against the Sikhs and presented a high profile report that the only way out to tackle the Khalistan movement was to storm the most prestigious and religiously motivated Sikh Temple, the Golden Tample in Indian Punjab as all the top Sikh separatists were hiding and operating from there. This prompted Indira Gandhi to ordered the most infamous military operation by Indian army, code-named *Operation Blue Star* in which thousands of innocent Sikhs were butchered by Indian army troops.

RAW, MOSSAD, NDS BEHIND TERRORISM IN PAKISTAN

Intelligence agencies of India, Afghanistan and Israel are involved in terrorist activities in various parts of Pakistan. Reliable sources told WAQT NEWS on Saturday that in Karachi mostly Research and Analysis Wing (RAW) of India was involved in killings. In Balochistan, RAW and Afghan intelligence agency, NDS, have joined hands to encourage separatists. At a broader level, it becomes a troika with Mossad as its third wing. Daily killings in Karachi have become a serious challenge to the government and the steps taken by it so far have failed to bridle the criminals. "The security agencies have the evidence of RAW's involvement in Karachi terrorist activities," said the sources. According to them, after committing heinous acts, terrorists go to the RAW offices along the Afghan border, show the videos to the officials, collect money from them and get directions for further operations. Evidence about the RAW providing millions of dollars to such elements is available with the Pakistan Intelligence agencies.

The RAW, in collaboration with Afghan intelligence agency, NDS, is also actively providing covert financial and weapon support to Baloch militant groups, Balochistan Liberation Army (BLA), Baloch Republican Army (BRA) and Balochistan Liberation Front (BLF), for terrorist activities in the province. These outfits are pursuing the separatist agenda and are responsible for playing havoc with the province. "Irrefutable evidence" suggests that Baloch militants are being harboured at various places and training camps located at Kabul, Nimroz and Kandahar in Afghanistan by RAW in collaboration with NDS since 2006.

RAW is also providing sustained financial and monetary support to Baloch feudalists and militants, both in Afghanistan and Balochistan. Besides, RAW, with the complete support and patronage of Afghan authorities, is also providing arms and ammunition to Baloch militants for terrorist activities inside Pakistan. Sources privy to the situation also claim they have evidences that RAW is involved in providing fake identity and travel documents to Baloch militants for moving out of Afghanistan to India, UAE and Western countries.

"It is arranging visits of Baloch sub nationalists and militants to India for training purposes. In this regard, RAW arranged a visit of Riaz Gull Bugti (a leading militant commander of Brahamdagh Bugti) to India in September 2009, where he was trained by RAW for terrorist activities. In order to overcome the linguistic problems, RAW is also arranging Balochi language courses in India for Afghan intelligence operatives through Baloch instructors so that their expertise could be utilised to intensify terrorist activities in the province.

RAW, in collaboration with prominent Baloch sub-nationalists round the globe, is also persistently utilising various international forums, NGOs and think-tank organisations like United Nations Human Rights Council (UNHRC) to malign Pakistan through arranging stage events such as preplanned anti-Pakistan interventions, media briefings, protests and demonstrations. "Their convergence, facilitation and media coverage is managed and funded by RAW and other agencies through their operatives.

Tarek Fateh, a Canada-based political activist and sympathiser of Baloch sub-nationalists, after spitting venom against Pakistan during the UNHRC 22nd session at Geneva in February this year, visited India on RAW's sponsorship for future directions. He also held one-and-one meetings with RAW ex senior officers, Vikram Sood and AS Daulat.

According to the sources, the close relatives and friends of Hakim Ullah Mehsud, Maulana Fazlullah, frequently visits Afghanistan to meet RAW officers under diplomatic cover in their embassy and consulates, and collects money for terrorist activities in Pakistan.

The Swat militants are being harboured in camps in the areas of Kunar and Nuristan. They are imparted training and given weapons for organised militant actions against Pakistan's regular and civil armed forces in FATA areas. Maulana Fazlullah and his commanders openly travel in Afghanistan and visit Indian Embassy/consulates, RAW and NDS offices as if Afghanistan were their hometown. RAW and Mossad are also preparing plans against the nuclear installations of Pakistan.

9

Intelligence in Government Operations

Logically, intelligence means evaluated information gathering, may be in detail with data or particular information or fact. It is sometimes called active data or active intelligence. It is with regard to information on current plans, decisions and actions of people or may otherwise be considered valuable from the points of view of the intelligence-gathering organization. In Government operations, applications of intelligence are therefore necessary, and there are separate departments within the Government to look after the work relevant to them. This supply of information to the Government is the key need for operation of any Government.

In a sense, the usage of 'intelligence' at the national level may be somewhat associated with the concept of social intelligence which is tied to traditional politics, law and enforcement. Open source intelligence involves all-source collection, storage and indexing of data through intelligence officers of the Government department. However, security clearance may also be asked for. Government intelligence is usually assigned to intelligence agencies often with large budgets for which variety of techniques are applied to obtain information.

There are also specialist agencies for collecting various types of information that is crucial to the Government. RAW, CBI, IB are the most effective secret agencies in Inda. Depending on the national policy, some intelligence agencies engage in clandestine and covert activities such as political subversion, sabotage and assassination.

Other agencies strictly limit themselves to analysis.Military intelligence is an element of warfare which covers all aspects of gathering, analyzing and making use of information about enemy forces and the ground. It involves spying, lookouts, high-tech surveillance equipment and also secret agents.

Business intelligence denotes the public or secret information that an organization obtains about its competitors and markets. Intelligence trait serves for individual humans and animals.Intelligence collection is often controversial and seen as a threat to privacy but intelligence is essential for Government policy formulation and operations. It is a policy matter for individual Governments through which, though usually associated with warfare, it can also be used to preserve peace. The process of taking known information about situations and entities of strategic, operational or tactical importance, and with appropriate statements of probability is must for good operations for any Government. The descriptions are drawn from whatever matter is available in the form of deliberately deceptive information. The analysts must correlate the similarities among deceptions and extract a common truth. Although its practice is found in its purest form inside intelligence agencies, such as the Central intelligence Agency (CIA) in the US or the Secret Intelligence Service (SIS, M 16) in the UK, FBI in Pakistan, CBI & RAW in India, its methods are also applicable in fields such as business intelligence or competitive intelligence.

Intelligence analysis is a way of reducing the ambiguity of highly ambiguous situations, as such a situation which is often deliberately created by highly intelligent people with mindsets very different from those of the analysts, considering the facts of extreme risk to achieve minor gain. Above all, they are not in favor of cognitive traps for intelligence analysis projecting what they want the opponent to think, and using available information to justify that conclusion. Government authorities definitely maintain the facts for functioning their works smoothly and effectively but keeping their methods very much secret.

Moreover, present role of intelligence in governance has drastically changed due to interference of terrorists. Like India, intelligence in US Government operations has changed dramatically and is now more critical than ever to domestic security and foreign policy relying on a multitude of sources, including hundreds of official documents, detainee interrogation and homeland security intelligence.

Government of India in May 2000 had set up a group of Ministers (GoM) to study the recommendations of the Kargil Review Committee regarding India's Defense and intelligence functioning to study intelligence, defense management, internal security and border management. Accordingly, India has a Chief of Defense Staff (CDS), senior most from the Army, the Navy and the Air Force. But the CDS is responsible for command of intelligence service called the Defense intelligence Agency (DIA), which is overall responsible authority for coordinating the directorates of military, Naval and Air Force intelligence.

The wing called the intelligence Bureau (IB) has complete responsibility for internal security operations. The research and analysis wing (RAW) looks after significant external intelligence-gathering role. Besides, the J&K Police's special operations group (SOG0 in also involved in the task to prevent terrorist activates. The hard business of micro-intelligence gathering, running sources and producing actionable intelligence has been relegated to the background. Part of the reason is that, after the creation of the RAW, the IB was stripped of its technical intelligence assets. Now, IB is working independently, with communications capability in order to effectively monitor all forms of cellular, land-line, radio frequency and internet traffic.

It has its own cryptographic resources, along with direction-finding equipment to locate transmissions for deep penetration operations.The RAW, like the IB is more focused organization. It utilizes the services of paramilitary forces like the Shanti Suraksha Bal (SSB) and the Indo-Tibetan Border police along the border with China and are engaged for in-house security needs, gathering external intelligence and running transborder operations. Moreover, RAW retains the high-profile Aerial Recon-naissance Centre (ARC) which has been set up with the assistance of US in the wake of the India-China border conflict.

National societies seek a more assertive role in the response to needs in their country. They also seek better acknowledgement of their contribution and capacities on the part of the ICRC.*Truly Universal:* the ICRC and its 12,000 staff is under steady pressure due to the pace of global change and its multiple effects on people's safety, integrity, dignity and livelihoods. The approach it has advocated over the years-of taking into account the interaction between local, regional and global dimensions-becomes more important than ever. It is becoming truly universal in its thinking and action. It has become adaptable to the changing realities and needs of different contexts. The way the ICRC does not allow the manifold problems and constraints standing in its way to undermine its steadfast determination to discharge its responsibilities is truly admirable.

Military intelligence has also formed in the form of DIA which is most powerful bureau. Other two directly controlled agencies of Defense which are also powerful are the signals intelligence Directorate and the Defense Image Processing and Analysis Centre (DIPAC). They coordinate information to army corps commanders in areas where the Armed forces special powers Act is in force.At present India has only one joint tri-series command, located on the adaman and nicobar islands. It is the inter-services working which is headed by a Vice-Admiral and is Navy-dominated. It has an exemplary working style for overall control of all forces.

Coordination with and among each of the Government agencies and defense authorities is a must for protecting our motherland from any internal and external threats. More state-of-the-art weapons, modern gadgets, new technology usage with sincere efforts at this juncture is required to prevent any 26/11 type of attack in future.

INDIAN RAW INTELLIGENCE OPERATIONS IN SOUTH ASIAN COUNTRIES

India's premier intelligence outfit Research and Analysis Wing (RAW)'s operations against the regional countries are conducted with great professional skill and expertise. Central to the operations is the establishment of a huge network inside the target countries.

It uses and targets political dissent, ethnic divisions, economic backwardness and criminal elements within these states to foment subversion, terrorism and sabotage.

Having thus created the conducive environments, RAW stage-manage future events in these countries in such a way that military intervention appears a natural concomitant of the events. In most cases, RAW's hand remains hidden, but more often that not target countries soon begin unearthing those "hidden hand". A brief expose of RAW's operations in neighbouring countries would reveal the full expanse of its regional ambitions (Open Secrets. India's Intelligence Unveiled by M K Dhar. Manas Publications, New Delhi, 2005).

Indian intelligence agencies were involved in Bangladesh since early 1960s.In fact, the main purpose of raising RAW in 1968 was to organise covert operations in Bangladesh. As early as in 1968, RAW was given a green signal to begin mobilising all its resources for the impending surgical intervention in erstwhile East Pakistan. When in July 1971 General Manekshaw told Prime Minister Indira Gandhi that the army would not be ready till December to intervene in Bangladesh, she quickly turned to RAW for help. RAW was ready. Its officers used Bengali refugees to set up Mukti Bahini. Using this outfit as a cover, Indian military sneaked deep into Bangladesh. The story of Mukti Bahini and RAW's role in its organisation and training is now well-known. RAW never concealed its Bangladesh operations. Interested readers may have details in Asoka Raina's Inside RAW: the story of India's Secret Service published by Vikas Publishing House of New Delhi.

It was partly to put an end to the activities of the ISI in India's North-East from East Pakistan that Indira Gandhi decided to assist the Bengali-speaking people of East Pakistan in their efforts to separate from Pakistan and achieve an independent State to be called Bangladesh.

The IB before 1968 and the R&AW thereafter had built up a network of relationships with many political leaders and Government officials of East Pakistan.

The R&AW's role was five-fold: Provision of intelligence to the policy-makers and the armed forces; to train the Bengali freedom fighters in clandestine training camps; to network with Bengali public servants from East Pakistan posted in West Pakistan and in Pakistan's diplomatic missions abroad and persuade them to co-operate with the freedom-fighters and to help in the freedom struggle by providing intelligence; to mount a special operation in the CHT against the sanctuaries and training camps of the Naga and Mizo hostiles;and to organize a psychological warfare (PSYWAR) campaign against the Pakistani rulers by disseminating reports about the massacres of the Bengalis in East Pakistan and the exodus of refugees.

An American report confirmed RAW was directly involved in the secession of East Pakistan into Bangladesh and is currently engaged in similar activities. RAW has a long history of activity in Bangladesh supporting both secular forces and the area's Hindu minority masterminding the break up of Pakistan in 1971.

The main objective of the RAW is to create internal trouble in neighbouring countries and take benefit from the trouble that the neighbouring countries face (Machination of RAW in South Asia and Movement of RAW in Nepal/ by Dr Shastra Dutta Pant).

The analysis of Indian foreign policy trends shows that the Indian governments had adopted an aggressive attitude and covert means for attaining its two permanent foreign policy goals: (a) to attain a hegemonic position in South Asia; (b) to play a role in international system based on Kautilyan principles. Indian governments have used intelligence agencies, not only for monitoring the activities of neighbouring States, but also as a covert forward base to achieve its goals and to implement its hegemonic policies in the region. Over the years RAW become an important instrument for promoting the hegemonic influence of India in the Asian region and has also played a significant role in enhancing India's image as an important international actor. RAW has now acquired the important role of being the covert instrument of Indian national power and will remain decisive actor in furthering Indian interests and future Indian hegemonic ambitions in the region.

Ever since the partition of the sub-continent India has been openly meddling in Nepal's internal affairs by contriving internal strife and conflicts through RAW to destabilise the successive legitimate governments and prop up puppet regimes which would be more amenable Indian machinations. Armed insurrections were sponsored and abetted by RAW and later requests for military assistance to control these were managed through pro-India leaders. India has been aiding and inciting the Nepalese dissidents to collaborate with the Nepali Congress. RAW: An Instrument Of Indian Imperialism by Isha Khan.

India has been openly meddling in Nepal's internal affairs by contriving internal strife and conflicts through RAW to destabilize the successive legitimate governments & prop up puppet regimes which would be more amenable Indian mechanization. Armed insurrections were sponsored and abetted by RAW and later requests for military assistance to control these were managed through pro-India leaders. India has been aiding & inciting the Nepalese to collaborate with the Nepali Congress. For this they were supplied arms whenever the king or the Nepalese Government appeared to be drifting away from the Indian dictates & impinging on Indian hegemonic designs in the region. In fact under the garb of democratization process, the Maoists were actively encouraged by the RAW to collect arms to resort to open rebellion against the legitimate Nepalese governments.

Indian sources, including journalists, have put on record how much before 1971 RAW had established the network of a separatist movement through 'cells' and military training camps in Indian territory adjoining Bangladesh. The Mukti Bahini were all in place organisationally to take advantage of the political trouble in 1971 and carry out acts of sabotage against communication lines so that Indian forces simply marched in at the 'right' time. RAW agents provided valuable information as well as acting as an advance guard for conducting unconventional guerrilla acts against the Pakistani defence forces.

A Mukti Bahini activist, Zainal Abedin, has written a revealing book which includes his personal experience in Indian training camps, entitled RAW and Bangladesh. It was the post-fall of Dhaka period which exposed the Indians' true intentions and made Abedin realise that It was evident from the conduct of the Indian Army that they treated Bangladesh as a colony ... It is now evident that India had helped the creation of Bangladesh with the aim that it would be a step forward towards the total Indian subjugation. RAW has since been seeking to create Indian dominance culturally, ideologically and economically in Bangladesh. Following the independence of Bangladesh, it signed a seven-point secret treaty with India. According to the treaty, all types of employees including civil employees appointed during the Bangladesh civil war should be granted permanent status, other employees also could be appointed only by the Indian administrative service, a certain number of Indian soldiers will continue to remain in Bangladesh despite independence, Bangladesh will not have its own army, for its internal security, it will have only militias from among the freedom fighters who will work under the Indian military command, the trade between the two countries will be kept open and free, and matters pertaining to foreign affairs will be dealt only after close consultation with the Indian foreign ministry.

The treaty had two main points. India will have its control over foreign and defence matters and Bangladesh would open its market for Indian products. Even after this, Indian newspapers continued to lobby for the merger of Bangladesh into India.If European countries can become a united Europe, why can't India go to status-quo-ante, or the situation prior to 1947? Such were the views expressed in those newspapers.

In addition, RAW had also created another insurgency outfit, Shanti Bahini. This force comprises the Chittagong Hill Tracts Hindu and Buddhists tribesmen (the Chakmas) and the intention is to bleed the Bengali military and keep the border area tense.

The Chakma guerrillas had closely assisted RAW operatives. They were assisted during and after the liberation War. The Chakmas, after the change of govt in 1975, contacted the RAW. The Chakmas offered to infiltrate among the Mizo rebels and pass on information to the Indian govt in lieu of asylum. This offer was accepted.

In 1975, the RAW was instructed to assist the Chakma rebels with arms, supplies, bases and training. Training was conducted in the border camps in Tripura but specialized training was imparted at Chakrata near Dehra Doon. Shantu Larma's Shanti Bahini members were flown to Chakrata and then sent back to Tripura to infiltrate into Chittagong Hill Tracts. A RAW office and its operatives at Agartala monitored the progress of the trainees. In 1976, the Shanti Bahini launched its first attack on the Bangladesh force. A new insurgency had been born and India's secret war in the hills of Bangladesh had begun (South Asia's Fractured Frontier, by Binalaksmi Nepram, Mittal Pablishers, New Delhi, 2002, pp-153).

The RAW was involved in training rebels of Chakma tribes and Shanti Bahini to carry out subversive activities in Bangladesh (RAW's role in Furthering India's Foreign Policy, The New Nation, Dhaka, 31 August 1994). The Indian intelligence had collaborated the armed rebels of Chittagong Hill Tracts to destabilise the region (Indo-Bangladesh Relation, Motiur Rahman, daily Prothom Alo, 10 December 2002).

RAW retained a keen interest in Bangladesh even after its independence. Mr. Subramaniam Swamy, Janata Dal MP, a close associate of Morarji Desai said that Rameswar Nath Kao, former Chief of RAW, and Shankaran Nair upset about Sheikh Mujib's assassination chalked a plot to kill General Ziaur Rahman. However, when Morarji Desai came into power in 1977 he was indignant at RAW's role in Bangladesh and ordered operations in Bangladesh to be called off; but by then RAW had already gone too far. General Zia continued to be in power for quite some time but he was assassinated after Indira Gandhi returned to power, though she denied her involvement in his assassination (Weekly Sunday, Calcutta,18 September, 1988). It also unleashed a well-organized plan of psychological warfare and dissension among the political parties and religious sects, control of media, denial of river waters, and propping up a host of disputes in order to keep Bangladesh under a constant political and socio-economic pressure (" RAW and Bangladesh" by Mohammad Zainal Abedin, November 1995, RAW In Bangladesh: Portrait of an Aggressive Intelligence, by Abu Rushd, Dhaka).

RAW continues keeping effective contacts with the political personalities, parties and election process.

The Economist of London recently wrote: 'Ever since 2008, when the Awami League, helped by bags of Indian cash and advice, triumphed in general elections in Bangladesh, relations with India have blossomed.

A couple of years back an Indian journalist Rajesh Joshi had reported that a political party of a neighbouring country received a fund of Rupees 4.5 crore from RAW(Research and Analysis Wing, India's premier intelligence outfit) in 1991 but the party was defeated (The Indian Express, 28 April 1991). It may be mentioned here that elections were only held in Bangladesh in 1991 in the subcontinent and AL was defeated in that election. Years later weekly Sugandha had a similar story on 24 April 1996. Political parties, personalities and various outfits had received Indian fund, assistance, training etc in not too distant past. Some references:

'The involvement of RAW in East Pakistan is said to date from the 1960s, when RAW supported Mujibur Rahman, leading up to his general election victory in 1970'.

INDIAN SPY AGENCY RESERCH AND ANALYSIS WING OPERATION AND COMMANDING METHODS

The Research and Analysis Wing [RAW] is India's foreign intelligence agency. RAW has become an effective instrument of Indian national power, and has assumed a significant role in carrying out India's domestic and foreign policies. RAW has engaged in espionage against Pakistan and other neighbouring countries. It has enjoyed the backing of successive Indian governments in these efforts. Working directly under the Prime Minister, the structure and operations of the Research & Analysis Wing are kept secret from Parliament.

Founded in 1968, RAW focused largely on Pakistan. Its formation was initially motivated by reports of Pakistan supplying weapons to Sikh militants, and providing shelter and training to guerrillas in Pakistan.

Numerous missions were assigned to RAW upon its creation. These included monitoring political and military developments in neighbouring countries that affects Indian national security. Consequently, considerable attention is paid by RAW to Pakistan and China, countries that are traditional rivals of India. RAW has evolved from its origins as a part of the Intelligence Bureau to develop into India's predominant intelligence organization. In 1968, RAW had 250 agents and a budget of Rs. 2 crore. This has expanded to a 2000 total of an estimated eight to ten thousand agents and a budget that experts place at Rs. 1500 crore, alternately estimated at $145 million.

Pakistan has accused the Research and Analysis Wing of sponsoring sabotage in Punjab, where RAW is alleged to have supported the Seraiki movement, providing financial support to promote its activities in Pakistan and organizing an International Seraiki Conference in Delhi in November-December 1993. RAW has an extensive network of agents and anti-government elements within Pakistan, including dissident elements from various sectarian and ethnic groups of Sindh and Punjab. Published reports in Pakistan allege that as many as 35,000 RAW agents entered Pakistan between 1983-93, with 12,000 working in Sindh, 10,000 in Punjab, 8,000 in North West Frontier Province and 5000 in Balochistan.

RAW has a long history of activity in Bangladesh, supporting both secular forces and the area's Hindu minority. The involvement of RAW in East Pakistan is said to date from the 1960s, when RAW supported Mujibur Rahman, leading up to his general election victory in 1970. RAW also provided training and arms to the Bangladeshi freedom fighters known as Mukti Bahini. RAW's aid was instrumental in Bangladesh's gaining independence from Pakistan in 1971.

During the course of its investigation the Jain Commission received testimony on the official Indian support to the various Sri Lankan Tamil armed groups in Tamil Nadu. From 1981, RAW and the Intelligence Bureau established a network of as many as 30 training bases for these groups in India. Centers were also established at the high-security military installation of Chakrata, near Dehra Dun, and in the Ramakrishna Puram area of New Delhi. This clandestine support to the Liberation Tigers of Tamil Eelam (LTTE), some of whom were on the payroll of RAW, was later suspended. Starting in late 1986 the Research and Analysis

Wing focused surveillance on the LTTE which was expanding ties with Tamil Nadu separatist groups. Rajiv Gandhi sought to establish good relations with the LTTE, even after the Indian Peace Keeping Force [IPKF] experience in Sri Lanka. But the Indian intelligence community failed to accurately assess the character of the LTTE and its orientation India and its political leaders. The LTTE assassination of Rajiv Gandhi was apparently motivated by fears of a possible re-induction of the Indian Peace Keeping Force (IPKF) in Sri Lanka and a crackdown on the LTTE network in Tamil Nadu.

RAW was heavily criticized in 1999, following the Pakistani incursions at Kargil. Critics accused RAW of failing to provide intelligence that could have prevented the ensuing ten-week conflict that brought India and Pakistan to the brink of full-scale war. While the army has been critical of the lack of information they received, RAW has pointed the finger at the politicians, claiming they had provided all the necessary information. Most Indian officials believe that in order to prevent another such occurrence, communication needs to be increased between the intelligence agencies, which would require structural reform.

Most recently, RAW has gained attention for providing the US with intelligence on Al-Qaeda and Taliban targets for the war on terrorism in Afghanistan. Maps and photographs of terrorist training camps in Afghanistan and Pakistan, along with other evidence implicating Osama bin Laden in terrorist attacks, were given to US intelligence officials.

The objectives of RAW include:

To monitor the political and military developments in adjoining countries, which have direct bearing on India's national security and in the formulation of its foreign policy.

To seek the control and limitation of the supply of military hardware to Pakistan, mostly from European countries, the USA and China.

The chief of the RAW is designated Secretary (Research) in the Cabinet Secretariat, which is part of the Prime Minister's Office (PMO). Most of the position's occupants have been experts on either Pakistan or China. The head of the Research & Analysis Wing (RAW), the external intelligence agency, enjoys greater autonomy of functioning than their counterparts in the UK and US and has the same privileged direct access to the Prime Minister as their UK counterparts. The control of the Cabinet Secretary over the RAW is limited to administrative and financial matters, with very little say in operational and policy matters.

They also have the benefit of training in either US or the UK, and more recently in Israel. The Secretary (R) reports on an administrative basis to the Cabinet Secretary, who reports to the Prime Minister (PM). However, on a daily basis the Secretary (R) reports to the National Security Advisor. Reporting to the Secretary (R) are: Two Special Secretaries and one Special Director of the ARC, the Aviation Research Centre; Four Additional Secretaries, responsible for different geographical regions; A large number (above 40) Joint Secretaries, who are the functional heads of various desks.

The structure of the RAW is a matter of speculation, but brief overviews of the same are present in the public domain. Attached to the HQ of RAW at Lodhi Road, New Delhi are different regional headquarters, which have direct links to overseas stations and are headed by a controlling officer who keeps records of different projects assigned to field officers who are posted abroad. Intelligence is usually collected from a variety of sources by field officers and deputy field officers; it is either pre-processed (vetted) by a senior field officer or by a desk officer. The desk officer then passes the information to the Joint Secretary and then on to the Additional Secretary and from there it is disseminated to the concerned end user. The Director RAW is a member of the JIC Steering Committee and is authorized to brief the Prime Minister should the need arise.

Some officers of the RAW are members of a specialized service, the Research and Analysis Service (RAS), but several officers also serve on deputation from other services. The RAW has sub-organizations like the Aviation Research Center (ARC), the Radio Research Center (RRC) or the Electronics and Technical Service (ETS), which have considerable capacity for technical intelligence gathering. Another important branch under the operational control of the RAW is the Directorate General of Security (DGS). This agency has oversight over organizations like the Special Frontier Force (SFF), the Special Services Bureau (SSB) etc... Liaison with the military is maintained through the Military Intelligence Advisory Group and the Military Advisor to the Director RAW.

Though the RAW is primarily intended for collecting intelligence beyond India's national borders, it has over time come to have a strong presence in all fields of intelligence gathering. The RAW was brought into internal security issues during the Sikkim situation, it played a role in the events of the emergency of 1977-79, it was asked to operate in Punjab to counter-balance the presence of the ISI (and so also in Kashmir), and the RAW has provided the security for the India's nuclear program. Right from its formation in 18 September, 1968, R N Kao, the founding father of RAW, picked up the best men from within government and from outside for RAW. A combination of military, academicians, bureaucrats and policemen was a fine start for RAW which modelled itself on the lines of CIA.

INDIA NEEDS NATIONAL COUNTER TERRORISM CENTRE (NCTC)

State governments ruled by non-Congress party opposed the formation of the National Counter Terrorism Centre (NCTC) due to the apprehension of dominant authority and unilateral action of centre over states using the agency would challenge their authority. Consequently, Indian Government has planned to draft a more transparent and accountable proposal of NCTC to pacify the opposition, that the NCTC is kept out of Intelligence Bureau (IB) and states be given major role in counterterrorism activities.

The formation of NCTC is highly justified to coordinate counterterrorism efforts all the way through a vast country like India. Counterterrorism is shared responsibility of centre and states as terrorists do not distinguish between boundaries of states. As a nodal agency NCTC would operate closely with other law enforcement and investigating agencies and also state governments in seeking to counter terrorism threats from the neighbouring countries primarily from Pakistan and Bangladesh based terrorist groups; countering home grown Islamic extremists; internecine and separatist threats from north eastern states; threats from Maoist insurgency and last but not the least, nascent vigilantism from fringe Hindu groups. To undermine the ideological motivation, operational and strategic capabilities of terrorist groups, coordination between state and central agencies are very important. States have no such capacity and capability to weaken and destabilize the terrorist networks and their logistic lines within India. States are not also able to handle the terror activities with their imperfect and inadequate security infrastructure and of course with inherent lack of political will. For that reason NCTC is crucial and key to prevent perplexity and disorder concerning intelligence efforts, and also to ensure that it would be a focal point where intelligence is analyzed and draws operational conclusions.

The worth and significance of NCTC stems from three main drivers – gathering and analyzing the intelligence; coordinating the different intelligence and other security agencies and carrying out operations. The role of NCTC in gathering intelligence is the central and decisive in combating terrorism in India. The NCTC would play a key role in pr-emption and disruption of terrorist activity; in post-incident investigations; and its inputs to shielding and defensive security measures. Consequently, NCTC would get outlook – to identify those engaged in terrorism at all levels of involvement; to reveal their hide outs and resources of recruitment; tracking their weapons and channels of supply; to discover their methods for funding terrorism; warn against future attacks and thus prevent them; manage crisis situations by transmitting the information decision makers require; provide information necessary to carry out counterterrorism actions; disrupt terrorist organization's communication networks.

Coordination between intelligence agencies and security forces is a key to counter terrorism. According to counterterrorism experts, the plan's success relies not only on the type of intelligence obtained it's quality, but also on effective circulation in the shortest time possible among all agencies involved. Accordingly, NCTC has to come forward as an accommodating, supportive and centralized organization to allow for efficient and expeditious collection, analysis and dissemination of information regarding terror threats and terror activities to all the intelligence agencies and security forces involved. For this purpose the NCTC ought to be tasked with collecting intelligence in real time, to optimize intelligence flow and to coordinate between different agencies like the Research and Analysis Wing (RAW), Intelligence Bureau (IB), Defence Intelligence Agency (DIA), Department of Revenue Intelligence (DRI), National Information Grid (NATGRID), National Technical Research Organization (NTRO), etc. intelligence agencies of states and union territories and security forces involved in field operations.

The NCTC was granted the power to call for the services of the National Security Guard (NSG) or any other Central special forces. The new proposal envisages that state governments would also be able to apply for not only NSG, but also the Marine Commandos of the Navy, Para Commandos of the Army, Garud of the Air Force as well as the Special Frontier Force under RAW. However, it would be the most responsive, insightful and complicated ingredient of NCTC is to create an operations wing of its own, because without such operations division, NCTC would be fragmentary and incomplete. The operations division should develop elite special force similar to SEALS of United States (US) or *Sayeret Matkal* of Israel.

The operational methods to counter the terror threats NCTC must be investigating including collecting, collating, analyzing and assessing secret intelligence pertinent to the threat; stand-in to countering the threats, keeping the central and states governments and other important agencies informed about the threats; advising on the correct countermeasures, including protective security; and assisting: supporting other agencies and state governments. As far as investigation is concerned National Investigation Agency (NIA) would have to be brought under the overall control of NCTC.

NCTC certainly needs charismatic and dynamic leadership both at executive and political level. Indian Government should focus on revamping the counterterrorism architecture by making the NCTC an independent institution with executive powers working under the direction of an honest and robust executive, accountable to the country on all matters relating to internal security, whether from a military or police service must be one who has impeccable professional credentials and the capability to oversee intelligence, investigation and operations. In order to be accountable to Parliament, it would be coherent and rational to place the NCTC under a new Ministry of Internal Security, by appointing a highly qualified professional with vast experience in security related matters to direct and coordinate counterterrorism efforts.

The NCTC will integrate and explore intelligence pertaining to terrorism; track or direct other agencies to pursue the different leads; and coordinate with the existing agencies for an effective response. However, recognition and assurance of the human rights by the NCTC has been essential to keep population away from terrorists and their promises.

INDIAN SPY AGENCY: RAW - "RUSTED AND WASTED"

The once famous India's external intelligence agency - Research and Analysis Wing [RAW] has now become synonymous as dysfunctional and utterly incompetent. With no advance intelligence about China's designs, India was rather surprised by a Chinese full-fledged attack in 1962 [Thereby throwing Nehru's 'Hindi-Chini Bhai Bhai' slogan to dust], RAW was thus setup after the war to fix the gaping holes in its Intelligence gathering.

RAW was initially instrumental in some highly successful endevours envisaged by its founder R.N.Kao, over the years this agency also fell prey to Political mechanizations. RAW's heads are choose from IPS cadre from across the country - most of these would-be heads are in their final years of service. The current head of RAW Ashok Chaturvedi, is an IPS officer from Kerala, his tenure with RAW speaks volumes about RAW's ineptness in its handling of issues. Ashok Chaturvedi appointment itself is mired in controversy; he is related to a Cabinet secretary in the Central

Government who was know to have exerted recommendations to the Prime Minister's Office (PMO). The controversy does not end there, Chaturvedi in his retiring age mentality has single handedly brought RAW to its knees, with lack of Government will in cleaning up this agency, one controversy after other have surfaced in recent years.

1. The much publicized defection of a senior RAW agent, Rabinder Singh to USA, who is known to have left with several highly classified documents [He was most probably a CIA mole in RAW] continues to live grandly in his New Jersey home.
2. The utter Intelligence Failures or lack of Intelligence gathering operations in Pakistan and Bangladesh
3. Lack of Intelligence inputs from RAW with regard to the numerous terrorist attacks in India

One wonders why has an Intelligence agency created for the sole purpose of collecting external intelligence, counter-terrorism and covert operations has failed so miserably? Other questions that arise are:

Why cannot India act against its enemies who are causing death and mayhem on our soil?

Why cant the government clean up RAW - top to bottom and appoint younger generation from the Armed forces instead of appointing IPS candidates nearing retirement with no knowledge of external intelligence?

Why cant RAW indluge in Aggressive intelligence, in subversion and even sabotage against those who are directly responsible for causing innumerable deaths of Innocent people?

Why has RAW or for that matter the Government [Congress] has lost its Spine?

One simple example is the case of senior ULFA commanders staying in Dhaka hotels. It is by now a well known fact not only among Intelligence agencies but also ordinary populace that Paresh Barua the head of ULFA and his senior Terrorist commanders stay in Bangladesh and have made its Capital a nerve center for its operations in Assam, with a tacit approval from Bangladesh. Same goes with Dawood Ibrahim who is know to be staying in a posh bungalow in Karachi. What does RAW do, probably update the politicians in Delhi of what hotels they stay in, what they had for dinner etc. - That is where it all probably ends. And what do our politicians do? Nothing. Congress which is even reluctant to go against Illegal Bangladeshi immigrants and known terrorists in our country will never approve of covert operation in another country. And the outcome? A brazen terrorist organization which has grown stronger and stronger and its leader boldly issuing statements almost every month from his citadel in Dhaka. This is a NATIONAL SHAME. For its size India if not feared must at least be respected but in the present situation even countries like Bangladesh have taken us for granted.

If one reads about what Intelligence agencies of other countries facing a small percentile of our problems do then we are sure to be flabbergasted! Israel Mossad is dreaded by its enemies, Hezbollah leader for fear of Israeli missiles never has seen day light in years and moves every night to a different location for fear of assassination in HIS home country Lebanon. We hear of occasional bombs exploding under Terrorists or its sympathizers in Palestine or Syria - work of Mossad. Ofcourse Israel is an aberration with its radical mentality. But how about USA? The grand old democratic country with its list of Human rights and Geneva conventions upholder status - It also has secretly authorized attacks in ANY country that it deems dangerous. A Recent article in New York Times says that "The United States military since 2004 has used broad, secret authority to carry out nearly a dozen previously undisclosed attacks against Al Qaeda and other militants in Syria, Pakistan and elsewhere, according to senior American officials"

I wonder has the RAW chief had at any time even noticed that USA has reached out to the other end of the world in dealing a death blow to "Suspected" Terrorists - when Chaturvedi cannot even sanction a reprisal against known and well trenched terrorists in our own backyard - Bangladesh. Its time to act, to get rid of the RUST and WASTE that has piled on RAW, to make it shiny and dreadful once more, otherwise India will face an unprecedented level of attacks both from within and without its borders.

"NATIONAL SECURITY" FOR WHOM?

A secret Intelligence Bureau (IB) report (perhaps officially leaked) on the anti-development impact of non-governmental organisations (NGO) activities in India has come into the public domain and was debated extensively by the media. This has been quickly followed by the ugly role played by the IB in scuttling, no doubt at the behest of the government, the appointment of Gopal Subramaniam to the Supreme Court, a report again perhaps officially leaked.

Neither the IB nor the Research and Analysis Wing (RAW) or the other intelligence agencies in India have a clearly established and credible accountability mechanism. The IB lacks a proper legal framework and charter of duties. This led to many abuses during the Emergency (1975-77), which were exposed by the Shah Commission set up by the Janata Party government in 1977 after the electoral defeat of the Congress party. Abuses by the police were also exposed in the reports of the Commission. The Janata government set up the National Police Commission (1979-81) for police reforms and the LP Singh Committee (1981) for reforms of the IB and the Central Bureau of Investigation (CBI). However, the return to power by the Congress party in the elections of 1980 prevented the implementation of the recommendations.

What is "national security"?

The concept of "national security", uncritically used by the IB in its classified reports on various subjects, needs to be defined properly. The IB, a secret intelligence agency headed by generalist officers of the Indian Police Service (IPS), often strays into subjects without the required expertise.

The economic impact of NGO activities in the country are best examined by the concerned ministries such as the Ministry of Home Affairs, Ministry of Environment and Forests (MoEF) or by the Planning Commission. The report and recommendations of the committees set up by these ministries need not be classified. The 2008 Experts Group Report on "Development Challenges in Extremist Affected Areas" report published by the Planning Commission, dealing with Maoist violence in central India, was not a classified report and is available to the general public. However this report has been largely ignored by the MHA, in favour of a classified IB report characterising the Maoist violence as the "biggest internal security threat" in India. Based on the latter report, the MHA undertook massive deployment of central paramilitary forces in tribal India with far-reaching deleterious consequences.

History and development of the IB

Historically, the origins of the IB go back to the Thugee and Dakaiti (T&D) Department set up by William Sleeman in 1835 in the government of India. In 1887, two years after the formation of the Indian National Congress, the department was given the additional duty of collecting "secret and political" intelligence in a branch known as Central Special Branch (CSB). The IB of today is the natural development from the new and expanded functions of the T&D Department. The CSB collected, collated and interpreted intelligence gathered by Provincial Special Branches set up the same year in the provincial police headquarters. In 1920 for the first time the CSB was renamed the IB whose functions were briefly spelt out under Section 40(2) of the Government of India Act, 1919. On this basis in 1924, the IB was asked to work on matters related to the security of India and report directly to the governor-general. The Rowlatt Act of 1919 was based on the evidence marshalled by the Bengal and central units of the Special Branch. In 1935, Central Intelligence Officers (CIOs) were placed in selected provinces under the IB. In 1945, it was clarified that the IB was the intelligence agency of the government of India in the security field; that it exercised no police powers; and that its powers were vested in the director appointed by the governor-general who had special areas of authority under the Government of India Act 1935. When the Constitution of India 1950 came into force, the secret files of the central and provincial IBs were destroyed or sent abroad.

The director of the IB under Jawaharlal Nehru (1950-64), B N Mullik played a key role in the preventive detention of Sheikh Abdullah (1953); the deployment of the army in Nagaland (1955); the "forward policy" in the India-China border (1959); and the dismissal of the communist government in Kerala (1959). The role of the IB in these and other matters was graphically described by Mullik himself in his three-volume autobiographical account published in the 1970s described as the "most indiscreet memoirs" ever written by an intelligence official. The role of the IB in political developments under Indira Gandhi and after was colourfully brought out in 2005 in a book by M K Dhar, another top IB official. A later and more insightful book on the workings of the RAW was produced in 2007 by a senior official B Raman.

As a secret police organisation functioning in today's India, the work of the IB should be limited to police subjects such as terrorism, sabotage, subversion, espionage, counterintelligence and other law and order matters. It should avoid subjects such as economic consequences of NGO activities. Further, over-classification is one of the major problems of the IB, which led the former Home Secretary L P Singh to set up the R&P Division in the ministry to write independent reports. One of its earliest reports on Maoist violence was termed "Causes and Nature of Agrarian Tensions" (1969).The division fell on bad days after the departure of Singh and was eventually wound up depriving the ministry of vital policy inputs. The ministry earlier also dealt with the development and protection of scheduled castes and tribes, among other subjects. The ministry appears today to have deteriorated into an essentially paramilitary outfit.

The L P Singh Committee report (1981) recommended a charter of duties for the IB whose overall task was said to be to collect, collate and disseminate intelligence having a bearing on "national security", the security of the state and the protection of the Constitution. Its main activities were to include protection of the sovereignty and integrity of India from espionage, sabotage and subversion; prevent subversion of the loyalty of public servants; report on inter-state tensions, activities inimical to friendly relations with foreign states and so on. The committee's report failed to clearly specify the meaning of the concept of national security, which is now the need of the hour. Some senior intelligence officials erroneously argue that their work relating to loosely defined national security need not be bound by the Constitution of India.

They have even defended the extrajudicial executions of Ishrat Jahan and others by the Gujarat police. The CBI is investigating the case under the supervision of the Supreme Court.

Appointment of Gopal Subramaniam

In the case of Gopal Subramaniam's appointment to the Supreme Court, it is important to remember that there is an established procedure in India whereby "inputs" are obtained on a regular basis from IB/Central Bureau of Investigation about the prospective candidates for appointment as judges of the Supreme Court. This was perhaps part of the practice in British India in order to keep nationalist political influences out of the Indian judiciary at that time. The procedure is institutionalised in the MHA via a joint secretary who deals with judicial matters and coordinates with the Supreme Court.

This procedure has revealed its ugly features in the case of Gopal Subramaniam selected by the Supreme Court collegium for appointment as a judge. The government of India claims that Subramaniam's relations with lobbyist Niira Radia and his actions in connection with the 2G investigations were the factors behind their disinclination to go along with the Supreme Court collegium's preferred option. On the contrary Subramaniam himself claims that his role as amicus curiae in the Sohrabuddin fake encounter case in Gujarat and the resulting Supreme Court order preventing the BJP leader Amit Shah from entering his home state were the real political reasons behind the government's reluctance to approve his appointment. This is a first rate political controversy.

The collegium of the Supreme Court which selected Subramaniam for the post has remained intriguingly silent after the outbreak of the controversy. It was the Court itself, which had in the first place, appointed Subramaniam as amicus curiae in the Sohrabuddin case. It would therefore be appropriate for the Supreme Court collegium to stand up to the government and insist on having Subramaniam on the bench. This exhibition of weakness on their part affects the credibility of the highest court in the land.

MI5 – Secret service in the UK

A publication of the UK government (Her Majesty's Stationary Office, 1996) provides details of the activities of its secret service MI5 based on a clear and unambiguous legal framework, which includes a parliamentary oversight committee. The security service, as the MI5 is called, exists under the authority of the Home Secretary who answers to Parliament for the Service. The provisions of the Security Act 1989 were amended by the Intelligence Services Act 1994. The Director General of the MI5, appointed by the Home Secretary in consultation with the prime minister, is responsible for i) the ensuring the operations and efficiency of the service; ii) ensuring that it does nothing to further the interests of any political party; and iii) that it discloses information only in accordance with its functions; and iv) that it make an annual report to the prime minister and the Home Secretary. The internal mechanisms of the service are designed to ensure that i) the rule of law is paramount; ii) the methods of investigation must be proportionate to the threat; and iii) the more intrusive the means of investigation, the higher are the level of authorisation for its use.

The UK Intelligence Service Act (ISA) 1994 also established the Intelligence and Security Committee (or "Oversight Committee") to "examine the expenditure, administration and policy" of the Security Service, the Secret Intelligence Service (SIS) and the Government Communications Headquarters (GCHQ), The committee consists of nine members from both Houses of Parliament. The prime minister in consultation with the leader of the Opposition appoints the committee. No current minister can be a member. The committee's annual report is placed before Parliament subject to any exclusion on security grounds. The DG of the service has a statutory duty to provide the committee with any information required by it excluding "sensitive" information. The parliamentary oversight committee in the UK has worked well without damaging the operational secrecy of the intelligence agencies.

Way forward

In India in 1999, the National Security Council (NSC) system chaired by the prime minister was established. It includes the Strategic Policy Group (SPG) headed by the cabinet secretary; the National Security Advisory Board (NSAB) consisting of independent experts; and the National Security Council Secretariat (NSCS) responsible for evaluation of the performance of intelligence agencies. However there has been no significant change that has been implemented in the organisation itself.

The lack of professional autonomy within the IB is essentially the hand maiden of the ruling party of the day. It is a pity that the Supreme Court of India has not yet found a way of avoiding murky police enquiries, reminiscent of colonial-era practices, against its own fraternity and established independent procedures of selection of its judges on the basis of judicial lessons drawn from advanced countries such as the UK and US.

THE SAGA OF INDIA-ISRAEL INTELLIGENCE CO-OPERATION

In the present global world, intelligence co-operation has become a major pillar in bilateral relations of the states. History of intelligence sharing can be traced from the Second World War, when an intelligence alliance was established between Australia, Canada, New Zealand, UK, and USA, known as 'Five Eyes', all these countries were bound by "UKUSA agreement", a joint treaty of intelligence co-operation. A system administer of CIA Edward Snowden revealed that the NSA of the United States America shares raw intelligence with Israel. CIA's relationship with Jordanian intelligence agency mukhbarat is not hidden from the international community.

The common rising threat of global terrorism has created a strong strategic bond between India and Israel. India recognized the state of Israel in September 1950, but the history of their warm relationship starts from 1992, with the establishment of formal diplomatic relations with each other. Since the establishment of diplomatic relations, India and Israel have enlarged collaboration in defence and intelligence ventures. India has emerged as one of the biggest market for the arms export for Israel. It is providing India with most up-to-date weaponry such as surface-to-air missiles, sophisticated sensors to use in LOC areas of Jammu and Kashmir, remotely piloted drones and artillery. The common rising threat of global terrorism has created a strong strategic bond between the two. The robustness of India-Israel relations marked in the Israeli Prime Minister Benzamin Netanyahu's statement in a meeting with Indian Prime Minister Nerendra Modi on 29 September 2014 in New York, Netanyahu told Modi that "sky is the limit" as far as the prospects of India and Israel relationship goes. Israel's rapid response to India's request for military assistance during 1999 Kargil war increased Israel's trustworthiness as a dependable arms supplier and helped to strengthen the bilateral relationship.India's relations with Israel entered in a new era when Indian Prime minister invited Israeli Prime Minister Ariel Sharon on a three days visit to India in September 2003.

The Indo-Israeli rapprochement is not only limited to military equipments but moves further with intelligence sharing. Israel's highly developed spy satellite 'Polaris' was installed into space by an Indian space launch vehicle that would also permit India to use certain images from this satellite. Counter-terrorism and intelligence sharing are two significant field of India-Israel cooperation, according to Ashraf Javed intelligence agencies of the both of the countries have robustly followed close co-operation to achieve common strategic goals. In 1968 when the Research and Analysis Wing (Indian External Intelligence) established, Rameshwar Nath Kao was asked by Indira Gandhi to develop relationship with Mossad. A rediff story in 2003 covered that the RAW and Mossad are having secret military intelligence contact since 1960s, Israel was willing to help to the Indian army in its conflict with china and Pakistan. The relations between the two external intelligence agencies were an undisclosed saga until Morarji Desai came into power.

There is a lot to earn and more to learn for India from a very small country, who has managed to survive in the highly hostile atmosphere. Co-operation in the field of security no doubt will help to India in combating terrorism and saving the life of the civilians. After 9/11 attacks on USA, Israeli military and intelligence officials under the leadership National Security Advisor, Uzi Dayan met with their Indian counterpart to discuss the nations' common danger. Mumbai attack in 2008 paved a way to creation of a joint working group to fight against terrorism. Just after the attacks Israel offered India homeland security assistance and counter-terror capabilities, in response to this, Maharashtra government also sent a delegation to Israel. In December 2009 when Gen. Gabi Ashkenazi visited India to cement the military ties between the two nations. He promised that Israel will provide every help to India in fight against terrorism, which including intelligence sharing as well. In January 2010, Indian National Security Advisor M. K. Narayan held a meeting with his Israeli counterpart Uzi Arad, focus of this meeting was counterterrorism cooperation. In February 2014, India and Israel signed an agreement on Cooperation in Public and Homeland Security which also include intelligence sharing for Security of civilians.

The story moved further with the Israeli President Shimon Peres' visit to New Delhi last week, here he met with Indian Prime Minister Narendra Modi and briefly discussed about the various ways for co-operation to counter-terrorism, and other issues like infrastructure, water, agriculture, health, science, and technology. While talking about Counter-Terrorism, Mr. Peres said that "Terror is a common challenge to both Israel and India. We must fight those extremists who target innocent civilians in the name of religion". In October when National Security Advisor of Israel visited India, he also transmitted to his Indian colleagues about the Israel's willingness to expand co-operation in all fields and without any limits. The growing ties between India-Israel will be a positive move for India to utilize Israeli know- how in the field of military technology. There is a lot to earn and more to learn for India from a very small country, who has managed to survive in the highly hostile atmosphere. Co-operation in the field of security no doubt will help to India in combating terrorism and saving the life of the civilians.

INDIA'S INTELLIGENCE APPARATUS(RAW) CONDUCTS SECRET WARS AGAINST GEOPOLITICAL FOES

The doctrine of the Indian secret agency, Research and Analysis Wing (RAW) is based on the principle of waging continuous secret battles through its agents. Since its creation in 1968, RAW has assumed a significant status in formulation of Indian foreign policy.

While waging their secret battles, RAW's agents have their presence in almost all regional countries, implementing various tactics of psychological warfare. In this context, M. K Dhar in his book, "Open Secrets, India's Intelligence Unveiled" points out, "RAW's operations against the regional countries are conducted with great professional skill and expertise, which include the establishment of a huge network inside the target countries. It has used propaganda, political dissent, ethnic divisions, economic backwardness and criminal elements to foment subversion and terrorism to weaken these states in consonance with Indian regional ambitions." However, application of these nefarios designs vary from country to country as RAW's secret batlles in the following countries proves.

Sikkim was the easiest prey for RAW and India annexed it in mid-1970s. The King of Bhutan has been reduced to the nominal position by acting upon Indian dictates.

Under a well-orchestrated plan of RAW, on November 30 1988, 400 well-trained mercenaries infiltrated and stormed the capital of Maldives. Indian Prime Minister Rajiv Gandhi reacted promptly by sending about 1600 combat troops who flushed out the attackers from the streets. In this way, Maldives was totally brought under Indian influence.

Sri Lanka offers an unprecedented example of incursion by RAW's agents as violence kept on going in the country for a long time. In this regard, Jain Commission revealed that since 1981, RAW established 30 training bases in India for clandestine support to the Liberation Tigers of Tamil Elam (LTTE), some of whom were already on the payroll of this agency. In the recent past, Indian Prime Minister Manmohan Singh had told Sri Lankan President Mahinda Rajapaksa that rights and safety of the Tamil community in Sri Lanka should be upheld.

For many years, India has openly been meddling in Nepal's internal affairs by contriving internal strife through RAW in order to destabilize the successive governments and prop up puppet regimes. In 2001, RAW had played a key role in the massacre of nine members of the Royal family of Nepal, when the former King tried to drift away from Indian hold.

In the recent past, Indian-backed monarchy in Nepal was abolished after a long struggle of the Maoists who won the elections in April 2008. Now Nepal's leadership has forsaken India and has tilted towards China whom New Delhi considers its strategic rival in Asia. But despite the victory of the Maoists, Nepali Congress and the former had been unable to reach a deal on power-sharing. Availing the opportunity, RAW's agents who were well-penetrated in Nepali Congress and various government departments have been manipulating the situation so as to create lawlessness to bring Nepal back to Indian influence.

In the recent past, RAW-supported Tibetans in Nepal have held protests against China's rule over Tibet. In this regard, on March 10, 2008 when anti-government protests by Buddhist monks had erupted in Tibet, flaring in nearby provinces. Dalai Lama, the spiritual leader of Tibet who has lived in exile in India along with his 120,000 followers has been tacitly encouraged by RAW's secret warriors—enabling him to mobilize armed groups and international support to create instability in Tibetan regions of China.

As regards Bagladesh, surprisingly, RAW had also created insurgency force: The Shanti Bahini (Fighters for Peace). The agency has been involved in training rebels of Chakma tribes (Hindu and Buddhists tribesmen) and Shanti Bahini to carry out subversive activities in Bangladesh.

In August 17, 2005, RAW's elusive masterminds rocked various districts of Bangladesh with 370 explosions. Indian security agencies and media advised the central government to force Khaleda Zia to clamp down on Islamic fundamentalist outfits. A study of the post-blast behaviour of New Delhi indicated that those blasts were conducted by Indian intelligence agency, RAW to destablize a pro-China Bangladesh.

So far as Pakistan is concerned, the country has become a special target of RAW's secret battles. In this connection, fundamentalist Hindus give credit to Indira Gandhi who in the late 1970s gave RAW a new role to suit her Indira Doctrine specifically asking it to undertake covert operations in Pakistan. RAW mobilised all its resources by exploiting political turmoil in East Pakistan in 1971 which it had created through its agents. Nevertheless, its intrigues culminated in the dismemberment of Pakistan.

At present, New Delhi has established more than 200 foreign offices and training camps in Afghanistan where RAW's intelligence officials with the help of Khad and tactical support of CIA are doing their utmost to weaken Pakistan by sending weapons to the separatist elements in Balochistan and particularly to the insurgents of FATA regions. In Wakhan, a religious Madrassa of the Indian Muslim clerics is functioning under the patronage of RAW and Mossad. Very young boys including Afghans, recruits are mostly from Central Asia, bordering Afghanistan. Thus more than 20,000 ideologically motivated terrorists are intermittently being infiltrated into troubled spots of Pakistan. Posing as volunteers, they join the Taliban militants to fight against Pakistan's security forces. These miscreants also conducted a number of suicide attacks, bomb blasts and targeted killings in Pakistan, killing a number of innocent persons and personnel of the security forces. In Kurram Agency, RAW's Afghan agents were also actively involved in the sectarian conflict. However, their main plot is to create chaos in our country.

Even in Afghanistan, acting upon the old policy of divide and rule, it is owing to the tactics of RAW that Muslims are killing the Muslims either they belong to Afghan forces or Taliban.

The campaign of RAW's battles sharpens as violence takes some other dimensions in case of Kashmir. As regards the current phase of Indian state terrorism, it began on August 12, 2008 when Indian forces killed Hurriyat Conference leader Sheikh Abdul Aziz in the occupied Kashmir. At present, indefinite curfews, crackdowns and killings by the Indian security forces keep on going against the non-violent mass uprising of Kashmiris. More than 1000 innocent people have been killed by the Indian forces so far. Nevertheless, since 1989, Indian military troops backed by RAW's clandestine moves have been using all inhuman methods of ethnic cleansing to disturb the majority population of the

Kashmiris. In the recent years, hundreds of unidentified graves with at least 2000 bodies have been discovered in the Indian-held Kashmir. These Kashmiris were tortured to death by RAW.

One of the important roles of RAW is to thwart Sino-Pak strategic relations. In this context, fast growing economic power of China coupled with her rising strategic relationship with the Third World has irked the eyes of Americans and Indians. Owing to this jealousy, support of the US to India for a permanent seat in the U.N. Security Council and US-India nuclear agreement are part of American desire to make India a major power to counterbalance China in Asia.

Nevertheless, Beijing and Islamabad cannot neglect their common defence when their adversaries are following a covert strategy. In this respect, Pakistan and China have signed a number of agreements to enhance bilateral cooperation in diverse sectors including energy, telecommunication, trade and space technology. China also agreed to supply nuclear reactors to Pakistan.

China will also be able to use the Karakoram Highway and ports of Gwadar (which links C. Asia) and Karachi for transporting its goods to the Middle East and Africa.

It is mentionable that on April 18, 2008, Foreign Minister Shah Mehmood Qureshi had openly claimed that "some external forces were trying to weaken Pak-China strategic ties by creating misunderstandings."

Nonetheless, in New Delhi, it does not matter who is at the helm of affairs, policy of manipulation and subversion in neighbouring states through RAW's secret battles in order to extend Indian regional hegemony, continues unabated.

PAKISTAN, INDIA, AND THE SECRET WAR FOR AFGHANISTAN

The Soviet invasion of Afghanistan in 1979 and the Iranian Islamic Revolution of 1978 helped to re-shape the politics of the Greater Middle East. The latter created the concept of Shi'a political Islam, both within Iran and other parts of the Mideast with significant Shi'a population. In the meantime, the occupation of Afghanistan by the Red Army resulted in the emergence of political

Wahhabi Sunni jihadists – backed by the Central Intelligence Agency and Saudi Arabia, coordinated by the Inter-Services Intelligence of Pakistan. In a sense, these two political events lead to the rebirth of the centuries-old Shia-Sunni conflict, and they also reinvigorated Sunni political Islam, or pan-Islamism ideologies in the Muslim world. Iran has become the base for Shia political Islam and the Sunnis wanted to defeat the Soviet Army in Afghanistan in order to establish a base for Sunni political Islam in Afghanistan. This Wahhabi/Sunni dream became truth with the emergence of the Taliban movement from 1994 to 2001. However, The NATO-led invasion of Afghanistan in 2001, with the assistance of the Northern Alliance, has ended the dream – at least for now.

Without regard to what happens in the near future in Afghan politics, the government of Pakistan, with the help of the Inter-Services Intelligence (ISI), is committed to dominating Afghan politics and shaping it in a way that favors Pakistani interests. For instance, the Peshawar Seven formed in 1985 with the assistance of ISI and Saudi Arabia aimed to promote Islamist fundamentalism in Afghanistan.

This Peshawar Seven is a group of political parties within Afghanistan, all of which report back to ISI and seek its FINANCIAL and military assistance. It is important to understand that Pakistan was created in 1947 on the basis of Islam and not ethnicity. Thus, promoting Islamist ideology in neighbouring Afghanistan will balance the power of its long-term rival, India and also allow Pakistan to remain stable.

Pakistan also has a large Pashtun ethnic group and maintaining Afghanistan under a Pashtun leadership will deter nationalism sentiment among the Pakistani Pashtuns. Pakistan's involvement in Afghanistan aimed to create a safer border between both states and to integrate Pakistani Pashtuns in the Pakistani government. In other words, Pakistan sought to diminish Pashtun nationalism within Pakistan by giving them more political power in the Pakistani government and higher governmental positions.

Pakistan's interests in Afghanistan:

1. Limit and lessen India's sphere of influence in Kabul.

2. Keep India from establishing a closer relationship with Afghanistan, which could in the long run encircle Pakistan and weaken the Pakistani central government in Islamabad.
3. Promote and finance the Haqqani network and Taliban insurgents in Afghanistan to conduct attacks on Indian interests in Kabul. For instance, the Indian embassy in Kabul was attacked twice in 2008 and 2009 and the ISI was rumored to be behind the attacks.
4. Prevent Pashtun nationalism in Afghanistan, which could endanger Pakistani territorial integrity by promoting Pakistani disintegration along ethnic lines. For instance, a strong Afghan government under Pashtun leadership can re-claim the Durand line.
5. Establish economic relations with the oil-rich states of Central Asia by financing a government in Kabul that favors Pakistani interests.
6. Contain the neighbouring states from projecting their sphere of influence into Afghanistan.
7. 7Make sure Pakistan plays an important role in the Afghan peace process, particularly in any post-2014 negotiations with the Taliban. For instance, Pakistan supported the idea of creating a Taliban office in Qatar, Doha in-order to maintain the presence of Taliban in Afghan politics after the NATO withdrawal.

India's Perspective

The Indian government has been quite supportive of the NATO-led ISAF mission in Afghanistan, as foreign troops saved the country from becoming a safe haven for terror groups led by Islamabad against New Delhi. India seeks to work closely with its Afghan counterparts in reconstruction and economic development projects across the country. India wants Afghanistan to become economically prosperous and capable of limiting Pakistani influence in Afghan domestic affairs. It also wants to prevent the country from becoming a safe haven for Al-Qaeda and the Taliban once again. In October 2011, the Indian government signed a Strategic Partnership with the Afghan government. India agreed to train the Afghan National Army and Afghan National Police, INVEST massively in Afghan mining, energy, communications, and transportation sectors and provide an additional aid package of $500 million in reconstruction and development projects. India is an emerging economy along with the rest of the BRICS states; thus India needs to extract Afghan natural, mineral, and energy resources in order to drive its economic growth.

India's interests in Afghanistan:

1. Keep Afghanistan from being used as a base for Pakistan to train and coordinate terror attacks against Indian cities.
2. Weaken and limit Pakistani and Taliban/Pashtun influence over Afghan politics.
3. Establish a network to access oil-rich regions of Central Asia via Afghanistan for pipeline projects and assure energy security.
4. India is seeking great power status, thus the Indian government should foster its sphere of influence across South Asia to promote regional stability.
5. Maintain a certain level of political influence in Afghan politics.
6. Deliver FINANCIAL aid in order to maintain some sort of economic influence over the Afghan economy.

ENFORCEMENT AGENICES AND INVESTIGATIONS

As said in the preceding chapter; we all know that a legal system constitutes of a set of legal principles and norms which protect and promote a secure living to all subjects in a cultured and civilized society. Unlike animals; in the case of man, it is from his own very species that he faces the greatest threat to his life, limb and property. In primitive society indigenous groups of men devised their own methods of security from opposing groups of men. As the civilization advanced, these primitive devices proved powerless. Then came the legal system and the government into the scenario. It was legal system which recognized rights, prescribed duties and provided the ways and means of enforcing the same. It became the function of the government to provide security to the people which was to be provided by the ¯Police System. There is a machinery termed as the ¯Law Enforcing Machinery which is responsible for implementing various methods for enforcing law. ¯Law Enforcement Machinery implements the objective of secure living of citizens through ¯Law Enforcement Agencies which are the tools of ¯Law Enforcement Machinery. They prevent crime and maintain peace. The police system is one of the most important part of segment or ¯Law Enforcement Agencies.

Since man is a social being and in order to survive, he has to come into contact with other social beings. There may be matters of both kinds i.e. matters which are in his interest and ones which are not in his interest. Thus there begins the role of enforcement agencies. They are agencies which maintain harmony between the conflicting parties. These ¯Law Enforcement Agencies are of various forms.

Investigating agencies are one of them. Further a more particular term has been accredited to them known as Special Investigating Agencies. They are termed as Special Investigating Agencies because of the much complicated nature of tasks they perform.

Law enforcement in India is conducted by numerous law enforcement agencies. At the Union (federal) level, the agencies are part of the Union Ministry of Home Affairs and support the states in their duties. Since the federal nature of the

Constitution in India mandates law and order as a subject of State, the bulk of the policing lies with the respective states and territories of India. Cities which are very large also operate Metropolitan Police which is also under the State Govt. All senior police officers in the state police forces as well as those in federal agencies are members of Indian Police Services.39

Enforcement Agencies: Let us get into the depth of this concept ¯Enforcement Agencies and know the meaning of the word ¯Enforce. Enforce means:-

(a) To compel observance of or obedience to40
(b) To impose (a kind of behavior) e.g. to enforce military discipline

(c) To give force to; reinforce:

According to another source, enforce has the following meaning

(a) To put or keep in force;

(b) To impose (a course of action) upon a person

(c) To obtain (payment, obedience, etc.) by force or compulsion.

(d) To support (a demand claim, etc.) by force

(e) To impress or urge (an argument, contention etc.) forcibly; lay stress upon

In literal terms its means to bring into the working of any rule or law. In the same way ¯Enforcement means the act of enforcing or any control exerted by group action. Enforcement agencies means agencies which are responsible for insuring obedience to the laws.42 Enforcement agencies have the power given to them by the government in order to maintain its existence and to regulate the life of the people according to the constitution. No state can have existence which is divested of enforcement agencies. The role of enforcement agencies is quite similar to that of a public welfare body. One of the most important agency of enforcement agencies since ages have been the *police*. Police power has been utilized for their own selfish interest by the governmental machinery since times immemorial. The Britishers utilized the police power to control and suppress the revolutionary activities of the Indians and now after independence respective governments at the centre and in the States used the police power for their own interests Consistent interference by the government in day to day functioning of the police and other investigating agencies have become a matter of great concern. It is the general public who is affected the most by this ridiculous act of government.

Law enforcement agencies need to have a mission statement, it gives their officers the drive to protect country and the people in it. Law enforcement agencies are the backbone of a civilized society. Both law enforcement and crime prevention is principally intended to create an environment where a spontaneous law abiding disposition prevails amongst the citizens. To further prevent misuse of powers by the enforcement agencies, they are given powers only to prosecute and not to punish.

¯The Executive Committee on Indian Country Law enforcement improvements, created in response to a white house directive, has labeled the law enforcement problems in Indian country as ¯*Severe* and acknowledge that ¯the most glaring deficiency is a chronic lack of law enforcement resources.

Law enforcement agencies protect and promote fundamental rights and this is possible only when the nation has an efficient law enforcement machinery. It is only through proper enforcement of rules and laws, that an orderly civilized society can function. The quality and manner of law enforcement is often indicative of the quality of governance. It is aptly said that:-

¯The difference between the democracy and dictatorship is not in the laws but in the manner of enforcement of the laws *

In a democratic system laws have to be enforced not only firmly but also with due regard to the rights of the citizens. Effective law enforcement is possible only when there are trained and efficient keepers of the law, obliging the human rights norms. Law enforcement in India is conducted by numerous law enforcement agencies. Like many federal structures, the nature of the constitution of India mandates law and order as a subject of the state. Therefore the bulk of the policing lies with the respective states and territories of India. At the federal level, many agencies are part of the Union Ministry of Home Affairs and support the states in their duties. Larger cities also operate metropolitan police forces, under respective governments.

Types of Law Enforcement Agencies:

1. Local Law Enforcement Agencies: They have no jurisdiction outside the city where they are employed e.g. police force.
2. State Law Enforcement Agencies: They have jurisdiction in the entire state e.g. water police, marine and harbor control officers.
3. The Border Patrol: Enforces immigration laws and provides surveillance of the border states. Law enforcement is a broad term which encompasses any setup that is put in place to promote adherence to law in an organized manner by identifying and punishing people who violate the rules

and norms of the society. Enforcement agencies is more often referred to those govt. agencies which directly engage in patrolling or surveillance to detect and dissuade various criminal acts or investigate criminal cases and apprehended those who violate law.

Each nation has its own law enforcement agencies, and every state of that nation may have a law enforcement agency of its own. Similarly there can be more than one law enforcement agency within the nation or state which may be dealing with a specific type of crime such as economic offences, drug related crimes etc. It is important to note that law enforcement is just a part of the broad concept of policing and not the concept as a whole.

Some of the federal Law enforcement agencies which are under the Centre Government and are known as Central Agencies are:-

1. Central Bureau of Investigation (CBI)
2. Border Security Force (BSF)
3. Central Industrial Security Force
4. Central Reserve Police Force
5. Directorate of Revenue Intelligence
6. Indo-Tibetan Border Police (ITBP)
7. National Security Guards (NSG)
8. National Investigating Agency (NIA)
9. Railway Protection Force (RPF)
10. Special Protection Group
11. Seema Suraksha Bal
12. Narcotics Control Bureau (NCB)
13. National Central Bureau (Interpol), New Delhi.

Then comes the organizations under the centre government. They are:-

1. Bureau of Police Research & Development (BPR&D)
2. National Crime Records Bureau (NCRB)
3. Central Forensic Science Laboratory (CFSL)
4. National Institute of Forensic Sciences (NIFC)

Further the law enforcement agencies have been classified on the basis of security, intelligence / investigation and Armed Police Forces. Let us look into the classification based on security.

Internal Security:

1. Intelligence Bureau
2. Joint Intelligence Committee
3. Central Bureau of Investigation
4. Criminal Investigation Department
5. All India Radio Monitoring Service

External Security:

1. Research and Analysis Wing
2. National Technical Research Organisation
3. Radio Research Center
4. Electronics and Technical Services.

Based on intelligence, the law enforcement agencies are further classified into defence intelligence and Economic Intelligence.

Defence Intelligence:

1. Directorate of Military Intelligence
2. Defence of Intelligence Agency
3. Directorate of National Intelligence
4. Directorate of Air Intelligence
5. Image Processing and Analysis Centre
6. Directorate of Signals Intelligence
7. Joint Cipher Bureau.

Economic Intelligence:

1. Directorate of Revenue Intelligence
2. Economic Intelligence Council
3. Directorate of Income Tax Investigation
4. Narcotics Control Bureau
5. Central Economic Intelligence Bureau
6. Directorate of Economic Enforcement
7. Directorate of Anti-Evasion.

Based on the Armed Police Forces, the Classification is such as:-

Central Armed Police Forces:

1. Border Security Force (BSF)
2. Central Industrial Security Force (CISF)
3. Central Reserve Police Force (CRPF)
4. Indo Tibetan Border Police (ITBP)
5. National Security Guards (NSG)
6. Railway Protection Force (RPF)
7. Special Protection Group (SPG)
8. Sashashtra Seema Bal/ Armed Border Force.

The above mentioned are Central (Federal) Agencies

The State Police Consists of:

1. Organisation
2. Metropolitan Police
3. Traffice Police
4. State Armed Police Forces

The topic of our concern is investigation. The classification of Special Investigating Agencies is as below:-

Central Investigation and Intelligence Agencies:

1. Central Bureau of Investigation
2. National Investigating Agency
3. Central Vigilance Commission
4. National Central Bureau (Interpol) New Delhi.
5. Narcotics Control Bureau
6. Indian Income Tax Department (Investigation)
7. Directorate of Revenue Intelligence
8. Research and Analysis Wing
9. Enforcement Directorate.

Special Investigating Agencies:

1. CBI
2. NIA
3. National Central Bureau (Interpol) New Delhi
4. Research and Analysis Wing (RAW)
5. Enforcement Directorate

6. Directorate of income Tax (Investigation)

Sociology in Law Enforcement

The essential interaction between sociology and law enforcement is very necessary. Sociology is simply the study of society while law enforcement concerns the prevention of and struggle against crime within the same society. For effective law enforcement, the study of society may provide invaluable information. In order to eradicate the roots of crime, this information is essential. After all, by understanding why crime takes place within society, law enforcement agencies will be able to enhance their efforts to fight crime.

There is a branch of sociology referred to as the sociology of law, investigating the interaction of society with law. This sub discipline of the study of society may help law enforcement agencies to understand the effect that they have on society. From this we can gather that social change affects law enforcement. So, we can say that enforcement agencies need different laws at different times in order to curb crime. Same laws at different situations of crime are not helpful in fighting crime. A law enforced by enforcement agency in times of peace may not be sufficient at the times of revolution. Another important use of sociology to law enforcement agencies is the understanding that lead people to commit crime. By increasing their knowledge about, when and where crimes may happen, law enforcement agencies would naturally enhance their effectiveness. Sociology may thus guide law enforcement agencies would naturally enhance their effectiveness. Sociology may thus guide law enforcement agencies in their work.

Problems and Challenges Faced by Enforcement Agencies

Law enforcement officers are in our country's front line in the fight against crime and they perform a difficult and dangerous job with skill and dedication, but the nation's law enforcement officers constantly face extraordinary new challenges with limited resources. With the passage of time serious problems in law enforcement began to surface. ¯Prof. David Bayley has quoted.

¨In India, today a dual system of criminal justice has grown up- the one of law the other of politics

Law enforcement officers, throughout India have grown into the habit of appealing to political figures for remission from the sanctions of law.

David Bayley also observed that

¨The rule of law in modern India, the frame upon which justice hangs, has been undermined by the rule of politics. Supervision in the name of democracy has eroded the foundations upon which impartiality depends in a Criminal Justice System.

India has a federal system, established by the constitution and this poses as another problem for law enforcement. Since public order and police are State subjects but when the police poses as a failure, this issue is raised in the parliament. There are variations between the centre and state Government Judgements. As a result the enforcement officers find it difficult to satisfy both of them.

With the passage of time, there is escalation of crime and lawlessness. Main objective of effective law enforcement is to maintain peace and tranquility in the country so that people can pursue their vocations without having any fear of crime and lawlessness. With the passing of every decade, there is steady increase of crime. After war, crime is the biggest threat in modern societies.

Another very serious threat on the efficiency of law enforcement agencies is the *non registration of cases*. It has a very negative impact on law enforcement. The National Police Commission in its 4th Report stated that:

This malpractice of non registration arises from several factors, including the extraneous influences and corruption that operate in the system, besides the disinclination of the staff to take on additional load of investigational work in the midst of heavy pressure of several other duties. Among all such factors the most important one which, in our view, accounts for a substantial volume of crime going unregistered, is the anxiety of the political executive in the State Govt. to keep the recorded crime figures low so as to claim before the State Legislatures, the public and the press that crime is well controlled and is even going down as a result of efficient' police administration under their charge. The Chiefs of Police and other senior police officers also find it easy and convenient to toe the line of the Govt. in developing such a statistical approach for assessing the crime situation and evaluating police performance. As a consequence, this attitude permeates the entire hierarchy down the line and is reflected at the police stations in their reluctance and refusal to register cases as and when crimes are brought to their notice.

In a survey of police society relationship, it was revealed that from the starting of lodging a complaint in the police station, one has to take the help of a political person without which no complaint would be registered.

This survey makes it clear that how badly our enforcement officers are caught in the web of political people and other influential persons, thus making the conditions of working of law enforcement officers more than pathetic.

Another hindrance for effective law enforcement is *over proliferation* of laws. There are a vast number of old and outdated laws, cultured in our statute books. Even after committing a heinous crime a criminal is allowed to move out of prisons on paying a very nominal fees, thus the feeling of deterrence is totally missing in criminals. Enforcement agencies officers puts his day and night in order to curb crime and criminals, but to no avail. This hard work is eroded away when he sees the same criminal out of the bars after paying a nominal sum of rupees. It lowers down the morale of the enforcement officers, thus also lowering the efficiency of enforcement agencies.

Enforcing law is not just the job of a law enforcement agency but it is a whole way of a total commitment.

We need to understand that policing is not an easy job, it requires a lot of sacrifices as well as going out of way many a times to perform ones duty. Even if the enforcement officers try to change laws or the way things are done, they have to face the consequence of confronting the institutions which have made those laws. Doing the job of an enforcement officer is a challenging and sometimes a dangerous choice. Maintaining law and order is not catwalk as it requires 24x7 commitment and readiness from the officers.

Further the problems and challenges can be categorized into (a) technical (b) legal and (c) operational challenges.

Technical Challenges

These are technology related challenges which are faced by the law enforcement agencies. Where a hacker disrupts a traffic control at a local airport or a child pornographer sends computer files over the internet or when credit card numbers are stolen from a company engaged in e-commerce, investigators must locate the source of communication They have to trace the ¯electronic trail leading from the victim to the perpetrator in almost every case.

To succeed in identifying and tracing global communications, investigators have to work across border, not only with one's counterpart but also with industry to preserve critical evidence such as log files, emails etc. before it is altered or deleted. Besides, while less sophisticated cyber criminals may leave electronic ¯finger prints, more experienced criminals know how to conceal their tracks in cyber space.

Internet telephony, strong encryption and wireless and satellite communication and other technological advances have made it possible for international criminals and terrorist to target victims in unprecedented ways. One of the problems/challenges faced by enforcement agencies is the cyber crime.

The use of computers has grown exponentially during the last few years. Financially networks, communication systems, power stations, depend on computers. It is therefore not surprising that computer technology is involved in a growing number of crimes. These are generally taken to include theft of computer services, software piracy and the alteration and theft of electronically stored information, extortion committed with the help of computers, obtaining unauthorized access to record from banks, credit card issuers or customer reporting agencies, traffic in stolen passwords and transmission of destructive viruses or commands. With the physical growth of the internet over the past few years, a number of new generation crimes affecting the LAN, WAN and Internet such as theft of information piracy, forgery, counter feiting, dissemination of offensive materials, terrorism have also grown. Hacking computer, network breaches, copyright, piracy, software piracy, child pornography are some of the new terms in average criminal investigator's dictionary. Highly intelligent persons commit these new generation crimes leaving hardly any trace and making investigation highly difficult and complicated.

Computer crimes are now a matter of growing concern. Traditional barriers to crime faced by criminals are being obliterated by digital technologies. In a digital world, there are no state or international borders. Bits of information flow effortlessly around the globe. In the past the culprit had to be physically present to commit a crime. Robbing a bank or an armoured vehicle of cash would pose problems of transportation and storage whereas transfer of money poses no such problems in the digital world.

Cyber crimes have become a reality in India too. Law enforcement agencies today face a number of challenges in the investigation of such cases.

Legal Challenges

Deterring and punishing computer criminals requires a legal structure that will support detection and prosecution of offenders. Yet the laws defining computer offences and the legal tools needed to investigate criminals using the internet, often lag behind social and technological changes, creating legal challenges to law enforcement agencies.

In India, however the I.T. Act 2000 has been enacted in pursuance to the General Assembly of United Nations resolution A/RES/51/162 dated the 30th Jan 1997. The I.T. Act 2000 elaborates upon digital signature, electronic governance attribution, acknowledge and dispatch of electronic records, secure electronic records etc. It specifies that Electronic Signatures will be valid and legally enforceable only if the e-transactions is done through ¯public key cryptography the Act delineates two separate types of penal provisions : contraventions and information technology offences. While contravention results in monetary penalty, I.T. Offences result in the offender being imprisoned or fined or both.

Amendments have also been made to the IPC, Indian Evidence Act the Banker's Book Evidence Act and R.B.I. Act to facilitate investigation and prosecution of cyber crime.

Operational Challenges

There is need to have high tech crime units that respond to quick investigation and assist law enforcement agencies faced with computer crimes. The police have to be made cyber sensitive by imparting adequate training.

The investigation of computer crime requires a team effort of police, forensic scientists, lawyers and programmers or system administrators. Police may not know much about computers and thus not know what evidence to look for. Whereas programmers may know a great deal about computers, networks and how they work, but may not know about legal procedural requirements regarding the presentation of evidence.

Forensic scientists may know how to deal with evidence but like the police, may not know what to look for when dealing with digital evidence or how to apply real world forensic methods to it. But now since cyber crimes re increasing, the police and law enforcement agencies have to learn how to handle digital evidence, use it to generate investigative leads and to know when to call in an expert for assistance.

Even the lawyers have to learn to dig up digital evidence, defend it against common arguments and determine whether it is admissible or not. Even forensic scientists have to become intimately familiar with every aspect of digital evidence so that they can process it to support an investigation.

The Central Bureau of Investigation (CBI) has recently created a cyber crime research and development unit which maintains close liaison with international agencies like the Federal Bureau of Investigation (FBI), Interpol and other foreign police agencies to share skills and techniques in investigating cyber crimes. The officers of the Central Bureau of Investigation (CBI) associated in this exercise share their expertise with the state police forces through regional training programmes held periodically.

Concept of Investigation in Law Enforcement Agencies

A complex society faces an increasing array of crime and loss issues. Theft, fraud, terrorism and accidents must all be investigated. Investigation is a complex undertaking. Investigation can be defined quite simply as a *systematic fact finding and reporting process*. It is derived from the Latin Word *Vestigere,* to ¯track or trace, and encompasses a patient, step-by-step inquiry. Investigation is finding facts; it is akin to research conducted in the academic arena. It is a multi-disciplined field of study. It encompasses the law, the sciences, communications and a host of other things. It requires an inquisitive mind coupled with an attention to detail. As we know that on account of the fact, in most cases, the police do both the duties of being a specialist and investigating crimes, which makes it difficult for the police to handle different cases with perfection Usually the police has less time for routine investigation work. Here the question arises, what is Investigation?

Investigation is basically ¯an art of unearthing hidden facts with the purpose of linking up of different pieces of evidence for successful prosecution. Investigation requires specialization and professionalism of a type not yet fully achieved by the police agencies.

For the very reason Malimath Committee referred to the 154th report of the Law Commission which recommended separation of investigation agency from the law and order wing for the following reasons:-

1. It will bring investigation agencies under the protection of judiciary and reduce external influences.
2. It will reduce the possibility of unjustified and unwarranted prosecution.
3. It will result in speedier investigations and disposal of cases.
4. It will increase the expertise of investigation officers.
5. Investigating police in plain clothes will have greater rapport with police.

The word ¯Investigation has been defined in Criminal Procedure Code (Criminal Procedure Code (Cr.P.C.) all the proceedings under this code for the collection of evidence conducted by a police officer or by any person (other than a Magistrate) who is authorized by a Magistrate in this behalf. It primarily consists of verification of facts and circumstances of the case after the First Information Report (FIR) is registered, though the law nowhere says that investigation cannot be started till a formal First Information Report FIR is drawn up. Indeed an investigation is a question of fact and can start even before registration of a First Information Report FIR. Whenever a serious crime is committed public expect prompt results. Prompt and speedy investigation can be done only by identifying the specific areas of investigation.

Thus for a successful investigation of cases, one has to concentrate on three specific areas of investigation i.e.

1. Collection of incriminating and relevant material from the scene of offence and from other places.
2. Collection of intelligence/information through the process of interview/interrogation.
3. Careful and meticulous documentation undertaken with an eye on the court process.

While taking up the investigation time has to be spent on planning and coordination in the different aspects of the investigation. It must be well planned and coordinated.

Definition of investigation:

1. The act or process of investigating or the condition of begin investigated.
2. A searching inquiry for ascertaining facts, detailed or careful examinations.
3. An investigation is a systematic minute and thorough attempt to learn the facts about something complex or hidden, it is often formal and official. Some synonyms for investigation are:-
4. Scrutiny, exploration examination, inquiry, research. According to the

Thesaurus Investigation means:

(a) An inquiry into unfamiliar or questionable activities

(b) The work of inquiring into something thoroughly and systematically. All these terms express the idea of an active effort to find out something.

An examination is an orderly attempt to obtain information about or to make a test of something often something presented for observation. For example a physical examination. An inquiry is an investigation made by asking questions rather than by inspection or a study of available evidence. A research is careful and sustained investigation.

Extensive definition of Investigation

It is the process of inquiring into a matter through research follow up, study or formal procedure of discovery. The term may refer to any of the following:

- Academic or intellectual investigation aimed at discovering, interpreting of knowledge.
- Private investigation undertaken by a private investigator or a detective.
- Investigation carried under official authority by law enforcement personnel.

Kinds of Investigation

Investigation is a process of conducting research, discovery, study, observation into any matter to find facts. It helps people in gathering vital information required for specific purpose.

Investigations are a very important part of law enforcement. They are very helpful in curbing crime which is mushrooming at the speed of light. In order to make the society evil free and a place where the society can reside without the fear of any criminal activities, we need to make the investigation process effective and a complete success.

There are many kinds of investigations that become a part of the routine of an investigator. The first and the foremost are the Criminal Investigations beginning of the Criminal investigation is unknown, but there is reason to believe that it came into existence in a very rudimentary form with the origin of legal trials. Law has vested ample powers to the investigating agencies to carryout the investigations. Under the Chapter XII of the Criminal Procedure Code, the police has a statutory right to carry on an investigation. Further the functions of the police and the Judiciary are complimentary, and the combination of individual liberty with a due observation of law and order is only to be obtained by leaving each to exercise its own function. The policy of non interference in the investigation was well explained by the Primary Council in King Emperor Vs. Khawaja Nazir Ahmad in the following terminology:

...... just as it is essential that everyone accused of crime should have free access to the court of Justice\, so that he may be duly acquitted, if found not guilty of the offence of which he is charged, so it is of utmost importance that the Judiciary should not interfere with the police in matters which are within their province and into which law imposes on them the duty of inquiry....

On realizing the difficulties of the investigation agencies, the Law Commission in its report observed:

A report under section 173 of the Criminal Procedure Code (Cr.P.C.), is normally the end of an investigation, Sometimes, however the police officer after submitting the report, comes upon evidence bearing on the guilt or innocence of the accused.

We should heave thought that police officer can collect that evidence and send it, to the Magistrate concerned. It appears that the courts have sometimes taken narrow view that, once a final report has been submitted the police cannot touch the case again and reopen the investigation.

The Criminal Investigation is aims at looking for the techniques used by the criminals to commit a crime besides the grounds and the reasons. It also involves confirming the right criminals and victims through exploring and interrogating the witnesses.

By using various methods it is ensured that correct identification of a criminal is made who has committed an offence. The skilled and professional criminals have a tendency to follow a definite technique, committing the offence at certain types of place with specific style leaving behind a certain trademark. In such cases, the criminal investigation departments work on the basis of the accumulated data, and have ready access to such public records. Information flows in to the *Investigating Agencies* more or less continuously. Interrogation of suspects is one of the most important functions of Criminal Investigation. Investigators work either for the victim or for the defendant or his attorney in criminal proceedings. Serious crimes, which may lead to arrest and conviction of a subject are the sources of cases for the legal/ criminal investigator.

Investigations, here are related to different crimes. If an illegal action takes place, like murder, robbery, dacoit, homicide etc. then the police and legal investigators come in to action to find the facts behind the crime and to nab the criminals. Investigations in such cases goes on till the case is solved and the offender is caught and punished.

Let us try to analyse the meaning of criminal investigations. Criminal investigations is defined by a group of scholars as looking into police work, as the collection of information and evidence for identifying, apprehending and convicting suspected offenders.

A criminal investigation is the reconstruction of a past event. It is an official effort to uncover information about a crime. There are generally three ways that a person can be brought to justice for a criminal act.

The first way, which is probably the least likely, is that the individual confesses to his criminal act. Second, the officer of law can catch him in the act and the third way i.e. the last is the most common way i.e. a criminal investigation can identify him as a suspect, after which he may confess or be convicted by trial.

In most cases, when a crime is committed, the officials have two primary concerns. One is, they want to know who committed the crime and the other is what the motive was. The reason why a person breaks a law is called the motive.

It is not a must that the motive comes after identifying the perpetrator in a criminal investigation. Sometimes the motive is suspected or known and used to catch the criminal. This often happens in the crimes such as kidnapping and murders. Notes or other forms of evidence may be left that reveal why the crime has been committed. Criminal investigations are usually conducted by the police.

There are other official agencies that have the authority to investigate and launch criminal charges. In India C.B.I., i.e. Central Bureau of Investigation is the main agency for doing criminal investigations.

While in U.S.A. it is the Federal Bureau of investigation i.e. F.B.I. and the Internal Revenue Service (I.R.S.). Police and other officials may use a variety of methods to conduct criminal investigations. Various scientific techniques such as fingerprint and ballistics analysis are often used.

In U.S.A., sometimes the method of employing informants is used, which is quite a controversial investigation method. Many people disagree with this practice because these individuals are generally criminals who are looking to get out of trouble or to reduce their punishment. It is therefore argued that they can be influenced to say or do whatever will please those investigating the case.

There are some parts of a criminal investigation that police may not be able to handle. It is because some cases require investigation techniques that demand specialized knowledge or training that the investigators may not have.

This means that the police may have to employ others to help them. This is especially true with deoxyribonucleic acid (DNA) testing. Although this technique is popular, it is often performed by third parties.

A criminal investigation does not always yield results. Sometimes suspects are accused only for it to be determined later that they are not guilty. At other times, an extensive criminal investigation may not produce any suspects. This can mean that no one will be punished for the crime that was committed.

Civil Investigations

These type of investigations involve law suits in which questions of money or property are to be settled. Violations of law are usually not included. A civil investigation is an investigation related to a civil matter. A civil matter is a court action (or pending court action) that is not criminal in nature. Let me cite an example for this.

An investigation related to the care of a child is a civil investigation if the opposing parent is trying to prove that their ex-spouse is not taking good care of the child.

A civil investigation helps uncover and assemble the information needed for a civil trial. A civil trial is the opposite of a criminal trial. In most cases, this type of court case involves two individuals who are arguing about an issue that relates to their rights as citizens. A civil investigation can help, gather the evidence that is essential to such a trial. A civil investigation usually begins with an analysis.

There are many kinds of civil investigations, with some of the more common ones being:-

- Missing person investigations.
- Child custody and child abuse investigations.
- Marital investigations
- Workers compensation investigations
- Personal injury investigations
- Domestic abuse investigations
- Back ground checks.

Apart from criminal and civil investigations, there are two other types of investigations, which are very important. Lately their influence on society and need for the society have grown at a rapid rate. They are background investigation and an undercover investigation.

Background Investigation

It is a kind of civil investigation. It depends on the level of the background. Back Ground investigation can consist of looking into somebody's credit to see if they are the kind of person that is irresponsible, their driving record, to criminal history, if they have been arrested or been prosecuted for crimes. The goal is to find the truth. Any person who is interested or been prosecuted for crimes. The goal is to find the truth. Any person who is interested in the other person, with whom he wants any kind of investment can go for such background investigation. It splits the chaff from the grains i.e. takes out the real truth of the person being investigated.

Undercover investigation

This is an important form of investigation. An undercover investigation is specifically to inject yourself into the particular entity you are investigating.

An undercover investigation is conducted by injecting yourself into that situation. The goal of an undercover investigation is to gather information as truthfully as possible.

Observation is a critical technique used in undercover investigation. The key thing is that you have to observe the situation without others knowing that you are investigating. This is called Subrosa Investigation. A subrosa is an old Latin term meaning under the nose.

Elements Of Effective Investigation

Since the primary job of a researcher is to investigate, so to that end a researcher usually collects and analysis data and draws conclusions. Long time ago, the researchers were not trained, infact they lacked the basic techniques related to date collection and analysis. In order, that the Special Investigating Agencies conduct effective and objective investigation, the investigators need to keep some points in their minds for conducting good investigation.

Elements of effective investigation

The first and the foremost thing, for an effective investigation is that the person investigating should have creative thinking. By creative thinking, we mean that the investigator should think in a way that the other people do not. Creative thinking helps an investigator come up with better results and get to them faster.

(i) Creative thinking cannot be taught, infact it is inborn but can be learnt to a great extent. Though the creativity of a person can be brought out by explaining him examples of other creative solutions. The second thing which an effective investigation should have is:-

(ii) Knowledge of data analysis and statistics: This is a very crucial part of any effective and objective investigation. Without this knowledge there is no objectivity and for sure no efficiency. We need to distinguish between the three things and also know how to integrate them in order to have an effective investigation. What is Statistical Thinking? Statistical thinking simply means understanding variability and knowing how to deal with it. It is a mode of thinking that includes both logical and analytical reasoning. It evaluates the whole of a problem as well as its component parts and attempts to assess the effects on the whole of changing one or more variables and it attempts to understand not only problems and solutions but the process involved. Some experts define statistical thinking to include skills of problem identification, process reasoning, questioning of premises, conclusions and data, problem solving and explanation of the problem, the solution and the processes involved.

Statistical thinking is a philosophy of learning and action based on the following fundamental principles;-

- All work occurs in a system of interconnected processes.
- Variation exists in all processes and
- Understanding and reducing variation are keys to success.

Coming to data analysis, as the name implies, it means when we have obtained a set of data and need to bring out the information hidden in it. It is a process of inspecting, cleaning, transforming and modeling data with the goal of highlighting useful information, suggesting conclusions and supporting decision making.

Data analysis has multiple facets and approaches, encompassing diverse techniques under a variety of names, in different business, science and social science domains.

Let me simplify it, it is the process of evaluating data using analytical and logical reasoning to examine each component of the data provided. Then comes statistical analysis data analysis. It is the collection, enumeration, summarization, manipulation and interpretation of quantitative data to discover its underlying casus, patterns, relationships and trends. Some basic knowledge of the statistical theory behind these methods is definitely useful.

The third important constituent of an effective investigation is:

Knowledge of the subject matter

It is equally important in investigation. It is the guiding light that helps the investigator know how to define the problem, what to experiment on, what data to collect, what to expect and how to make sense of the data analysis results. The more the investigator knows about the subject matter the faster and more economically too they get to the results. One implication is that the less knowledge of subject matter in research, the more time, money and resources are allocated to the problem. In any study, the design of data collection should start with the knowledge of subject matter and end with drawing conclusions, that too guided by the knowledge of subject matter.

Last but not the least the Fourth Constituent of an effective investigation is the Basic Skills. Basic skills are those that help any person in all aspects of life, work or personal needs. What is considered as a basic skill varies with problem, job, place and is changing with time also.

Let me cite an example. The ability to communicate is a very important skill in many U.S., Industries.

Many years ago it was essential for an engineer to know how to work with a slide rule. Today the same engineer need to be versed in a variety of computer packages and know how to use internet. Basic knowledge of any subject is considered as basic skills, depending on the person where a person is conducting on the research. Thus these elements are a must for an effective investigation.

Suggestins For Enforcement Agencies

We know that law enforcement agency is an agency responsible for insuring obedience to the laws, ACC to Webster's Dictionary.

Whether the law enforcement agencies are a friend or foe is entirely a matter of faith. Undeniably, the police and other law enforcement agencies have garnered a bad reputation as is evidenced by any news report or survey.

However low a main sinks he never reaches the level of the police "Quetin crisp. This means, unfortunately, the general public has lost faith in the enforcement agencies. They are looked at as corrupt, bribe taking, lackadaisical, insensitive and inefficient. The enforcement agencies often claim that the portrayal is exaggerated, but the truth is that instances of apathy exist and the faith of the public remains shaken and this makes us mistrust our law enforcement agencies and shy away from reporting or aiding them.

Some suggestions for the enforcement agencies are cited below, in order to win back the faith of the general public.

1. It is the foremost duty of the enforcement agencies to lodge an First Information Report (FIR). The police should never be reluctant to do so in a genuine case.
2. The cases which relate to women's special rights and offences pertaining thereto should be handled with a very high level of sensitivity.
3. The police should publish literature regarding various rights of the individual and related procedure for their curbing.
4. The police can venture into other avenues, like targeting specific crime and launching schemes to tackle them which involves interaction with the community of potential victims.
5. Investigations should not be lackadaisical. They should be sharp, precise and effective.
6. The number of all women police stations should be increased with documentation being made easy and quick.
7. Trials in cases involving the dignity of women should be handled with care and sensitivity.
8. The police should abandon the habit of always being late on the scene.

9. Establishment of Fast Track Courts should be given significant encouragement to ensure negative gratification for criminals in the form of sentences.
10. Last but not the least, for effective investigation by the enforcement agencies, scientific ways of investigation are very necessary, Hence, modern scientific ways of investigation of crimes are very much necessary in order to make progress in the working of investigation agencies.

The suggestions of the National Anti Corruption Strategy Draft should be looked into and should also be implemented.

10

R&AW Operates as an Invisible Force in Nepali Politics

To be released tomorrow in Delhi, Prashant Jha's book 'Battles of The New Republic: A Contemporary History of Nepal' tells the story of the country's transition from war to peace, monarchy to republic, a Hindu kingdom to a secular state. This extract details how India Research and Analysis Wing plays a critical role in Kathmandu politics.

2003-05: I asked a former RAW [Research and Analysis Wing, India's overseas intelligence organisation] official, who was well acquainted with Nepal's affairs and even served as the organization's head at one point, about India's initial engagement with the Maoists. Sitting on the top floor of one of Delhi's premium hotels, he said, 'My organization's engagement with the Maoists began in 2003. It was also the time when they were in talks with the king's nominated government back in Nepal.' But didn't declaring the rebel group as terrorists and supporting Nepal's security forces, yet keeping channels of communication open with the Maoists and allowing the top leaders to stay in India, reflect conflicting objectives at best and devious intent at worst? The Palace, generals of the army, and a dominant section of the NC [Nepali Congress party] saw Indian 'doublespeak' as the primary reason for the Maoists' success, and blamed Delhi for covertly supporting the rebels. The former intelligence official responded,

'This is not true at all. We had links, we had communication. But that is the nature of intelligence organizations. We keep in touch with the enemy and we establish channels so that if at any point, our policy-makers shift tracks, there is a pathway to implement it.'

He may have been right, about agencies developing ties and relationships with actors across the ideological and political spectrum. But there was surely more to it if the engagement was happening with a group that was supposedly hostile to India's interests. Analysts have long pondered the connection between India and the Maoists.

It was also a time when everyone was talking to everyone else in Nepal. The RAW official I spoke to emphasized this point and argued that India could not be behind the curve. 'We knew the Palace and Maoists had been in touch in the early years of the war and still retained contact through intermediaries. We knew that both factions in the NC — Sher Bahadur Deuba and Koirala — kept channels open with the Maoists. We knew that various Left leaders had met Maoists in India. We had consistently asked all parties and the Palace to work together against the Maoists, but they just did not understand the gravity of the situation. It was clear to us that, eventually, a political solution would need to be found. In statecraft, you build up leverage when you can.'

Those who were then serving in the Indian establishment take great pains to emphasize that being in touch could not be construed as support. And as proof, they point to how several Maoist leaders were arrested in India during that period. C. P. Gajurel 'Gaurav' was picked up in Chennai when he was travelling on a fake passport to England. The party's ideologue, and Prachanda's political guru, Mohan Vaidya 'Kiran', was arrested in Siliguri. The Maoist leader from the Madhes, Matrika Yadav, was arrested and handed over to Nepal. (Yadav's arrest seems to have been a result of a difference in outlook between the IB [India's Intelligence Bureau] and RAW. The RNA [Royal Nepalese Army] had passed on information about Yadav to an IB official who was visiting Nepal with an Indian minister's entourage; and a RAW functionary once mentioned to me how IB had 'messed up' by arresting a key source.) Upendra Yadav, who was known to be close to the Maoists, though his exact relationship with the party remained ambiguous, was picked up, but then mysteriously let off. Suresh Ale Magar, the ethnic theorist for the Maoist party, was arrested and so were Ram Karki, who had served as an important link of the party with India's radical movements, and Bamdev Chhetri. Cases were filed against many Maoist cadres. It became a lot more difficult for the top leadership to travel in India as compared to the late 1990s.

The arrests caused a ripple within the Maoist organization. Despite the sporadic communication his party representatives had with Delhi, Prachanda was now convinced that the principal contradiction of the people was with the 'expansionists', meaning India. Worried about their safety, both he and Bhattarai returned to Rolpa in 2004 and began living in their base areas. Prachanda even announced that they would eventually have to fight a war with India, and called for trenches to be dug for that purpose. Bhattarai was uncomfortable with the rhetoric, for he continued to view the Palace and the monarchy as the key problem, the enemy which needed to be vanquished, not India. The tension had historical roots, with different schools of the Nepali Left prioritizing either 'nationalism' or 'democracy'.

2009-10: Like many other Nepalis, I was angered by India's policy, actions and behaviour in that period. Having covered the political process day in and out, I had seen the depths to which the Indian establishment had plunged to isolate the Maoists, with little regard for the notions of sovereignty, democratic norms and processes, or political ethics. India's actions appeared to confirm long-held apprehensions in Nepal that Delhi was not comfortable with any domestic force with a sizeable mass base, and one which refused to take dictation from the babus of South Block. Delhi's desire to be in control of events and actors in Kathmandu has often preceded any other objective. In 1960, the Nehru-B. P. Koirala relationship had become uneasy when Koirala had struck out and asserted his strong and independent personality. In the 1990s, minor incidents disrupted India's ties with the NC which eventually benefited the Palace. And now, India had a problem with the two forces who had been most successful in the 2008 elections—the

Maoists nationally, and the Madhesi Janadhikar Forum (MJF) in the plains. It seemed India really wanted pliant agents, and was just not mature enough to deal with autonomous political agents in a neighbouring country.

I asked a thoughtful RAW official why they could not let go and allow domestic processes in Nepal to play out, irrespective of outcomes, without meddling. 'If you have an open border, there has to be a special security relationship. We could have lived with a Maoist dictatorship if it was 5,000 miles away but, across an open border, we cannot risk it.'

What India was attempting with the Maoists was not a simplistic strategy of isolation, though. It was emulating a highly sophisticated tradition of statecraft it had practiced, with mixed results, in Kashmir with the Hurriyat Conference and, in the Northeast, with the National Socialist Council of Nagaland (Isak-Muivah). Engage, coerce, divide, frustrate, exhaust, corrupt, lure, repeat the cycle, and give nothing. It had never stopped talking to the Maoists even when the war of words was at its worst. It had isolated them to show them the high costs of not listening to advice. It had encouraged Baburam Bhattarai as a counter to Prachanda in order to sharpen the divisions within the party.

It had created a situation where the leadership could deliver nothing to the cadre, frustrating them and increasing the gulf between the top and the bottom. It offered inducements and showed the benefits of cooperating and playing along with the existing political-economic networks. And it kept up the strategies until the incentives for the other side changed, and caused a transformation in its behaviour which suited the establishment.

[...] this time, India was intervening not in favour of universal values but to influence outcomes in a fragmented but democratic political landscape. There was no reason for Delhi to play favourites among Nepali politicians, for no one—including the Maoists—had harmed India's security interests. They could have let domestic political processes take their own course instead of preventing a natural equilibrium from emerging. For a neighbour to actively intervene in order to try and kill another country's elected institution, and target one political force, went beyond any acceptable norm of inter-state relations. But the Nepali Maoists, despite this baggage, had come around to the new political reality. They had participated in the elections and won legitimately. Despite sporadic incidents, they had allowed a free and extremely critical press to flourish. They had given up their base areas and opened it up to political competition so that other political parties could operate there. They had dissolved their parallel courts and had agreed to have their former army put into cantonments. Prachanda had resigned when faced with an uncomfortable political situation, and was making a bid to return to power by gaining a majority on the floor of the house.

2011: There was also a change of personnel in the Indian establishment. And as we had seen in 2005-06, individuals played a major role in shaping policy. Sanjeev Tripathi had taken over RAW in January 2011, and he was understood to be in favour of reengaging with the Maoists. Alok Joshi had taken over as special secretary who looked after key neighbouring countries. Joshi had served as the station chief in Nepal between 2008 and 2010. A product of JNU, and an Indian Police Service officer from the Haryana cadre, he had sharp political sense and knew the lay of the land in Nepal.

RAW did not believe in giving the Maoists a blank cheque and recognized the importance of challenging them in order to get them to deliver on commitments. But it could also see that the experiment of keeping the Maoists out of power had perhaps outlived its utility, and the Indian position needed revision. It argued to the national security advisor, Shiv Shanker Menon, that the Maoists should be given 'one final chance'.

Rakesh Sood had left Kathmandu for Paris, and the new ambassador, Jayant Prasad, had not yet arrived in Kathmandu. A soft-spoken, brilliant diplomat, with uncanny political sense and a commitment to basic democratic ethos, Prasad had an old Nepal connection. His father, Bimal Prasad, a former professor in JNU [Jawaharlal Nehru University], had been India's envoy to Kathmandu in the early 1990s and had a reputation of being close to the NC. But Jayant Prasad had visited Nepal only once during his father's tenure and carried little baggage. A 'free-thinker' in his student days in JNU, where he distinguished himself academically, Prasad could empathize with broad socialist and Left political thinking, but carried no dogma. While Prasad did not take charge till August-end, Sood's departure had already helped to partially detoxify the India-Maoist relationship.

Prachanda had met senior Indian intelligence officials during his trips to various Southeast Asian cities through the summer of 2011. In early August, they met in Kuala Lumpur where Prachanda once again committed to completing the peace process as soon as the Maoists led the government. He briefed them on internal tensions within the party, and said that after Khanal resigned, the Maoists would put forward Baburam Bhattarai as the party's prime ministerial candidate. Indian officials are learnt to have told him that they would not object if the Maoists observed all democratic processes and mustered a majority on the floor of the house. This was a significant meeting in rebuilding the relationship between the two sides. While the mistrust was deep, both sides were slowly inching back to the more nuanced approach they had with each other between 2005 and 2008. To borrow Prachanda's metaphor, the warmth may not have returned, but there was a thaw. A rapprochement was on the horizon.

Would it finally enable the successful accommodation of the Maoists into the formal power structure? Would it help integrate the Maoist combatants into the NA [Nepalese Army] — an issue which was at the heart of the tensions over the UN's role in Nepal, over General Katawal's dismissal, over the Maoists' re-entry into government, and the yardstick for whether the rebels had indeed transformed into a democratic force? Would it finally push forward the Constitution-writing project, which had been in limbo as power games overwhelmed Kathmandu politics? Would the renewed engagement between India and the Maoists bring back the focus on the core political goal of restructuring the Nepali state and Nepali nationalism?

The NC was now in panic mode. Ambassador Sood had completed his tenure in Kathmandu and had left a few months earlier. This had weakened the voice of the MEA within the establishment, which was more averse to giving the Maoists a chance. RAW, on the other hand, had veered towards allowing the Maoists another chance. They had not encouraged the Madhesi parties—but the 'agency', as Kathmandu politicians called RAW, had not discouraged them either. Left to domestic factors, the NC realized that there was little that would stop the Madhesi parties from choosing the more attractive option.

The NC now used all its political capital to get India involved on their side. The former party leader, and now President, Ram Baran Yadav, shared a personal equation with finance minister and old political warhorse Pranab Mukherjee—the only senior political leader in Delhi who really paid attention to Nepal. They spoke to each other in Bangla—Yadav had attended school in Calcutta. President Yadav warned Mukherjee that the Maoists' return to power would be dangerous, and they must help stop the Madhesis from voting for Bhattarai.

An Indian embassy official, upset with the [Nepali] President's attempt to undercut the local mission and reach out directly to the political leadership, told me about this conversation and said that it had rattled Delhi. Surya Bahadur Thapa, the former prime minister who had excellent ties with Delhi's political and bureaucratic elite, called up his interlocutors with a similar warning. Thapa's grandson Siddhartha had become a close friend and, over coffee at Babar Mahal, Siddhartha expressed deep unease at the evolving Indian stance, as they saw it. Shekhar Koirala, G. P. Koirala's nephew who had played an active role in the run-up to the signing of the 12-point Understanding, shared cordial ties with National Security Advisor Shiv Shankar Menon. They had known each other since Menon's time as a joint secretary handling Nepal in the mid-1990s. Koirala called up his old friend, urging India to get the Madhesis to support Poudel. He warned India that having the Maoists in power at this time would ensure that they remained in office if the CA ended without a Constitution having been finalized and that would have adverse consequences for Delhi. I met Koirala in the CA [Constituent Assembly] compound a few days later, and he confirmed to me that he had reservations about India's position and felt that Delhi was making a mistake.

Delhi seems to have become worried by the multiple messages

from friendly interlocutors. The political section of the Indian embassy now got into the act. They warned the Madhesi parties that the Maoists would deceive them, that their commitment to federalism was opportunistic, and that the parties of the plains must reconsider their options. The pressure could either have been born out of a desire to show to the NC that India was doing its bit, or born out of a genuine policy line to block the Maoists once again. Delhi ordered RAW, which was more open to the Maoists, to step back from the process.

Bibliography

Asoka Raina: *Inside RAW: The Story of India's Secret Service*, Vikas Publishing, New Delhi,1981.

Ayesha Siddiqa-Agha: *Military Inc.: Inside Pakistan's Military Economy*, London: Pluto, 2007.

Chengappa, Raj: *Weapons of peace : the secret story of India's quest to be a nuclear power*. New Delhi: Harper Collins Publishers, India. 2000.

Dhar, Maloy Kri. : *Mission to Pakistan: An Intelligence Agent in Pakistan*, Manas Publication, 2002.

Ganguly, Sumit : *"Avoiding War in Kashmir"*, Foreign Affairs, New York, Winter 1990.

Gupta, J.B. Das : *Islamic Fundamentalism and India* : Hope India Publications, Delhi, 2002.

Hussain Mushahid: *Pakistan: Problems of Governance*, Vanguard 1993.

Kumar, Dinesh : *"What it took and the run up to Operation Vijay'*, Times of India, New Delhi, 1999.

Maloy Krishna Dhar : *Open Secrets: India's Intelligence Unveiled*, New Delhi, Manas Publication, 2005.

Multani, R K P : *Islamic Fundamentalism in South Asia* : Sumit Enterprises, Delhi, 2007.

Parkash, Pahuja, Om : *India: A Nuclear Weapon State*. Prabhat Prakashan. 2012.

Perkovich, George: *India's nuclear bomb: the impact on global proliferation*. University of California Press. 2002.

Sagar, Tariq Ismail : *RAW: Research and Analysis Wing*, Sagar Publication, 2007.

Saleem, Muhammad : *RAW: Global and Regional Ambitions*, Islamabad Policy Research Institute, Asia Printers, Islamabad, 2005

Shuja Nawaz: *Crossed Swords: Pakistan, Its Army, and the Wars Within*, Karachi: Oxford University Press, 2008.

Singh, Major General Sujan : *Phatoms of Chittagong; The Fifth Army in Bangladesh*, Allied Publishers, 1985, New Delhi.

Sumit Ganguly: *Conflict Unending: India-Pakistan Tensions since 1947*, New York: Columbia University Press, 2001.

Sunanda K Datta-Ray: *Smash and grab: Annexation of Sikkim*, Tranquebar, 1984

Index

N

O

R

S

T

❑❑❑